Evangelical Lutheran Augustana Synod

Hymnal for Churches and Sunday-Schools of the Augustana Synod

Evangelical Lutheran Augustana Synod

Hymnal for Churches and Sunday-Schools of the Augustana Synod

ISBN/EAN: 9783337089702

Printed in Europe, USA, Canada, Australia, Japan

Cover: Foto ©Thomas Meinert / pixelio.de

HYMNAL

FOR

CHURCHES AND SUNDAY-SCHOOLS

OF THE

AUGUSTANA SYNOD.

ROCK ISLAND, ILL.
LUTHERAN AUGUSTANA BOOK CONCERN.

CONTENTS.

Page.

ORDER OF SERVICE FOR THE SUNDAY SCHOOL.

I. ORDER FOR OPENING.

After singing an appropriate Hymn, the School standing, the Superintendent shall say:

In the Name of the Father, and of the Son, and of the Holy Ghost. Amen.

Oh, come, let us worship and bow down; let us kneel before the Lord our Maker, for He is our God.

If we say that we have no sin, we deceive ourselves, and the truth is not in us.

If we confess our sins, God is faithful and just to forgive us our sins, and to cleanse us from all unrighteousness.

Then the Superintendent and the School together shall say:

Have mercy upon me, O God, according to Thy lovingkindness: according unto the multitude of Thy tender mercies blot out my transgressions. Wash me throroughly from mine iniquity, and cleanse me from my sin. Against Thee, Thee only, have I sinned, and done this evil in Thy sight.

Create in me a clean heart, O God; and renew a right spirit within me. Cast me not away from Thy presence; and take not Thy Holy Spirit from me. Restore unto me the joy of Thy salvation; and uphold me with Thy free Spirit.

The School shall sing:

Glory be to the Father, and | to the | Son, || and | to the | Holy | Ghost: || as it was in the beginning, is now, and | ever shall be, || world without | end. A- | men.||

Then the Superintendent shall say the following Collect, or some other Collect appropriate to the day:

Grant us, we beseech Thee, Almighty God, Heavenly Father, a steadfast faith in Jesus Christ, a cheerful hope in Thy mercy, and a sincere love to Thee and to all our fellowmen, through Jesus Christ our Lord.

The School shall sing:

Then the Superintendent and the School responsively shall read the Bible Lesson.

After the reading of the Lesson, the Superintendent and the School together shall say the Apostles' Creed.

I believe in God the Father Almighty, Maker of Heaven and earth.

And in Jesus Christ His only Son, our Lord; who was conceived by the Holy Ghost, Born of the Virgin Mary; Suffered under Pontius Pilate, Was crucified, dead, and buried; He descended into hell; The third day He rose again from the dead; He ascended into heaven, And sitteth on the right hand of God the

Father Almighty; from thence He shall come to judge the quick and the dead.

I believe in the Holy Ghost; The holy Christian Church, the Communion of Saints; The forgiveness of sins; The Resurrection of the body; and the Life everlasting. Amen.

Then, the School sitting, a Hymn shall be sung, after which the Class Instruction shall begin.

II. ORDER FOR CLOSING.

The Class Instruction ended, and the School having been called to order, a Lesson Review, or Questions on the Catechism may follow, after which all necessary Announcements shall be made.

A Hymn having been sung, the Superintendent, the School standing, shall say the following General Prayer (Instead of this Prayer a free Prayer may be used):

O Lord our God, most loving and merciful Savior, who didst call little children to come unto Thee, and didst lay Thy hands upon them, look upon us we humbly beseech Thee, and bless us Thy children, dedicated to Thy service in holy Baptism. Bestow upon us Thy saving grace, and make us to remember our Creator in the days of our youth. Teach us the fear of God which is the beginning of wisdom.

Bless, O Lord, the instruction which we have received this hour, and grant that Thy precious Word may be so grafted into our hearts as to bring forth the fruits of righteousness to the honor and glory of Thy name.

Teach us truly to believe in Thee, to love Thee with all our heart, to worship Thee and give Thee thanks, to obey Thy commandments, to reverence Thy holy Name and Word, and to serve Thee faithfully all the days of our lives.

Be gracious unto all of us here before Thee. Preserve us from all danger, and deliver us from the power of the evil one and from the wickedness that is in the world. Defend us by day and by night. Unite us in the bonds of Christian love, and receive us at last unto Thyself in Thy heavenly kingdom. These and all things else necessary for us, and for the whole Church, we humbly beg in the Name and for the sake of Jesus Christ our Lord, Who liveth and reigneth with Thee and the Holy Ghost, ever one God, world without end. Amen.

Then the Superintendent and the School together shall say:

Our Father, who art in heaven; Hallowed be Thy name; Thy kingdom come; Thy will be done on earth, as it is in heaven; Give us this day our daily bread; And forgive us our trespasses, as we forgive those who trespass against us; And lead us not into temptation; But deliver us from evil; for Thine is the kingdom, and the power, and the glory, forever. Amen.

The Superintendent shall say:

Let us thank and praise the Lord.

The School shall sing:

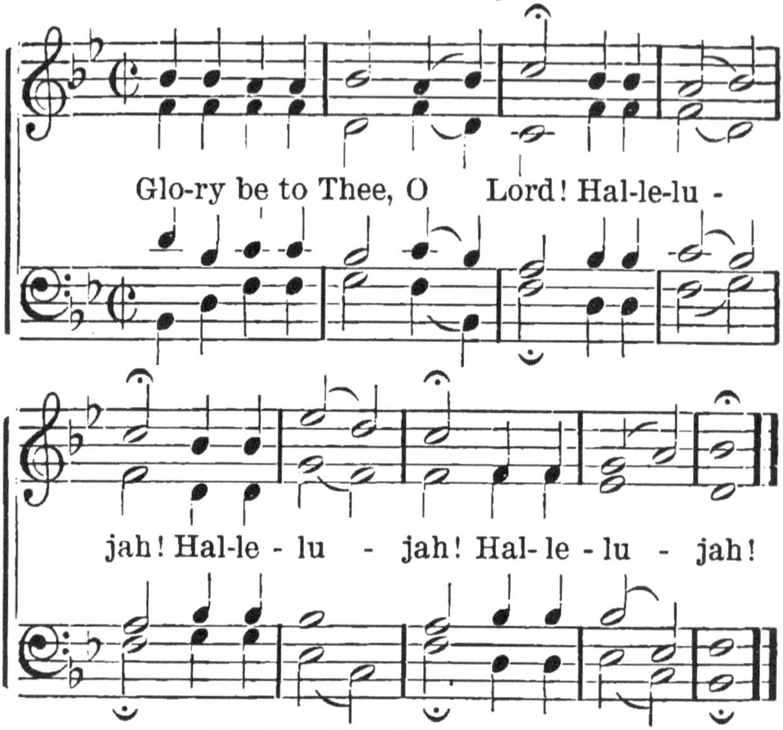
Glo-ry be to Thee, O Lord! Hal-le-lu -
jah! Hal-le - lu - jah! Hal- le - lu - jah!

The Superintendent shall say:

The grace of the Lord Jesus Christ, and the love of God, and the communion of the Holy Ghost, be with you all. (Amen).

The School shall sing:

A - men! A - men! A - - - men!

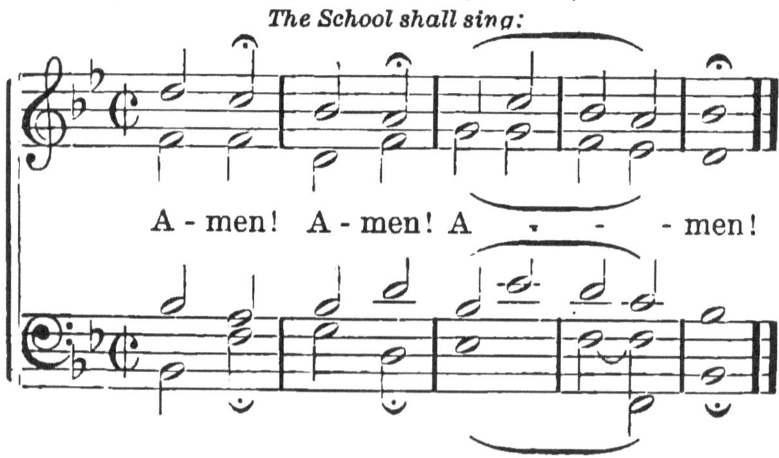

MORNING SERVICE.

The Service shall begin with a Hymn appropriate to the day. The Minister having in the meantime advanced to the Altar, shall turn to the Congregation and proceed thus:

Holy, holy, holy, is the Lord of Hosts: the whole earth is full of His glory. The Lord is in His holy temple; His throne is in heaven. The Lord is nigh unto them that are of a humble and broken spirit. He heareth the supplications of those who truly repent and inclineth to their prayers. Let us therefore come boldly unto the throne of grace and confess our sins.

The Minister, together with the Congregation, shall pray:

We poor miserable sinners, conceived and born in sin, with all our heart confess unto Thee, holy and righteous God, merciful Father, that we, in manifold ways during all our life, have offended against Thee. We have not loved Thee above all things, nor our neighbor as ourselves. Against Thee and Thy holy commandments have we sinned by thought, word, and deed, and we humbly acknowledge before Thee that, according to Thy justice and our sins, we have deserved eternal condemnation. But Thou, Heavenly Father, hast promised to receive with tender mercy all penitent sinners, who return unto Thee and with living faith flee for refuge to Thy fatherly compassion and to the merits of our Savior Jesus Christ. Their transgressions Thou wilt not regard, nor impute unto them their sins.

Relying upon Thy promise, we poor sinners confidently beseech Thee to be merciful and gracious unto us and forgive us all our sins to the praise and glory of Thy holy Name.

May the Almighty, Everlasting God, in His infinite mercy and for the sake of our Savior Jesus Christ, forgive all our sins, and grant us grace that we may amend our lives, and finally with Him obtain eternal life. Amen.

The Minister and the Congregation, standing, shall sing:

Lord, have mercy upon us!
Christ, have mercy upon us!
Lord, have mercy upon us!

Then shall the Minister sing or say:

Glory be to God on high, and on earth peace, good will toward men.

The Congregation shall sing, the Minister turning to the Altar:

All glory be to God on high,
Who hath our race befriended!
To us no harm shall now come nigh,
The strife at last is ended;
God showeth His good will to men,
And peace shall reign on earth again;
Oh, thank Him for His goodness.

Or

We praise Thee, we bless Thee, we worship Thee, we glorify Thee, we give thanks to Thee for Thy great glory, O Lord God, Heavenly King, God the Father Almighty.

O Lord, the Only-begotten Son, Jesus Christ; O Lord God, Lamb of God, Son of the Father, that takest away the sin of the world, have mercy upon us. Thou that takest away the sin of the world, receive our prayer. Thou that sittest at the right hand of God the Father, have mercy upon us.

For Thou only art holy; Thou only art the

Lord; Thou only, O Christ, with the Holy Ghost, art most high in the glory of God the Father. Amen.

Or

We praise Thee, we worship Thee, we give thanks to Thee for Thy great glory, O Lord God, Heavenly King, God the Father Almighty! O Lord, the Only-begotten Son, Jesus Christ! Holy Ghost, Spirit of grace and of truth and of peace! Amen.

The Minister, turning to the Congregation, shall sing or say:

The Lord be with you.

The Congregation shall sing:

And with thy spirit.

Then the Minister shall say:

Let us pray.

The Minister, turning to the Altar, shall say the following Collect, or another Collect appropriate to the day:

GENERAL COLLECT.

Grant us, we beseech Thee, Almighty God, Heavenly Father, a steadfast faith in Jesus Christ, a cheerful hope in Thy mercy, and a sincere love to Thee and to all our fellowmen; through Jesus Christ our Lord.

The Congregation shall sing:

Amen.

Then the Minister, turning to the Congregation, shall read the Epistle for the day, saying:

The Epistle for (here he shall name the day) is written in the...... Chapter of......, beginning at the...... verse.

The Epistle ended, the Congregation, sitting, shall sing an appropriate Hymn. The Hymn ended, the Minister shall continue:

Lift up your hearts unto the Lord and hear the Gospel for the day as it is written in the

.... Chapter of St.............., beginning at the...... verse.

Here the Congregation shall arise. The Gospel ended, the Minister and the Congregation shall say the Apostles' Creed.

I believe in God the Father Almighty, Maker of Heaven and earth.

And in Jesus Christ His only Son, our Lord; Who was conceived by the Holy Ghost, Born of the Virgin Mary; Suffered under Pontius Pilate, Was crucified, dead, and buried; He descended into hell; The third day He rose again from the dead; He ascended into heaven, And sitteth on the right hand of God the Father Almighty; From thence He shall come to judge the quick and the dead.

I believe in the Holy Ghost; The holy Christian Church, the Communion of Saints; The Forgiveness of sins; The Resurrection of the body; And the Life everlasting. Amen.

Here a Selection by the Choir may be sung. Then shall follow an appropriate Hymn. In the meantime the Minister shall enter the pulpit.

THE SERMON.

The Sermon ended, the Minister shall say:

Praised be the Lord, and blessed to all eternity, Who, by His Word has comforted, instructed, and admonished us. May His Holy Spirit confirm the Word in our hearts that we be not forgetful hearers, but daily increase in faith, hope, love, and patience unto the end, and be saved through Jesus Christ our Lord. Amen.

Here the Announcements may be made, after which the Minister shall say:

The grace of the Lord Jesus Christ, and the love of God, and the communion of the Holy Ghost be with you all. Amen.

Or

The God of all grace, who hath called us unto His eternal glory by Christ Jesus, after that ye have suffered a while; make you perfect, stablish, strengthen, settle you. To Him be glory and dominion for ever and ever. Amen.

Then shall the Congregation sing a short Hymn, during which the offerings shall be made. Then the Minister, in the meantime having gone before the Altar, shall turn to the Congregation and sing or say:

The Lord be with you.

The Congregation, standing, shall say:

And with thy spirit.

The Minister shall say (Instead of the following General Prayer, during Lent or on special occasions, the Litany may be used):

Let us pray

(the minister turning to the Altar):

Almighty and Everlasting God, the Creator and Preserver of all things, we implore Thee that Thou wouldst be gracious unto us for the sake of Jesus Christ, and that Thou wouldst not remember our sins! Sanctify and guide us with Thy Holy Spirit and give us grace that me may lead a holy life according to Thy Word! Gather, strengthen, and preserve Thy Church through the Word and the holy Sacraments! Have mercy, O Lord, on all the nations that sit in darkness and the shadow of death, and cause the saving and life-giving light of Thy Gospel to shine graciously upon them.

For Synodical and Conference Meetings.

Bless those who are now assembled to deliberate concerning the welfare of Thy Church, so that their counsels may further Thy glory and the upbuilding of Thy kingdom among us.

Grant also health and prosperity to all in authority, especially to the President [and Congress] of the United states, the Governor [and Legislature] of this Commonwealth, and to all our Judges and Magistrates; and endue them with grace to rule after Thy good pleasure, to the maintenance of righteousness, and to the hindrance and punishment of wickedness, that we may lead a quiet and peaceable life, in all godliness and honesty. Cause also the needful fruits of the earth to prosper, and bless all lawful occupations. Sanctify and bless O Lord, our homes; keep the baptized children in Thy covenant and give all parents and teachers grace to nurture them in Thy fear.

May Thy blessing rest on all institutions of learning, and make them nurseries for Thy kingdom.

For Catechumens. Remember graciously our Catechumens, and grant unto them a good understanding and sincere faith that they as Thy disciples may continue faithful in Thy truth.

For Communion. Bless also the guests at Thy holy table, in order that they may be strengthened in faith and love and the hope of eternal life.

Help and comfort the sick and poor, the afflicted and dying! Graciously protect all widows and orphans; support us in our last hour, and after the close of this corruptible life, vouchsafe unto us eternal blessedness through Jesus Christ, Thy Son our Lord.

The Congregation shall sing:

Amen.

The Minister shall continue:

Our Father, who art in heaven; Hallowed be Thy Name; Thy kingdom come; Thy will be done on earth, as it is in heaven; Give us this day our daily bread; And forgive us our trespasses, as we forgive those who trespass against us; And lead us not into temptation; But deliver us from evil; For Thine is the kingdom, and the power, and the glory, forever. Amen.

The Minister, turning to the Congregation, shall sing or say:

Let us thank and praise the Lord.

The Congregation shall sing:

Glory be to Thee, O Lord!
Hallelujah! Hallelujah! Hallelujah!

Then shall the Minister say:

Bow your hearts to God, and receive the benediction.

The Lord bless thee, and keep thee.

The Lord make His face shine upon thee, and be gracious unto thee.

The Lord lift up His countenance upon thee, and give thee peace.

In the Name of the Father, and of the Son, and of the Holy Ghost. Amen.

The Congregation shall sing:

Amen! Amen! Amen!

The Service shall close with silent prayer.

THE HOLY COMMUNION.

Without the Full Morning Service.

The Service shall begin with a suitable Hymn. The Minister standing before the Altar, shall turn to the Congregation and say:

In the Name of the Father, and of the Son, and of the Holy Ghost.

Here shall follow an appropriate Address, closing with the Confession of Sins, as follows:

We poor miserable sinners, conceived and born in sin, with all our heart confess unto Thee, holy and righteous God, merciful Father, that we, in manifold ways during all our life have offended against Thee. We have not loved Thee above all things, nor our neighbor as ourselves. Against Thee and Thy holy commandments have we sinned by thought, word and deed, and we humbly acknowledge before Thee that, according to Thy justice and our sins, we have deserved eternal condemnation. But Thou, Heavenly Father, hast promised to receive with tender mercy all penitent sinners, who return unto Thee and with living faith flee for refuge to Thy fatherly compassion and to the merits of our Savior Jesus Christ. Their transgressions Thou wilt not regard, nor impute unto them their sins. Relying upon Thy promise, we poor sinners confidently beseech Thee to be merciful and gracious unto us and forgive us all our sins to the praise and glory of Thy Holy Name.

Then the Minister, standing, shall pronounce the Absolution:

If this be your sincere confession, and if with penitent hearts you earnestly desire the forgiveness of your sins for the sake of Jesus Christ, God, according to His promise, forgiveth you all your sins; and I, by the authority of God's Word and by the command of our Lord Jesus Christ, announce to you that God, through His grace hath forgiven all your sins: In the Name of the Father, and of the Son, and of the Holy Ghost. Amen.

After the Absolution the Minister shall say:

Let us pray:

We render unto Thee heartfelt thanks that Thou hast forgiven our sins, and we pray Thee by Thy Holy Spirit to prepare us that we in true penitence and faith may receive the Sacrament of the Body and Blood of Thy Son Jesus Christ, and be strengthened in Christian faithfulness and in the hope of everlasting life; through Jesus Christ our Savior. Amen.

Then the Announcements may be made. A suitable Hymn shall be sung, during which the Collection shall be taken. While the Hymn is being sung, the Minister shall prepare for the administration of the Holy Sacrament.

Turning to the Congregation, he shall sing or say:

Lift up your hearts to God.

The Congregation, standing, shall sing:

We lift them up unto the Lord our God.

The Minister shall sing or say:

Let us give thanks unto the Lord.

The Congregation shall sing:

It is meet and right so to do.

The Minister, turning to the Altar, shall say:

It is truly meet and right, becoming and salutary, that we should at all times, and in all places, give thanks unto Thee, O Lord, Holy

Father, Almighty, Everlasting God, through Jesus Christ, our Lord: who is our Paschal Lamb offered for us, the innocent Lamb of God, who taketh away the sin of the world; who hath conquered death, is risen again, and liveth forever more. Therefore, we who trust in Him shall also through Him be victorious over sin and death, and inherit eternal life. And in order that we may keep in remembrance His unspeakable mercy, He hath instituted His Holy Supper.

Then shall the Minister consecrate the Elements, saying:

Our Lord Jesus Christ, in the night in which He was betrayed, took bread; and when He had given thanks, He brake it and gave it to His disciples, saying, Take, eat; this is My Body, which is given for you; this do in remembrance of Me.

After the same manner, also, when He had supped, He took the cup, and when He had given thanks, He gave it to them, saying, Drink ye all of it, this Cup is the New Testament in My Blood, which is shed for you, and for many, for the remission of sins; this do, as oft as ye drink it, in remembrance of Me.

The Minister shall continue:

Our Father, who art in heaven; Hallowed be Thy Name; Thy kingdom come; Thy will be done on earth as it is in heaven; Give us this day our daily bread; And forgive us our trespasses, as we forgive those who trespass against us; And lead us not into temptation; But deliver us from evil; For Thine is the kingdom, and the power, and the glory, forever. Amen.

Then shall the Minister and the Congregation together sing:

Holy, holy, holy, Lord God of Sabaoth; Heaven and earth are full of Thy glory; Hosanna in the highest.

Blessed is He that cometh in the Name of the Lord. Hosanna in the highest.

The Minister, turning to the Congregation, shall sing or say:

The peace of the Lord be with you alway.

Then shall be sung the Agnus Dei as follows, while the Communicants kneel at the Altar:

O Christ, Thou Lamb of God, that takest away the sin of the world, have mercy upon us.

O Christ, Thou Lamb of God, that takest away the sin of the world, have mercy upon us.

O Christ, Thou Lamb of God, that takest away the sin of the world, grant us Thy peace. Amen.

After the singing of the Agnus Dei, a Communion Hymn shall be sung, while the Distribution proceeds.

When the Minister gives the Bread, he shall say:

Take and eat; this is the Body of Christ, given for thee.

When he gives the Cup, he shall say:

Take and drink; this is the Blood of Christ, shed for thee.

In dismissing the Communicants, the Minister shall say:

The Lord Jesus Christ, whose true Body and Blood you have now received, strengthen and preserve you unto everlasting life. Amen.

When the Distribution of the Holy Supper is ended, the Minister shall say:

Let us pray.

Turning to the Altar, the Minister shall say:

We thank Thee, Almighty Father, who, through Thy Son Jesus Christ, for our consolation and salvation, hast instituted this Holy Supper; we pray Thee, grant us grace so to commemorate the death of Christ that we may be partakers of the great Supper in heaven.

The Congregation shall sing:

Amen.

The Minister, turning to the Congregation, shall sing or say:

Let us thank and praise the Lord.

The Congregation, standing, shall answer:

Glory be to Thee, O Lord!
Hallelujah! Hallelujah! Hallelujah!

Then the Minister shall say:

Bow your hearts to God and receive the benediction.

The Lord bless thee, and keep thee.

The Lord make His face shine upon thee, and be gracious unto thee.

The Lord lift up His countenance upon thee, and give thee peace.

In the Name of the Father, and of the Son, and of the Holy Ghost. Amen.

The Congregation shall sing:

Amen! Amen! Amen!

The Service shall close with silent prayer.

THE HOLY COMMUNION.

With the Full Morning Service.

The Service shall begin with a suitable Hymn. The Minister, standing before the Altar, shall turn to the Congregation and say:

In the Name of the Father, and of the Son, and of the Holy Ghost.

Here shall follow an appropriate Address, closing with the Confession of Sins, as follows:

We poor miserable sinners, conceived and born in sin, with all our heart confess unto Thee, holy and righteous God, merciful Father, that we, in manifold ways during all our life have offended against Thee. We have not loved Thee above all things, nor our neighbor as ourselves. Against Thee and Thy holy commandments have we sinned by thought, word and deed, and we humbly acknowledge before Thee that, according to Thy justice and our sins, we have deserved eternal condemnation. But Thou, Heavenly Father, hast promised to receive with tender mercy all penitent sinners, who return unto Thee and with living faith flee for refuge to Thy fatherly compassion and to the merits of our Savior Jesus Christ. Their transgressions Thou wilt not regard, nor impute unto them their sins. Relying upon Thy promise, we poor sinners confidently beseech Thee to be merciful and gracious unto us and forgive us all our sins to the praise and glory of Thy Holy Name.

Then the Minister, standing, shall pronounce the Absolution.

If this be your sincere confession, and if with penitent hearts you earnestly desire the forgiveness of your sins for the sake of Jesus Christ, God, according to His promise, forgiveth you all your sins; and I, by the authority of God's Word and by the command of our Lord Jesus Christ, announce to you that God, through His grace hath forgiven all your sins: In the Name of the Father, and of the Son, and of the Holy Ghost. Amen.

Then shall the Minister sing or say:

Glory be to God on high, and on earth peace, good will toward men.

The Congregation, standing, shall sing (the Minister turning to the Altar):

All glory be to God on high,
  Who hath our race befriended!
To us no harm shall now come nigh,
  The strife at last is ended;
God showeth His good will to men,
And peace shall reign on earth again:
  Oh, thank Him for His goodness.

Or

We praise Thee, we bless Thee, we worship Thee, we glorify Thee, we give thanks to Thee for Thy great glory, O Lord God, Heavenly King, God the Father Almighty.

O Lord, the Only-begotten Son, Jesus Christ; O Lord God, Lamb of God, Son of the Father, that takest away the sin of the world, have mercy upon us. Thou that takest away the sin of the world, receive our prayer. Thou that sittest at the right hand of God the Father, have mercy upon us.

For Thou only art holy; Thou only art the Lord; Thou only, O Christ, with the Holy

Ghost, art most high in the glory of God the Father. Amen.

Or

We praise Thee, we worship Thee, we give thanks to Thee for Thy great glory, O Lord God, Heavenly King, God the Father Almighty! O Lord, the Only-begotten Son. Jesus Christ! Holy Ghost. Spirit of grace and truth and of peace! Amen.

The Minister, turning to the Congregation, shall sing or say:

The Lord be with you.

The Congregation shall sing:

And with thy spirit.

Then the Minister shall say:

Let us pray.

The Minister, turning to the Altar, shall say the following Collect, or another Collect appropriate to the day:

GENERAL COLLECT.

Grant us, we beseech Thee, Almighty God. Heavenly Father, a steadfast faith in Jesus Christ, a cheerful hope in Thy mercy and a sincere love to Thee and to all our fellowmen; through Jesus Christ our Lord.

The Congregation, standing, shall sing:

Amen.

Then the Minister, turning to the Congregation, shall read the Epistle for the day, saying:

The Epistle for (here he shall name the day) is written in the...... Chapter of......, beginning at the...... verse.

The Epistle ended, the Congregation, sitting, shall sing an appropriate Hymn.

The Hymn ended, the Minister shall continue:

Lift up your hearts unto the Lord and hear the Gospel for the day as it is written in the .... Chapter of St. .. .., beginning at the .... verse.

Here the Congregation shall arise. The Gospel ended, the Minister and the Congregation shall say the Apostles' Creed:

I believe in God the Father Almighty, Maker of Heaven and earth.

And in Jesus Christ His only Son, our Lord; Who was conceived by the Holy Ghost, Born of the Virgin Mary; Suffered under Pontius Pilate, Was crucified, dead, and buried; He descended into hell; The third day he rose again from the dead; He ascended into heaven, And sitteth on the right hand of God the Father Almighty; From thence He shall come to judge the quick and the dead.

I believe in the Holy Ghost; The holy Christian Church, the Communion of Saints; The Forgiveness of sins; The Resurrection of the body; and the Life everlasting. Amen.

Here a Selection by the Choir may be sung. Then shall follow an appropriate Hymn. In the meantime the Minister shall enter the pulpit.

THE SERMON.

The Sermon ended, the Minister shall say:

Praised be the Lord, and blessed to all eternity, Who, by His Word, has comforted, instructed, and admonished us. May His Holy Spirit confirm the Word in our hearts that we be not forgetful hearers, but daily increase in faith, hope, love, and patience unto the end, and be saved through Jesus Christ our Lord. Amen.

Here the Announcements may be made, after which the Minister thall say:

The grace of the Lord Jesus Christ, and the love of God, and the communion of the Holy Ghost be with you all. Amen.

Or

The God of all grace, who hath called us unto His eternal glory by Christ Jesus, after that ye have suffered a while, make you perfect, stablish, strengthen, settle you. To Him be glory and dominion for ever and ever. Amen.

Then shall the Congregation sing a short Hymn, during which the offerings shall be made. Then the Minister in the meantime having gone before the Altar, shall turn to the Congregation and sing or say:

The Lord be with you.

The Congregation, standing, shall sing:

And with thy spirit.

The Minister shall say (Instead of the following General Prayer, during Lent or on special occasions, the Litany may be used):

Let us pray

(the Minister turning to the Altar):

Almighty and Everlasting God, the Creator and Preserver of all things, we implore Thee that Thou wouldst be gracious unto us for the sake of Jesus Christ, and that Thou wouldst not remember our sins! Sanctify and guide us with Thy Holy Spirit and give us grace that we may lead a holy life according to Thy Word! Gather, strengthen, and preserve Thy Church through the Word and the holy Sacraments! Have mercy, O Lord, on all the nations that sit in darkness and the shadow of death, and cause the saving and life-giving light of Thy Gospel to shine graciously upon them.

For Synodical and Conference Meetings. Bless those who are now assembled to deliberate concerning the welfare of Thy Church, so that their counsels may further Thy glory and the upbuilding of Thy kingdom among us.

Grant also health and prosperity to all in authority, especially to the President [and Congress] of the United States, the Governor [and Legislature] of this Commonwealth, and to all our Judges and Magistrates; and endue them with grace to rule after Thy good pleasure, to the maintenance of righteousness, and to the hindrance and punishment of wickedness, that we may lead a quiet and peaceable life in all godliness and honesty. Cause also the needful fruits of the earth to prosper, and bless all lawful occupations. Sanctify and bless, O Lord, our homes; keep the baptized children in Thy covenant and give all parents and teachers grace to nurture them in Thy fear.

May Thy blessing rest on all institutions of learning, and make them nurseries for Thy kingdom.

For Catechumens. Remember graciously our Catechumens, and grant unto them a good understanding and sincere faith that they as Thy disciples may continue faithful in Thy truth.

For Communion. Bless also the guests at Thy holy table, in order that they may be strengthened in faith and love and the hope of eternal life.

Help and comfort the sick and poor, the afflicted and dying! Graciously protect all widows and orphans; support us in our last hour, and after the close of this corruptible life, vouchsafe unto us eternal blessedness through Jesus Christ, Thy Son our Lord.

The Congregation shall sing:

Amen.

Then a suitable Hymn shall be sung. While the Hymn is being sung, the Minister shall prepare for the administration of the Holy Sacrament. Turning to the Congregation, he shall sing or say:

Lift up your hearts to God.

The Congregation, standing, shall sing:

We lift them up unto the Lord our God.

The Minister shall sing or say:

Let us give thanks unto the Lord.

The Congregation shall sing:

It is meet and right so to do.

The Minister, turning to the Altar, shall say:

It is truly meet and right, becoming and salutary, that we should at all times, and in all places, give thanks unto Thee, O Lord, Holy Father, Almighty, Everlasting God, through Jesus Christ, our Lord; who is our Paschal Lamb offered for us, the innocent Lamb of God, who taketh away the sin of the world; who has conquered death, is risen again, and liveth for evermore. Therefore, we who trust in Him shall also through Him be victorious over sin and death, and inherit eternal life. And in order that we may keep in remembrance His unspeakable mercy, He hath instituted His Holy Supper.

Then shall the Minister consecrate the Elements, saying:

Our Lord Jesus Christ, in the night in which He was betrayed, took bread; and when He had given thanks, He brake it and gave it to His disciples, saying, Take, eat; This is My

Body, which is given for you; this do in remembrance of Me.

After the same manner, also, when He had supped, He took the Cup, and when He had given thanks, He gave it to them, saying, Drink ye all of it; this Cup is the New Testament in My Blood, which is shed for you, and for many, for the remission of sins; this do, as oft as ye drink it, in remembrance of Me.

The Minister shall continue:

Our Father, who art in heaven; Hallowed be Thy Name; Thy kingdom come; Thy will be done on earth as it is in heaven; Give us this day our daily bread; And forgive us our trespasses, as we forgive those who trespass against us; And lead us not into temptation; But deliver us from evil; For Thine is the kingdom, and the power, and the glory, forever. Amen.

Then shall the Minister and the Congregation together sing:

Holy, holy, holy, Lord God of Sabaoth;
Heaven and earth are full of Thy glory;
Hosanna in the highest.
Blessed is He that cometh in the Name of the Lord. Hosanna in the highest.

The Minister, turning to the Congregation, shall sing or say:

The peace of the Lord be with you alway.

Then shall be sung the Agnus Dei as follows, while the Communicants kneel at the Altar:

O Christ, Thou Lamb of God, that takest away the sin of the world, have mercy upon us.

O Christ, Thou Lamb of God, that takest away the sin of the world, have mercy upon us.

O Christ, Thou Lamb of God, that takest away the sin of the world, grant us Thy peace. Amen.

After the singing of the Agnus Dei, a Communion Hymn shall be sung, while the Distribution proceeds.

When the Minister gives the Bread, he shall say:

Take and eat; this is the Body of Christ, given for thee.

When he gives the Cup, he shall say:

Take and drink; this is the Blood of Christ, shed for thee.

In dismissing the Communicants, the Minister shall say:

The Lord Jesus Christ, whose true Body and Blood you have now received, strengthen and preserve you unto everlasting life. Amen.

When the Distribution of the Holy Supper is ended, the Minister shall say:

Let us pray.

Turning to the Altar, the Minister shall say:

We thank Thee, Almighty Father, who, through Thy Son Jesus Christ, for our consolation and salvation, hast instituted this Holy Supper; we pray Thee, grant us grace so to commemorate the death of Christ that we may be partakers of the great Supper in heaven.

The Congregation shall sing:

Amen.

The Minister, turning to the Congregation, shall sing or say:

Let us thank and praise the Lord.

The Congregation, standing, shall answer:

Glory be to Thee, O Lord!
Hallelujah! Hallelujah! Hallelujah!

Then the Minister shall say:

Bow your hearts to God and receive the benediction.

The Lord bless thee, and keep thee.

The Lord make His face shine upon thee, and be gracious unto thee.

The Lord lift up His countenance upon thee, and give thee peace.

In the Name of the Father, and of the Son, and of the Holy Ghost. Amen.

The Congregation shall sing:

Amen! Amen! Amen!

The Service shall close with silent prayer.

EVENING SERVICE.

The Service shall begin with a short Hymn. The Minister, having in the mean time advanced to the Altar, shall turn to the Congregation and say:

Grace be unto you, and peace from God our Father, and from the Lord Jesus Christ. Amen.

Oh, come, let us worship and bow down; let us kneel before the Lord our Maker, for He is our God.

Then the Minister shall say:

O most merciful God and Father, whose grace endureth from generation to generation! Thou art patient and longsuffering, and forgivest all who are truly penitent their sins and transgressions. Look with compassion upon Thy people and hear their supplications. We poor sinners confess unto Thee that we are by nature sinful and unworthy of Thy goodness and love. Against Thee have we sinned and done wickedness in Thy sight. Remember not our transgressions; have mercy upon us; help us, O God, our Savior! For Thy Name's sake, grant us remission of all our sins and save us. Give us the grace of Thy Holy Spirit that we may amend our sinful lives and obtain with Thee everlasting life; through Thy Son Jesus Christ our Lord. Amen.

The Blood of Jesus Christ cleanseth us from all sin. He that believeth, and is baptized, shall be saved. Grant us, O Lord, this salvation.

All standing to the end of the Creed, the Minister and the Congregation shall sing:

Glory be to the Father, and to the Son, and to the Holy Ghost; as it was in the beginning, is now, and ever shall be, world without end. Amen.

Then shall the Minister read the Scripture Lesson for the day; after which shall be said either the Apostles' Creed or the Nicene Creed:

THE APOSTLES' CREED.

I believe in God the Father Almighty, Maker of Heaven and earth.

And in Jesus Christ His only Son, our Lord; Who was conceived by the Holy Ghost, Born of the Virgin Mary; Suffered under Pontius Pilate, Was crucified, dead, and buried; He descended into hell; The third day He rose again from the dead; He ascended into heaven, And sitteth on the right hand of God the Father Almighty; From thence He shall come to judge the quick and the dead.

I believe in the Holy Ghost; The holy Christian Church, the Communion of Saints; The Forgiveness of sins; The Resurrection of the body; And the Life everlasting. Amen.

THE NICENE CREED.

I believe in one God, the Father Almighty, Maker of Heaven and earth, and of all things visible and invisible.

And in one Lord Jesus Christ, the Only-begotten Son of God, Begotten of His Father before all worlds, God of God, Light of Light, Very God of very God, Begotten, not made, Being of one substance with the Father, By whom all things were made; Who, for us men, and for our salvation, came down from heaven, And was incarnate by the Holy Ghost of the Virgin Mary, And was made man; And was crucified also for us under Pontius Pilate. He suffered and was buried; And the third day He rose again, according to the Scriptures; And ascended into heaven, And sitteth on the right hand of the Father; And He shall come again with glory to judge both the quick and the dead; Whose kingdom shall have no end.

And I believe in the Holy Ghost, The Lord and Giver of Life, Who proceedeth from the Father and the Son, Who with the Father and the Son together is worshipped and glorified, Who spake by the Prophets. And I believe one holy Christian and Apostolic Church. I acknowledge one Baptism for the remission of sins; And I look for the Resurrection of the dead; And the Life of the world to come. Amen.

Then shall be sung a Hymn or a Selection by the Choir, after which shall follow the Sermon.

THE SERMON.

The Sermon ended, the Minister shall say:

The grace of the Lord Jesus Christ, the love of God, and the communion of the Holy Ghost, be with you all. Amen.

While the Congregation sing a Hymn, the Minister shall go to the Altar and at the close of the Hymn shall sing or say:

The Lord be with you.

The Congregation, standing to the end of the Benediction, shall sing:

And with thy spirit.

Then shall the Minister say:

Let us pray.

Turning to the Altar, he shall say:

O Lord, our Heavenly Father, watch over us and protect us from all evil; and grant that we may this night rest secure under Thy care. Preserve and bless Thy Church and our Government. Look in tender mercy upon them that are in sickness, in need, or in danger. Have mercy upon all men. And finally, when our last evening shall come, let us depart in peace; through Jesus Christ, Thy Son, our Lord.

Our Father, Who art in heaven, Hallowed be Thy Name; Thy kingdom come; Thy will be done on earth, as it is in heaven; Give us this day our daily bread; And forgive us our trespasses, as we forgive those who trespass against us; And lead us not into temptation; But deliver us from evil; For Thine is the kingdom, and the power, and the glory, forever. Amen.

Then may be sung the Nunc Dimittis:

Lord, now lettest Thou Thy servant depart in peace: according to Thy Word;

For mine eyes have seen Thy salvation: which Thou hast prepared before the face of all people;

A light to lighten the Gentiles: and the glory of Thy people Israel.

Glory be to the Father, and to the Son, and to the Holy Ghost;

As it was in the beginning, is now, and ever shall be, world without end. Amen.

Then the Minister, turning to the Congregation, shall pronounce the Benediction:

The Lord bless thee, and keep thee.

The Lord make His face shine upon thee, and be gracious unto thee.

The Lord lift up His countenance upon thee, and give thee peace.

In the Name of the Father, and of the Son, and of the Holy Ghost. Amen.

The Congregation shall sing:

Amen! Amen! Amen!

The Service shall close with silent prayer.

OH, COME, LET US SING UNTO THE LORD: LET US MAKE A JOYFUL NOISE TO THE ROCK OF OUR SALVATION.

LET US COME BEFORE HIS PRESENCE WITH THANKSGIVING: AND MAKE A JOYFUL NOISE UNTO HIM WITH PSALMS. *Ps. 95: 1, 2.*

HYMNS.

I. THE CHURCH YEAR.

ADVENT.

1. 8.7.8.7.7.7.8.8.

1 COMFORT, comfort ye my people,
  Speak ye peace, thus saith our God;
Comfort those who sit in darkness,
  Mourning 'neath their sorrows' load;
Speak ye to Jerusalem
Of the peace that waits for them;
Tell her that her sins I cover,
And her warfare now is over.

2 For the Herald's voice is crying
  In the desert far and near,
Bidding all men to repentance,
  Since the kingdom now is here.
Oh, that warning cry obey,
Now prepare for God a way!
Let the valleys rise to meet Him,
And the hills bow down to greet Him.

3 Make ye straight what long was crooked,
Make the rougher places plain:
Let your hearts be true and humble,
As befits His holy reign;
For the glory of the Lord
Now o'er earth is shed abroad,
And all flesh shall see the token
That His Word is never broken.

John Olearius.

2.

7.6.7.6.7.7.6.6.

1 PREPARE the way, O Zion!
Ye awful deeps, rise high,
Sink low, ye towering mountains;
The Lord is drawing nigh:
The righteous King of glory,
Foretold in sacred story.
Oh, blest is He that came
In God the Father's Name!

2 O Zion, He approacheth,
Thy Lord and King for aye!
Palm-branches strew with gladness,
Spread garments in His way.
God's promise faileth never,
Hosanna sound forever!
Oh, blest is He that came
In God the Father's Name!

3 Fling wide thy portals, Zion,
And hail thy glorious King;
His tidings of salvation
To every people bring,

Who, waiting yet in sadness,
Would sing His praise with gladness.
Oh, blest is He that came
In God the Father's Name!

4 He cometh not with warriors,
And not with pomp and show;
Yet smiteth He with terror
Sin, death, and every foe.
The Spirit's sword He wieldeth,
Not e'en to death He yieldeth.
Oh, blest is He that came
In God the Father's Name!

5 Give heed, thou sinful people,
Thy King and Savior own:
The kingdom which He foundeth
Is not an earthly one;
No power can overthrow it,
Nor earthly wisdom know it.
Oh, blest is He that came
In God the Father's Name!

6 The throne which He ascendeth
Is fixed in heaven above:
His sanctified dominion
Is light alone and love.
With grace and peace abounding
His praise be ever sounding.
Oh, blest is He that came
In God the Father's Name!

7 Jerusalem is fallen,
And closed its temple-door;
Its sacrifices ended;
Its scepter is no more.
Christ's kingdom never ceaseth,
Its glory still increaseth.
Oh, blest is He that came
In God the Father's name!

F. M. Franzen.

3.

L. M. D.

1 LIFT up your heads, ye mighty gates!
Behold the King of glory waits;
The King of kings is drawing near,
The Savior of the world is here;
Life and salvation He doth bring,
Wherefore rejoice, and gladly sing:
All praise and glory be to Thee,
Lord Jesus Christ, eternally.

2 The Lord is just, a Helper tried,
Mercy is ever at His side;
His kingly crown is holiness,
His scepter, pity in distress,
The end of all our woe He brings;
Wherefore the earth is glad and sings:
All praise and glory be to Thee,
Lord Jesus Christ, eternally.

3 Oh, blest the land, the city blest,
Where Christ the Ruler is confest!
Oh, happy hearts and happy homes
To whom this King in triumph comes!

The cloudless Sun of joy He is,
Who bringeth pure delight and bliss.
All praise and glory be to Thee,
Lord Jesus Christ, eternally.

4 Fling wide the portals of your heart;
Make it a temple, set apart
From earthly use for heaven's employ,
Adorned with prayer, and love, and joy;
So shall your Sovereign enter in,
And new and nobler life begin.
All praise and glory be to Thee,
Lord Jesus Christ, eternally.

5 Redeemer, come! I open wide
My heart to Thee; here, Lord, abide!
Let me Thine inner presence feel,
Thy grace and love in me reveal;
Thy Holy Spirit guide us on,
Until our glorious goal be won.
All praise and glory be to Thee,
Lord Jesus Christ, etern lly.

George Weissel.

4.

6 6 7.7 8.7.

1 O BRIDE of Christ, rejoice!
Exultant raise thy voice
To hail the day of glory
Foretold in sacred story.
Sing hosanna, praise, and glory,
Our King, we bow before Thee.

2 Let shouts of gladness rise
Triumphant to the skies.
Here comes the King most glorious
To reign o'er all victorius.
Sing hosanna, etc.

3 He wears no kingly crown,
Yet as a king He's known;
Though not arrayed in splendor,
He still makes death surrender.
Sing hosanna, etc.

4 The weak and timid find
Him gentle, good, and kind;
To them He gives a treasure
Of bliss beyond all measure.
Sing hosanna, etc.

5 Then go thy Lord to meet;
Strew palm-leaves at His feet;
Thy garments spread before Him,
And honor and adore Him.
Sing hosanna, etc.

6 Thy heart now open wide,
Bid Christ with thee abide;
He graciously will hear thee,
And be forever near thee.
Sing hosanna, etc.

7 E'en babes with one accord
With thee shall praise the Lord,

And every Gentile nation
Respond with exultation.
Sing hosanna, etc.

J. O. Wallin.

5.

8.7.8.7.8.8.7.

1 THOU, Jesus Christ, didst man become
From death us to deliver;
Thy pitying eye beheld our doom,
That we were lost forever;
Thou gavest hope in direst need
When death and hell with gaping greed
Were ready to devour us.

2 Thou couldst not bear that Satan's might
Had in its grasp enslaved us;
In pity Thou didst for us fight,
And hast in mercy saved us.
From heaven Thou cam'st for our release,
To purchase our eternal peace
By bitter death and suffering.

3 And Thou hast taught us in Thy Word
That faith shall life inherit,
For Thou art merciful, O Lord,
And sav'st us by Thy merit,
If we but simply do believe
That all Thy children shall receive
The blessings Thou hast promised.

4 Our brother Thou art now become—
An honor beyond measure!

Thou wouldst our life with mercy crown,
And give us richest treasure.
The world's contempt we need not fear,
God's Son is now our brother dear:
What power can now destroy us?

5 All praise to Thee eternally,
For all Thy gracious favor;
We are God's children now with Thee,
Lord Jesus Christ, our Savior!
Well may we one and all rejoice,
And praise our God with heart and voice;
He is our gracious Father.

O. Petri.

6.

C. M.

1 HARK, the glad sound, the Savior comes,
The Savior promised long!
Let every heart prepare a throne,
And every voice a song.

2 On Him the Spirit, largely poured,
Exerts His sacred fire;
Wisdom, and might, and zeal, and love
His holy breast inspire.

3 He comes the prisoners to release,
In Satan's bondage held:
The gates of brass before him burst,
The iron fetters yield.

4 He comes from thickest films of vice
To clear the mental ray,

And on the eyeballs of the blind
  To pour celestial day.

5 He comes, the broken heart to bind,
  The bleeding soul to cure,
And with the treasures of His grace
  To enrich the humble poor.

6 Our glad hosannas, Prince of Peace!
  Thy welcome shall proclaim;
And heaven's eternal arches ring
  With Thy beloved Name.

Philip Doddridge.

7. C. M.

1 ARISE, the kingdom is at hand,
  The King is drawing nigh;
Arise with joy, thou faithful band,
  To meet the Lord most high.

2 Look up, ye souls weighed down with care,
  The Sovereign is not far;
Look up, faint hearts, from your despair,
  Behold the morning star!

3 Look up, ye drooping hearts, to-day!
  The King is very near:
Oh, cast your griefs and fears away,
  For lo, your Help is here!

4 Hope, O ye broken hearts, at last!
  The King comes on in might;
He loved us in the ages past,
  When we lay wrapt in night.

5 Now fear and wrath to joy give place,
Now are our sorrows o'er,
Since God hath made us in His grace
His children evermore.

6 Oh, rich the gifts Thou bringest us!
Thyself made poor and weak;
Oh, love beyond compare that thus
Can foes and sinners seek!

7 For this we raise a gladsome voice
On high to Thee alone,
And evermore with thanks rejoice
Before Thy glorious throne.

John Rist.

8.

7.6.7.6.D.

1 HAIL to the Lord's Anointed,
Great David's greater Son!
Hail, in the time appointed,
His reign on earth begun!
He comes to break oppression,
To set the captive free;
To take away transgression,
And rule in equity.

2 He comes with succor speedy
To those who suffer wrong;
To help the poor and needy,
And bid the weak be strong;
To give them songs for sighing;
Their darkness turn to light,
Whose souls, condemned and dying,
Were precious in His sight.

3 He shall come down like showers
Upon the fruitful earth;
And love, joy, hope, like flowers,
Spring in His path to birth.
Before Him, on the mountains,
Shall peace, the herald, go;
And righteousness, in fountains,
From hill to valley flow.

4 For Him shall prayer unceasing
And daily vows ascend;
His kingdom still increasing,
A kingdom without end.
The tide of time shall never
His covenant remove;
His Name shall stand for ever;
That Name to us is Love.

James Montgomery.

9.

7.6.7 6.D.

1 OH! how shall I receive Thee,
How greet Thee, Lord, aright?
All nations long to see Thee,
My Hope, my heart's Delight!
Oh! kindle, Lord most holy,
Thy lamp within my breast,
To do in spirit lowly
All that may please Thee best

2 Thy Zion palms is strewing,
And branches fresh and fair;
My heart, its powers renewing,
An anthem shall prepare.

My soul puts off her sadness
Thy glories to proclaim;
With all her strength and gladness
She fain would serve Thy Name.

3 I lay in fetters groaning,
Thou com'st to set me free:
I stood, my shame bemoaning,
Thou com'st to honor me.
A glory Thou dost give me,
A treasure safe on high,
That will not fail nor leave me
As earthly riches fly.

4 Love caused Thine incarnation,
Love brought Thee down to me;
Thy thirst for my salvation
Procured my liberty.
Oh, love beyond all telling,
That led Thee to embrace,
In love all love excelling,
Our lost and fallen race!

5 Rejoice, then, ye sad-hearted,
Who sit in deepest gloom,
Who mourn o'er joys departed,
And tremble at your doom:
He who alone can cheer you,
Is standing at the door;
He brings.His pity near you,
And bids you weep no more.

Paul Gerhardt.

10.

7s.

1 COME, Thou Savior of our race,
Choicest Gift of heavenly grace!
O Thou blessed Virgin's Son,
Be Thy race on earth begun.

2 Not of mortal blood or birth,
He descends from heaven to earth:
By the Holy Ghost conceived,
Truly man to be believed.

3 Wondrous birth! O wondrous Child!
Of the Virgin, undefiled!
Though by all the world disowned,
Still to be in heaven enthroned.

4 From the Father forth He came.
And returneth to the same;
Captive leading death and hell,—
High the song of triumph swell!

5 Equal to the Father now,
Though to dust Thou once didst bow,
Boundless shall Thy kingdom be;
When shall we its glories see?

6 Brightly doth Thy manger shine!
Glorious is its light divine:
Let not sin o'ercloud this light,
Ever be our faith thus bright.

Ambrose. Martin Luther.

11.

8.7.8.7.D.

1 COME, Thou long-expected Jesus,
Born to set Thy people free;
From our fears and sins release us,
Let us find our rest in Thee.
Israel's Strength and Consolation,
Hope of all the earth Thou art;
Dear Desire of every nation,
Joy of every longing heart.

2 Born Thy people to deliver;
Born a Child, and yet a King;
Born to reign in us for ever,
Now Thy gracious kingdom bring.
By Thine own eternal Spirit,
Rule in all our hearts alone;
By Thine all-sufficient merit,
Raise us to Thy glorious throne.

C. Wesley.

12.

7.6.7.6.D.

1 REJOICE, all ye believers.
And let your lights appear;
The evening is advancing,
And darker night is near.
The Bridegroom is arising,
And soon He draweth nigh.
Up! pray, and watch, and wrestle—
At midnight comes the cry!

2 The watchers on the mountain
Proclaim the Bridegroom near;

Go meet Him as He cometh,
  With hallelujahs clear.
The marriage-feast is waiting,
  The gates wide-open stand;
Up, up, ye heirs of glory,
  The Bridegroom is at hand!

3 Ye saints, who here in patience
  Your cross and sufferings bore,
Shall live and reign for ever,
  When sorrow is no more.
Around the throne of glory
  The Lamb ye shall behold,
In triumph cast before Him
  Your diadems of gold!

4 Our Hope and Expectation,
  O Jesus, now appear;
Arise, Thou Sun so longed for,
  O'er this benighted sphere!
With hearts and hands uplifted,
  We plead, O Lord, to see
The day of earth's redemption,
  That brings us unto Thee!

Laurentius Laurenti.

CHRISTMAS.

13.

No. 47; 108.

1 ALL hail to thee, O blessed morn!
To tidings, long by prophets borne,
Hast thou fulfillment given.
O sacred and immortal day,
When unto earth, in glorious ray,
Descends the grace of heaven!
Singing | Sounds are blending,
Ringing | Praises sending
Unto heaven
For the Lord to mankind given.

2 'Tis God's own Image and, withal,
The Son of Man, that mortals all
May find in Him a brother.
He comes, with peace and love to bide
On earth, the erring race to guide,
And help, as could no other;
Rather | Closer, fonder.
Gather | Sheep that wander,
Feed and fold them,
Than let evil powers hold them.

3 He tears, like other men, will shed,
Our sorrows share, and be our aid,
Through His eternal power;
The Lord's good will unto us show,
And mingle in our cup of woe
The drops of mercy's shower;

Dying, | Through His passion
Buying | Our salvation.
And to mortals
Opening the heavenly portals.

4 He comes, for our redemption sent,
And by His glory heaven is rent
To close upon us never;
Our blessed Shepherd He would be,
Whom we may follow faithfully
And be with Him forever;
Higher, | Glory winging,
Nigher | Praises singing
To the Father
And His Son, our Lord and Brother.

J. O. Wallin.

14

L. M.

1 BEHOLD the joyful day is nigh,
And angels' voices from on high
Proclaim the news in early morn
That the Good Shepherd now is born.

2 In quiet splendor forth He comes,
The scattered sheep and tender lambs
He'll gather, and their fold prepare
With all a shepherd's tender care.

3 So meek and mild we Him behold;
And not with silver nor with gold,
But by His suffering and His death,
He saves us from eternal wrath.

4 His church, though small its seed may be,
Shall rise a tall and mighty tree,
With fruitful branches spreading o'er
The earth till time shall be no more.

5 His Word shall like a gentle rain
Make all the earth rejoice again,
And yield a rich and blest increase
In truth, and purity, and peace.

6 And heaven and earth shall pass away,
Yet shall His Word remain for aye;
All tongues shall soon with one accord
Proclaim Him Savior, God, and Lord.

7 Arise and shine, thy Light is come,
O humankind, O Christendom;
Thy glory and thy peace is here;
The Savior of the world draws near.

8 All praise and glory be to Thee
For wisdom, power, and majesty;
And for Thy grace and mercy, Lord,
Forever be Thy Name adored.

J. O. Wallin.

15.

7.6.7.6.D

1 REJOICE, rejoice, ye Christians,
With all your hearts, this morn!
Oh, hear the blessed tidings,
The Lord, the Christ, is born,

Now brought us by the angels
  That stand about God's throne;
Oh, lovely are the voices
  That make such tidings known!

2 Oh, hearken to their singing!
  This Child shall be your Friend;
The Father so hath willed it,
  That thus your woes should end.
The Son is freely given,
  That in Him ye may have
The Father's grace and blessing,
  And know He loves to save.

3 Nor deem the form too lowly
  That clothes Him at this hour;
For know ye what it hideth?
  'Tis God's almighty power.
Though now within the manger
  So poor and weak He lies,
He is the Lord of all things,
  He reigns above the skies.

4 Sin, death, and hell, and Satan
  Have lost the victory;
This Child shall overthrow them,
  As ye shall surely see.
Their wrath shall naught avail them;
  Fear not, their reign is o'er;
This Child shall overthrow them,—
  Oh, hear, and doubt no more!

From the German.

16.

L. M.

1 GOOD news from heaven the angels bring,
Glad tidings to the earth they sing:
To us this day a Child is given,
To crown us with the joy of heaven.

2 This is the Christ, our God and Lord,
Who in all need shall aid afford;
He will Himself our Savior be,
And from our sins will set us free.

3 To us that blessedness He brings,
Which from the Father's bounty springs:
That in the heavenly realm we may
With Him enjoy eternal day.

4 All hail, Thou noble Guest, this morn,
Whose love did not the sinner scorn:
In my distress Thou com'st to me,
What thanks shall I return to Thee?

5 Were earth a thousand times as fair,
Beset with gold and jewels rare,
She yet were far too poor to be
A narrow cradle, Lord, for Thee.

6 Ah, dearest Jesus, holy Child,
Make Thee a bed, soft, undefiled,
Within my heart, that it may be
A quiet chamber kept for Thee.

7 Praise God upon His heavenly throne,
Who gave to us His only Son:

For this His hosts, on joyful wing,
A blest New Year of mercy sing.

Martin Luther.

17.

L. M.

1 IMMANUEL, we sing Thy praise,
Thou Prince of Life, Thou Fount of Grace,
With all Thy saints, Thee, Lord, we sing;
Praise, honor, thanks, to Thee we bring.

2 E'er since the world began to be,
How many a heart hath longed for Thee!
And Thou, O long-expected Guest,
Hast come at last to make us blest!

3 Now art Thou here: we know Thee now;
In lowly manger liest Thou:
A Child, yet makest all things great;
Poor, yet is earth Thy robe of state.

4 Now fearlessly I come to Thee:
From sin and grief Thou set'st me free:
Thou bear'st the wrath, dost death destroy,
And turnest sorrow into joy.

5 Thou art my Head, my Lord divine:
I am Thy member, wholly Thine;
And by Thy Spirit's gracious power
Will seek to serve Thee evermore.

6 Thus will I sing Thy praises here,
With joyful spirit year by year:
And in Thy courts of joy above
Forever will I sing Thy love.

Paul Gerhardt.

18.

L. M.

1 THE happy Christmas comes once more,
The heavenly Guest is at the door,
The blessed words the shepherds thrill,
The joyous tidings: Peace, Good-will.

2 To David's city let us fly,
Where angels sing beneath the sky;
Through plain and village pressing near,
And news from God with shepherds hear.

3 Oh, let us go with quiet mind,
The gentle Babe with shepherds find,
To gaze on Him who gladdens them,
The loveliest flower of Jesse's stem.

4 The lowly Savior meekly lies,
Laid off the splendor of the skies;
No crown bedecks His forehead fair,
No pearl, nor gem, nor silk is there.

5 No human glory, might and gold,
The lovely Infant's form enfold;
The manger and the swaddlings poor
Are His, whom angels' songs adore.

6 Oh, wake our hearts, in gladness sing,
And keep our Christmas with our King,
Till living song, from loving souls,
Like sound of mighty waters rolls.

7 O holy Child, Thy manger streams
Till earth and heaven glow with its beams,
Till midnight noon's bright light has won,
And Jacob's Star outshines the sun.

8 Thou Patriarchs' joy, Thou Prophets' song,
Thou heavenly Day-Spring, looked for long,
Thou Son of man, Incarnate Word,
Great David's Son, great David's Lord!

9 Come, Jesus, glorious heavenly Guest,
Keep Thine own Christmas in our breast,
Then David's harp-strings, hushed so long,
Shall swell our Jubilee of song.

From the Danish.

19.

C. M.

1 JOY to the world; the Lord is come!
Let earth receive her King;
Let every heart prepare Him room,
And heaven and nature sing.

2 Joy to the earth; the Savior reigns!
Let men their songs employ;
While fields and floods, rocks, hills, and plains,
Repeat the sounding joy.

3 No more let sins and sorrows grow,
Nor thorns infest the ground;
He comes to make His blessings flow
Far as the curse is found.

4 He rules the world with truth and grace,
And makes the nations prove
The glories of His righteousness,
And wonders of His love.

Isaac Watts.

20.

11s.

1 COME hither, ye faithful, triumphantly sing;
Come see in the manger your Savior and King!
To Bethlehem hasten, with joyful accord;
Oh, come ye, come hither, to worship the Lord!

2 True Son of the Father, He comes from the skies;
To be born of a Virgin He does not despise:
To Bethlehem hasten, with joyful accord;
Oh, come ye, come hither, to worship the Lord!

3 Hark, hark to the angels, all singing in heaven,
"To God in the highest all glory be given!"
To Bethlehem hasten, with joyful accord;
Oh, come ye, come hither, to worship the Lord!

4 To Thee, then, O Jesus, this day of Thy birth,
Be glory and honor through heaven and earth.
True Godhead incarnate, omnipotent Word!
Oh, come, let us hasten to worship the Lord!

From the Latin. E. Caswall.

21.

7.6.7.6.

1 A GREAT and mighty wonder
Our Christmas Festal brings

On earth, a lowly Infant,
Behold the King of kings!

2 The Word is made incarnate,
Descending from on high;
And cherubim sing anthems
To shepherds, from the sky.

3 And we with them triumphant,
Repeat the hymn again:
"To God on high be glory,
And peace on earth to men!"

4 Since all He comes to ransom,
By all be He adored,
The Infant born in Bethlehem,
The Savior and the Lord!

5 And idol forms shall perish,
And error shall decay,
And Christ shall wield His sceptre,
Our Lord and God for aye.

Anatolius. John Mason Neale.

22.

8.7.8.7.

1 HARK! what mean those holy voices
Sweetly sounding through the skies?
Lo! the angelic host rejoices;
Heavenly hallelujahs rise.

2 Listen to the wondrous story,
Which they chant in hymns of joy:
"Glory in the highest, glory!
Glory be to God most high!

3 "Peace on earth, good-will from heaven,
Reaches far as man is found;
Souls redeemed, and sins forgiven;
Loud our golden harps shall sound.

4 "Christ is born, the great Anointed;
Heaven and earth His praises sing!
Oh, receive whom God appointed
For your Prophet, Priest, and King.

5 "Hasten, mortals, to adore Him;
Learn His Name, and taste His joy;
Till in heaven ye sing before Him,
Glory be to God most high!"

6 Let us learn the wondrous story
Of our great Redeemer's birth;
Spread the brightness of His glory,
Till it covers all the earth!

J. Cawood.

23.

8.7 8.7.4.7.

1 ANGELS, from the realms of glory,
Wing your flight o'er all the earth;
Ye, who sang creation's story,
Now proclaim Messiah's birth:
Come and worship,
Worship Christ, the new-born King.

2 Shepherds, in the fields abiding,
Watching o'er your flocks by night,
God with man is now residing,

Yonder shines the heavenly light:
Come and worship,
Worship Christ, the new-born King.

3 Sages, leave your contemplations;
Brighter visions beam afar:
Seek the great Desire of nations,
Ye have seen His natal star:
Come and worship,
Worship Christ, the new-born King.

4 Saints, before the altar bending,
Watching long in hope and fear,
Suddenly the Lord, descending,
In His temple shall appear:
Come and worship,
Worship Christ, the new-born King.

5 Sinners, wrung with true repentance,
Doomed for guilt to endless pains;
Justice now revokes the sentence,
Mercy calls you, break your chains:
Come and worship,
Worship Christ, the new-born King.

J. Montgomery.

24.

7s.

1 HARK! the herald angels sing
Glory to the new-born King!
Peace on earth, and mercy mild,
God and sinners reconciled!

2 Joyful, all ye nations, rise,
Join the triumph of the skies;
Universal nature say,
Christ the Lord is born to-day!

3 Veiled in flesh, the Godhead see,
Hail the incarnate Deity!
Pleased as Man with men to appear,
Jesus, our Immanuel here!

4 Hail, the heavenly Prince of Peace,
Hail, the Sun of Righteousness!
Light and life to all He brings,
Risen with healing in His wings.

5 Mild He lays His glory by,
Born that man no more may die;
Born to raise the sons of earth;
Born to give them second birth.

6 Come, Desire of nations, come,
Fix in us Thy humble home;
Oh, to all Thyself impart,
Formed in each believing heart!

C. Wesley. a.

25.

8.7. 12 lines

1 HARK, a burst of heavenly music
  From a band of seraphs bright,
Suddenly to earth descending
  In the calm and silent night!
And the shepherds of Judea,
  Watching in the earliest dawn,

Hear the glad and joyful tidings,
  "Jesus, Prince of Peace, is born!"
Sweet and clear those angel voices,
  Echoing through the starry sky,
As they chant the heavenly chorus,
  "Glory be to God on high!"

2 Slumbering in a lowly manger,
  Lies the mighty Lord of all;
And before the holy Stranger
  See the trembling shepherds fall.
He has come, the long-expected,
  Full of wisdom, love, and grace,
To redeem His ruined creatures,
  To restore our fallen race.
So let angels wake the chorus!
  So let ransomed men reply!
Chanting the celestial anthem,
  "Glory be to God on high!"

3 And this joyful Christmas morning,
  Breaking o'er the world below,
Tells again the wondrous story
  Shepherds heard so long ago.
Who shall still our tuneful voices,
  Who the tide of praise shall stem,
Which the blessed angels taught us
  In the fields of Bethlehem?
Hark! we hear again the chorus,
  Ringing through the starry sky,
And we join the heavenly anthem,
  "Glory be to God on high!"

26.

8.4.4.6.D.

1 ALL my heart this night rejoices,
As I hear,
Far and near,
Sweetest angel voices;
"Christ is born" their choirs are singing,
Till the air
Everywhere
Now with joy is ringing.

2 Come and banish all your sadness,
One and all,
Great and small,
Come with songs of gladness,
Love Him who with love is yearning;
Hail the star
That from far
Bright with hope is burning.

3 Hither come, ye heavy-hearted,
Who for sin,
Deep within,
Long and sore have smarted;
For the poisoned wounds you're feeling
Help is near,
One is here
Mighty for their healing.

4 Hither come, ye poor and wretched,
Know His will
Is to fill
Every hand outstreched;

Here are riches without measure,
Here forget
All regret,
Fill your hearts with treasure.

5 Faithfully Thee, Lord, I'll cherish,
Live to Thee,
And with Thee
Dying, shall not perish;
But shall dwell with Thee forever,
Far on high,
In the joy
That can alter never.

P. Gerhardt.

27.

7.6.7.6.

1 WHEN Christmas morn is dawning
In faith I would repair
Unto the lowly manger;
My Savior lieth there.

2 How kind, O loving Savior,
To come from heaven above!
From sin and evil save us,
And keep us in Thy love.

3 We need Thee, blessed Jesus,
Our dearest friend Thou art;
Forbid that we by sinning
Should grieve Thy loving heart.

From Hemlandssånger.

28.

7.6.8.6.D.

1 O LITTLE town of Bethlehem,
How still we see thee lie;
Above thy deep and dreamless sleep
The silent stars go by;
Yet in thy darkness shineth
The everlasting Light;
The hopes and fears of all the years
Are met in thee to-night.

2 For Christ is born of Mary,
And gathered all above,
While mortals sleep, the angels keep
Their watch of wondering love.
O morning stars, together
Proclaim the holy birth!
And praises sing to God our King,
And peace to men on earth.

3 How silently, how silently,
The wondrous gift is given!
So God imparts to human hearts
The blessings of His heaven.
No ear may hear His coming,
But in this world of sin,
Where meek souls will receive Him still,
The dear Christ enters in.

4 O holy Child of Bethlehem!
Descend to us, we pray;
Cast out our sin, and enter in,
Be born in us to-day.

We hear the Christmas angels,
  The great glad tidings tell:
Oh, come to us, abide with us,
  Our Lord Immanuel!

Phillips Brooks.

29.

6.6.8.9.6.

1 SILENT night! Holy night!
All is calm, all is bright,
Round yon Virgin Mother and Child;
Holy Infant, so tender and mild,
    Sleep in heavenly peace.

2 Silent night! Holy night!
Shepherds quake at the sight:
Glories stream from heaven afar;
Heavenly hosts sing alleluia,
  Christ, the Savior, is born!

3 Silent night! Holy night!
Son of God, love's pure light
Radiant beams from Thy holy face,
With the dawn of redeeming grace,
  Jesus, Lord, at Thy birth.

J. Mohr.

30.

7.6.7.6.D.

1 I LOVE to hear the story,
    Which angel voices tell;
  How once the King of glory
    Came down on earth to dwell;

I am both weak and sinful,
But this I surely know,
The Lord came down to save me,
Because He loved me so.

2 I'm glad my blessed Savior
Was once a child like me,
To show how pure and holy
His little ones should be;
And if I try to follow
His footsteps here below,
He never will forget me,
Because He loves me so.

3 To sing His love and mercy
My sweetest songs I'll raise;
And though I cannot see Him,
I know He hears my praise;
For He has kindly promised
That even I may go
To sing among His angels,
Because He loves me so.

Mrs. Miller.

31.

8.7.8.7.D.

1 NOW we bring our Christmas treasures,
Loving thoughts and deeds we bring,
Childlike hearts we gladly offer
To the Child, the children's King;
To the child, who, in the manger,
Lay upon that Christmas morn,
When the angels came to tell us
That the children's King was born.

2 And He lives, throughout the ages,
Lives and reigns in earth and sky;
Angel hosts still sing the glory
Of the children's King on high.
Yet He cares for children's praises:
So, with heart and voice we sing;
Glory in the highest, glory
To the Child, the children's King!

Maria H. Bulfinch.

32.

8.7.8.7.

1 HARK! what sounds are sweetly stealing,
Soft through Bethlehem's midnight air?
Louder yet, and louder pealing,
Angel accents sure are there.

2 See! a light from heaven is streaming,
Night and darkness quit the plain;
See! an angel brightly beaming,
Followed by a radiant train.

3 "Fear not, shepherds! glad my story,
Tidings of the greatest joy:
Christ is born, the Lord of Glory!
I proclaim a Savior nigh."

4 Thus the angel, then ascending,
Seeks again the realms of light;
Now the chorus faintly ending,
All is silence, all is night.

NEW YEAR.

33.

L. M.

1 LO! Jesus' Name rich comfort is,
Our haven safe, in all distress.
Through Jesus grace we do receive,
He best doth all our cares relieve.

2 God's only Son, O Jesus mild,
Forgive us, sinful and beguiled!
Thou seest and canst help our need,
Thou who art God and man indeed.

3 In Thee is all our righteousness,
In Thee all peace and happiness.
Who trusteth in Thy Holy Name,
He shall be saved from sin and shame.

4 We praise Thee for Thy living Word,
Baptismal grace, Thy table, Lord.
Grant us Thy help in all our strife,
And after death eternal life.

B. Förtsch.

34.

C. M.

1 HOW sweet the Name of Jesus sounds
In a believer's ear!
It soothes his sorrows, heals his wounds,
And drives away his fear.

2 It makes the wounded spirit whole,
And calms the troubled breast;
'Tis manna to the hungry soul,
And to the weary rest.

3 Dear Name! the Rock on which I build,
My Shield and Hiding-place;
My never-failing Treasury, filled
With boundless stores of grace.

4 By Thee my prayers acceptance gain,
Although with sin defiled:
Satan accuses me in vain,
And I am owned a child.

5 Weak is the effort of my heart,
And cold my warmest thought;
But, when I see Thee as Thou art,
I'll praise Thee as I ought.

6 Till then, I would Thy love proclaim
With every fleeting breath;
And may the music of Thy Name
Refresh my soul in death.

John Newton.

35.

7.6.7.6.8.8.7.7.

1 JESUS, Name all names above,
Jesus, best and dearest,
Jesus, Fount of perfect love,
Holiest, tenderest, nearest;
Jesus, Source of grace completest,
Jesus purest, Jesus sweetest,
Jesus, Well of power divine,
Make me, keep me, seal me Thine!

2 Thou didst call the prodigal;
Thou didst pardon Mary;

Thou whose words can never fall,
Love can never vary;
Thou whose wounds are ever pleading,
And Thy passion interceding,
From my misery let me rise
To a home in paradise!

3 Jesus, crowned with thorns for me,
Scourged for my transgression!
Witnessing, through agony,
That Thy good confession;
Jesus, clad in purple raiment,
For my evils making payment;
Let not all Thy woe and pain,
Let not Calvary, be in vain!

4 When I reach death's bitter sea,
And its waves roll higher,
Jesus, come, be near to me,
As the storm draws nigher:
Jesus, leave me not to languish,
Helpless, hopeless, full of anguish!
Tell me, — "Verily, I say,
Thou shalt be with Me to-day!"

Theoctistus of the Studium.

36.

7s.

1 JESUS, Name of wondrous love!
Name all other names above!
Name at which must every knee
Bow in deep humility!

2 Jesus, Name of priceless worth
To the fallen sons of earth!
For the promise that it gave:
"Jesus shall His people save."

3 Jesus, Name of mercy mild,
Given to the holy Child,
When the cup of human woe
First He tasted here below!

4 Jesus, only Name that's given
Under all the mighty heaven,
Whereby man, to sin enslaved,
Bursts his fetters, and is saved!

5 Jesus, Name of wondrous love!
Human Name of Him above!
Pleading only this we flee,
Helpless, O our God, to Thee.

William Walsham How. a.

37.

8.7.8.7. and Chorus.

1 TAKE the Name of Jesus with you,
Child of sorrow and of woe;
It will joy and comfort give you,
Take it, then, where'er you go.

Chorus—Precious Name, oh, how sweet,
Hope of earth and joy of heaven!
Precious Name, oh, how sweet,
Hope of earth and joy of heaven!

2 Take the Name of Jesus ever,
As a shield from every snare;
If temptations round you gather,
Breathe that holy Name in prayer.
Chorus—Precious Name, etc.

3 Oh, the precious Name of Jesus!
How it thrills our souls with joy,
When His loving arms receive us,
And His songs our tongues employ.
Chorus—Precious Name, etc.

4 At the Name of Jesus bowing,
Falling prostrate at His feet,
King of kings in heaven we'll crown Him,
When our journey is complete.
Chorus—Precious Name, etc.

Mrs. Lydia Baxter.

38.

8.7.8.7. Iambic, and Chorus.

1 THERE is no Name so sweet on earth,
No Name so sweet in heaven,
The Name before His wondrous birth
To Christ the Savior given.
Chorus—We love to sing around our King,
And hail Him blessed Jesus;
For there's no word ear ever heard
So dear, so sweet as Jesus.

2 His human Name they did proclaim
When Abram's son they sealed Him,

The Name that still by God's good will,
  Deliverer revealed Him.
    Chorus—We love to sing, etc.

3 And when He hung upon the tree,
  They wrote this Name above Him;
That all might see the reason we
  For evermore must love Him.
    Chorus—We love to sing, etc.

4 So now, upon His Father's throne,
  Almighty to release us
From sin and pains, in glory reigns
  The Prince and Savior Jesus.
    Chorus—We love to sing, etc.

5 To Jesus every knee shall bow,
  And every tongue confess Him,
And we unite with saints in light,
  To honor and to bless Him.
    Chorus—We love to sing, etc.

6 O Jesus, by that matchless Name,
  Thy grace shall fail us never;
To-day as yesterday the same,
  Thou art the same for ever.
    Chorus—Then let us sing, etc.

G. W. Bethune. a.

39. L. M.

1 THE old year now hath passed away,
  We thank Thee, O our God, to-day,

That Thou has kept us through the year,
When danger and distress were near.

2 We pray Thee, O Eternal Son,
Who with the Father reign'st as One,
To guard and rule Thy Christendom
Through all the ages yet to come.

3 Take not Thy saving Word away,
Our souls' true comfort, staff, and stay;
Abide with us and keep us free
From errors, following only Thee.

4 Oh, help us to forsake all sin,
A new and holier course begin;
Mark not what has been done amiss;
A happier, better year be this.

5 Grant us this year to live in Thee,
Or die if so Thy will shall be,
To rise again when Thou shalt come,
And enter our eternal home.

6 There shall we thank Thee, and adore,
With all the angels evermore;
Lord Jesus Christ, increase our faith
To praise Thy Name through life and death.

J. Steuerlein.

40.

9.8.9.8.8.8.

1 HELP us, O Lord, behold, we enter
Upon another year to-day;
In Thee our hopes and thoughts now center,

Renew our courage for the way:
New life, new strength, new happiness
We ask of Thee, oh, hear and bless!

2 May every plan and undertaking
This year be all begun with Thee,
When I am sleeping or am waking,
Still let me know Thou art with me;
Abroad do Thou my footsteps guide,
At home be ever at my side.

3 Be this a time of grace and pardon;
Thy rod I take with willing mind,
But suffer naught my heart to harden,
And let me now Thy mercy find;
In Thee alone, my God, I live,
Thou only canst my sins forgive.

4 And may this year to me be holy;
Thy grace so fill my every thought,
That all my life be pure and lowly
And truthful as a Christian's ought;
So make me, while yet dwelling here,
Faithful and blest from year to year.

5 Jesus, be with me and direct me;
Jesus, my plans and hopes inspire;
Jesus, from tempting thoughts protect me;
Jesus, be all my heart's desire;
Jesus, be in my thoughts all day,
Nor suffer me to fall away.

6 And grant, Lord, when the year is over,
That it for me in peace may close;
In all things care for me, and cover
My head in time of fear and woes;
So may I, when my years are gone,
Appear with joy before Thy throne.

J. Rist.

41.

L. M.

1 GREAT God, we sing that mighty Hand,
By which supported still we stand:
The opening year Thy mercy shows;
Let mercy crown it, till it close.

2 By day, by night, at home, abroad,
Still we are guarded by our God;
By His incessant bounty fed,
By His unerring counsel led.

3 With grateful hearts the past we own;
The future, all to us unknown,
We to Thy guardian care commit,
And, peaceful, leave before Thy feet.

4 In scenes exalted or deprest,
Be Thou our joy, and Thou our rest;
Thy goodness all our hopes shall raise,
Adored through all our changing days.

5 When death shall interrupt our songs,
And seal in silence mortal tongues;
Our Helper God, in whom we trust,
In better worlds our souls shall boast.

Philip Doddridge.

42.

7s.

1 FOR Thy mercy and Thy grace,
Faithful through another year,
Hear our song of thankfulness;
Father and Redeemer, hear.

2 In our weakness and distress,
Rock of strength, be Thou our stay:
In the pathless wilderness,
Be our true and living way.

3 Who of us death's awful road
In the coming year shall tread?
With Thy rod and staff, O God,
Comfort Thou his dying head.

4 Keep us fathful; keep us pure;
Keep us evermore Thine own.
Help, oh, help us to endure;
Fit us for the promised crown.

5 So within Thy palace gate
We shall praise, on golden strings,
Thee, the only Potentate,
Lord of lords, and King of kings.

Henry Downton.

43.

7s. D.

1 WHILE with ceaseless course the sun
Hasted through the former year,
Many souls their race have run,
Never more to meet us here;

Fixed in an eternal state,
They have done with all below;
We a little longer wait,
But how little, none can know.

2 As the winged arrow flies
Speedily, the mark to find;
As the lightning from the skies
Darts, and leaves no trace behind;
Swiftly thus our fleeting days
Bear us down life's rapid stream:
Upward, Lord, our spirits raise;
All below is but a dream.

3 Thanks for mercies past receive,
Pardon of our sins renew;
Teach us henceforth how to live
With eternity in view.
Bless Thy Word to young and old,
Fill us with a Savior's love;
And when life's short tale is told,
May we dwell with Thee above.

John Newton.

44.

S. M.

1 OUR times are in Thy hand.
O God, we wish them there;
Our life, our friends, our souls we leave
Entirely to Thy care.

2 Our times are in Thy hand,
Whatever they may be,

Pleasing or painful, dark or bright,
  As best may seem to Thee.

3 Our times are in Thy hand;
  Why should we doubt or fear?
A Father's hand will never cause
  His child a needless tear.

4 Our times are in Thy hand,
  Jesus, the Crucified,
The hand our many sins have pierced,
  Is now our guard and guide.

5 Our times are in Thy hand:
  We'll always trust on Thee,
Till we have left the weary land,
  And all Thy glory see.

W. F. Lloyd.

EPIPHANY.

45. 8.4.8.8.

1 A STAR is moving through the sky,
    Halleluia!
Before the wise men, wondrously.
    Halleluia! Halleluia!

2 They know by this that heaven's great King,
    Halleluia!
Good news to them on earth doth bring.
    Halleluia! Halleluia!

3 Thus came they unto Bethlehem,
Halleluia!
Thy lamp, O Lord, is lighting them.
Halleluia! Halleluia!

4 Gold, incense, myrrh, to Him they bear,
Halleluia!
And psalms, and hymns, and songs prepare.
Halleluia! Halleluia!

5 Thus should we also, all our days,
Halleluia!
To Jesus offer holy praise.
Halleluia! Halleluia!

6 Praise to the Father, and the Son,
Halleluia!
And Holy Ghost upon one throne.
Halleluia! Halleluia!

7 Praise to the Holy Trinity,
Halleluia!
From now to all eternity.
Halleluia! Halleluia!

?L. Jonae. J. O. Wallin.

46.

7s. 6 lines.

1 AS with gladness men of old
Did the guiding star behold;
As with joy they hailed its light,
Leading onward, beaming bright:
So, most gracious God, may we
Evermore be led by Thee.

2 As with joyful steps they sped
To that lowly manger-bed,
There to bend the knee before
Him whom heaven and earth adore;
So may we, with willing feet
Ever seek Thy mercy-seat.

3 As they offered gifts most rare
At that manger rude and bare;
So may we, with holy joy,
Pure, and free from sin's alloy,
All our costliest treasures bring,
Christ, to Thee, our heavenly King.

4 Holy Jesus, every day
Keep us in the narrow way;
And, when earthly things are past,
Bring our ransomed souls at last
Where they need no star to guide,
Where no clouds Thy glory hide.

5 In the heavenly country bright
Need they no created light:
Thou its Light, its Joy, its Crown,
Thou its Sun which goes not down;
There forever may we sing
Hallelujahs to our King.

William Chatterton Dix.

47.

No. 13, 108.

1 NOW Israel's hope in triumph ends,
With angels' glorious song ascends

A star of heavenly splendor.
O'er Bethlehem it shineth bright,
And people, walking in its light,
Shall come and homage render.
Great light, | Now descendeth,
Bright light | Darkness endeth,
Day beginneth,
Light to all the world it bringeth,

2 Among us dwells in truth and grace
The hidden God, who loves our race;
He brought us all salvation.
We now behold His majesty,
The only Son's true majesty,
And bow in adoration.
Draw near, | Every nation,
And hear, | Now salvation
God bestoweth,
And His love and mercy showeth.

3 Rejoice, my soul, and bless His Name
Who to the lost and fallen came,
To open heaven's portals.
Rejoice that God will mercy show,
The broken covenant renew
With us poor sinful mortals.
Now be | Ever given
Glory | God in heaven;
Peace unending
Be to earth from heaven descending.

S. J. Hedborn.

48.

11.10.11.10.

1 BRIGHTEST and best of the sons of the morning,
Dawn on our darkness, and lend us Thine aid;
Star of the East, the horizon adorning,
Guide where our infant Redeemer is laid.

2 Cold on His cradle the dewdrops are shining;
Low lies His head with the beasts of the stall:
Angels adore Him in slumber reclining,
Maker, and Monarch, and Savior of all!

3 Say, shall we yield Him, in costly devotion,
Odors of Edom, and offerings divine?
Gems of the mountain, and pearls of the ocean,
Myrrh from the forest, or gold from the mine?

4 Vainly we offer each ample oblation;
Vainly with gifts would His favor secure:
Richer by far is the heart's adoration;
Dearer to God are the prayers of the poor.

5 Brightest and best of the sons of the morning,
Dawn on our darkness, and lend us Thine aid;
Star of the East, the horizon adorning,
Guide where our infant Redeemer is laid.

R. Heber.

49.

C. M. D.

1 O THOU, who by a star didst guide
The wise men on their way,
Until it came and stood beside
The place where Jesus lay;
Although by stars Thou dost not lead
Thy servants now below,
Thy Holy Spirit, when they need,
Will show them how to go.

2 As yet we know Thee but in part;
But still we trust Thy Word,
That blessed are the pure in heart,
For they shall see the Lord.
O Savior, give us, then, Thy grace,
To make us pure in heart;
That we may see Thee face to face
Hereafter, as Thou art.

J. M. Neale.

50.

8.7.8.7.D.

1 HAIL, Thou Source of every blessing,
Sovereign Father of mankind!
Gentiles now, Thy grace possessing,
In Thy courts admission find.
Grateful now we fall before Thee,
In Thy church obtain a place;
Now by faith behold Thy glory,
Praise Thy truth, adore Thy grace.

2 Once far off, but now invited,
We approach Thy sacred throne;

In Thy covenant united,
  Reconciled, redeemed, made one.
Now revealed to eastern sages,
  See the star of mercy shine;
Mystery hid in former ages,
  Mystery great of love divine.

3 Hail, Thou all-inviting Savior!
  Gentiles now their offerings bring;
In Thy temple seek Thy favor,
  Jesus Christ, our Lord and King.
May we, body, soul, and spirit,
  Live devoted to Thy praise,
Glorious realms of bliss inherit,
  Grateful anthems ever raise.

B. Woodd.

51.

7.6.7.6.D.

1 LIGHT of the Gentile nations,
  Thy people's joy and love,
Drawn by Thy Spirit hither,
  We gladly come to prove
Thy presence in Thy temple,
  And wait with earnest mind,
As Simeon once had waited
  His Savior God to find.

2 Yes, Lord, Thy servants meet Thee,
  E'en now, in every place
Where Thy true Word hath promised
  That they should see Thy face.

Thou yet wilt gently grant us,
Who gather round Thee here,
In faith's strong arms to bear Thee,
As once that aged seer.

3 Be Thou our Joy, our Brightness,
That shines 'mid pain and loss,
Our Sun in times of terror,
The glory round our cross:
A glow in sinking spirits,
A sunbeam in distress,
Physician, Friend in sickness,
In death our happiness.

4 Let us, O Lord, be faithful
With Simeon to the end,
That so his dying song may
From all our hearts ascend:
"O Lord, let now Thy servant
Depart in peace for aye,
Since I have seen my Savior,
Have here beheld His day."

5 My Savior, I behold Thee
Now with the eye of faith:
No foe of Thee can rob me,
Though bitter words he saith;
Within Thy heart abiding,
As Thou dost dwell in me,
No pain, no death has terrors
To part my soul from Thee!

J. Franck.

52.

L. M.

1 O Christ, our true and only Light,
Illumine those who sit in night;
Let those afar now hear Thy voice,
And in Thy fold with us rejoice.

2 Fill with the radiance of Thy grace
The souls now lost in error's maze,
And all, O Lord, whose secret minds,
Some dark delusion hurts and blinds.

3 And all who else have strayed from Thee,
Oh, gently seek! Thy healing be
To every wounded conscience given,
And let them also share Thy heaven.

4 Oh, make the deaf to hear Thy Word,
And teach the dumb to speak, dear Lord,
Who dare not yet the faith avow,
Though secretly they hold it now

5 Shine on the darkened and the cold,
Recall the wanderers to Thy fold,
Unite those who now walk apart,
Confirm the weak and doubting heart.

6 So they with us may evermore
Such grace with wondering thanks adore.
And endless praise to Thee be given,
By all Thy church in earth and heaven.

John Heermann.

53.

7.8.7.8.7.7.

1 RISE, O Salem, rise and shine;
Lo! the Gentiles hail thy waking;
Herald of a morn divine,
See the Day-spring o'er us breaking,
Telling God hath called to mind
Those who long in darkness pined.

2 Ah, how blindly did we stray,
Ere this Sun our earth had brightened;
Heaven we sought not, for no ray
Had our wildered eyes enlightened:
All our looks were earthward bent,
All our strength on earth was spent.

3 But the Day-spring from on high
Hath arisen with beams unclouded,
And we see before it fly
All the heavy gloom that shrouded
This sad earth, where sin and woe
Seemed to reign o'er all below.

4 Thine appearing, Lord, shall fill
All my thoughts in sorrows hour;
Thine appearing, Lord, shall still
All my dread of death's dark power;
Whether joy or tears be mine,
Through them still Thy light shall shine.

5 Let me, when my course is run,
Calmly leave a world of sadness

For the place that needs no sun,
  For Thou art its light and gladness;
For the mansions fair and bright,
Where Thy saints are crowned with light.

John Rist.

LENT.

54. 8.7.8.7.7.7.7.7.

1 CHRIST the Life of all the living,
  Christ the Death of death our foe,
Who Thyself for us once giving
  To the darkest depths of woe,
Patiently didst yield Thy breath
But to save my soul from death,
Praise and glory ever be,
Blessed Jesus, unto Thee.

2 Thou, ah Thou, hast taken on Thee
  Bitter strokes, a cruel rod;
Pain and scorn were heaped upon Thee,
  O Thou sinless Son of God.
Only thus for me to win
Rescue from the bonds of sin;
Praise and glory ever be
Blessed Jesus, unto Thee.

3 Thou didst bear the smiting only
  That it might not fall on me;
Stoodest falsely charged and lonely,
  That I might be safe and free;

Comfortless that I might know
Comfort from Thy boundless woe.
Praise and glory ever be
Blessed Jesus, unto Thee.

4 Then for all that wrought our pardon,
For Thy sorrows deep and sore,
For Thine anguish in the garden,
I will thank Thee evermore;
Thank Thee with my latest breath
For Thy sad and cruel death,
For that last and bitter cry:
Praise Thee evermore on high.

Ernest Christopher Homburg.

55.

7s.D.

1 LORD, Thy death and passion give
Strength and comfort at my need.
Every hour while here I live
On Thy love my soul shall feed.
Thou didst death for me endure,
And I fly all thoughts impure;
Thinking on Thy bitter pains,
Hushed in prayer my heart remains.

2 Yes, Thy cross hath power to heal
All the wounds of sin and strife.
Lost in Thee, my heart doth feel
Sudden warmth and nobler life.
In my saddest, darkest grief,
Let Thy sweetness bring relief.
Thou who camest but to save,
Thou who fearest not the grave!

3 Lord, in Thee I place my trust,
Thou art my Defence and Tower;
Death Thou treadest in the dust,
O'er my soul he hath no power.
That I may have part in Thee,
Help and save and comfort me;
Give me of Thy grace and might,
Resurrection, life, and light!

4 Fount of good, within me dwell,
For the peace Thy presence sheds
Keeps us safe in conflict fell,
Charms the pain from dying beds.
Hide me safe within Thine arm,
Where no foe can hurt or harm;
Whoso, Lord, in Thee doth rest,
He hath conquered, he is blest.

John Heermann.

56.

8.7.8.7.

1 SUFFERING Son of man, be near me,
In my sufferings to sustain;
By Thy sorer griefs to cheer me,
By Thy more than mortal pain.

2 Call to mind that unknown anguish,
In Thy days of flesh below,
When Thy troubled soul did languish
Underneath a world of woe.

3 By Thy most severe temptation
In that dark Satanic hour;

By Thy last mysterious passion,
Screen me from the adverse power.

4 By Thy fainting in the garden,
By Thy dreadful death, I pray,
Write upon my heart Thy pardon;
Take my sins and fears away.

5 By the travail of Thy spirit,
By Thine outcry on the tree,
By Thine agonizing merit,
Gracious Lord, remember me!

C. Wesley. a.

57.

8.7.8.7.D.

1 JESUS, Refuge of the weary,
Object of the spirit's love,
Fountain in life's desert dreary,
Savior from the world above:
Oh, how oft Thine eyes, offended,
Gaze upon the sinner's fall!
Yet upon the cross extended,
Thou didst bear the pain of all.

2 Do we pass the cross unheeding,
Breathing no repentant vow,
Though we see Thee wounded, bleeding,
See Thy thorn-encircled brow?
Yet Thy sinless death has brought us
Life eternal, peace, and rest;
Only what Thy grace has taught us
Calms the sinner's stormy breast.

3 Jesus, may our hearts be burning,
With more fervent love for Thee;
May our eyes be ever turning
To Thy cross of agony;
Till in glory, parted never
From the blessed Savior's side,
Graven in our hearts for ever,
Dwell the cross, the Crucified.

Jerome Savonarola.

58.

7s.D.

1 SAVIOR, when in dust to Thee
Low we bend the adoring knee;
When repentant, to the skies
Scarce we lift our weeping eyes;
Oh, by all Thy pains and woe
Suffered once for man below,
Bending from Thy throne on high,
Hear our solemn Litany!

2 By Thy helpless infant years,
By Thy life of want and tears,
By Thy days of sore distress
In the savage wilderness;
By the dread mysterious hour
Of the insulting tempter's power;
Turn, oh, turn a favoring eye,
Hear our solemn Litany!

3 By Thine hour of dire despair,
By Thine agony of prayer;

By the cross, the nail, the thorn,
Piercing spear, and torturing scorn;
By the gloom that veiled the skies
O'er the dreadful sacrifice;
Listen to our humble cry,
Hear our solemn Litany!

4 By Thy deep expiring groan;
By the sad sepulchral stone,
By the vault whose dark abode
Held in vain the rising God;
Oh, from earth to heaven restored,
Mighty, reascended Lord,
Listen, listen to the cry
Of our solemn Litany!

Sir Robert Grant.

59.

C. M.

1 THERE is a fountain filled with blood,
Drawn from Immanuel's veins;
And sinners, plunged beneath that flood,
Lose all their guilty stains.

2 The dying thief rejoiced to see
That fountain in his day;
And there may I, as vile as he,
Wash all my sins away.

3 Dear dying Lamb, Thy precious blood
Shall never lose its power,
Till all the ransomed church of God
Be saved, to sin no more.

4 E'er since, by faith, I saw the stream
.Thy flowing wounds supply,
Redeeming love has been my theme,
And shall be till I die.

5 Then in a nobler, sweeter song,
I'll sing Thy power to save,
When this poor lisping, stammering tongue
Lies silent in the grave.

6 Lord, I believe Thou hast prepared,
Unworthy though I be,
For me a blood-bought free reward,
A golden harp for me.

7 'Tis strung and tuned for endless years,
And formed by power divine
To sound in God the Father's ears
No other name but Thine.

William Cowper, a.

60.

L. M.

1 ALL praise to Thee, our Savior good,
Who shedst for us Thy precious blood.
From Satan's might and wicked wiles
Thou hast us saved, O Jesus Christ.

2 We pray, true God and man, to Thee,
Us from the bonds of sin set free,
And comfort us, increase our faith,
And save us from eternal death.

3 Keep us from sin, from grief, and shame,
And help us by Thy mighty Name
To bear our cross without complaint,
And strengthen us when weak and faint.

4 O Jesus Christ, our Brother dear,
Thou ever wilt be with us here.
Remain with us, in peace, in strife,
And grant us everlasting life.

C. Vischer

61.

6.6.6.6.8.6.

1 I GAVE My life for thee,
My precious blood I shed,
That thou might'st ransomed be,
And quickened from the dead;
I gave, I gave My life for thee,
What hast thou given for Me?

2 My Father's house of light,
My glory-circled throne
I left, for earthly night,
For wandrings sad and lone;
I left, I left it all for thee,
Hast thou left aught for Me?

3 I suffered much for thee,
More than thy tongue can tell,
Of bitterest agony,
To rescue thee from hell;
I've borne, I've borne it all for thee,
What hast thou borne for Me?

4 And I have brought to thee,
Down from My home above,
Salvation full and free,
My pardon and My love;
I bring, I bring rich gifts to thee,
What hast thou brought to Me?

Frances R. Havergal.

62. L. M.

1 Ride on, ride on in majesty!
In lowly pomp ride on to die!
O Christ, Thy triumphs now begin
O'er captive death and conquered sin.

2 Ride on, ride on in majesty!
The angel armies of the sky
Look down with sad and wondering eyes,
To see the approaching Sacrifice.

3 Ride on, ride on in majesty!
Thy last and fiercest strife is nigh:
The Father on His sapphire throne
Expects His own anointed Son.

4 Ride on, ride on in majesty!
In lowly pomp ride on to die!
Bow Thy meek head to mortal pain,
Then take, O God, Thy power, and reign.

Henry Hart Milman. a.

63. 10s. 6 lines.

1 PASSION-WEEK memories sacred and blest,
Speak to my soul now of stillness and rest;

Slowly we go to Gethsemane's dale;
Show me the sufferer trembling and pale,
Treading forsaken a path full of thorns,
Loving the world, which in turn only scorns.

2 Now I perceive Him in shadows of night,
Putting the powers of darkness to flight,
Crushed 'neath the load of the sin of the world,
Death and damnation around Him are hurled.
Thorn-crowned and scourged still the sacrificed Lamb,
Lifting his brow, says: "A King yet I am."

3 Show me the cross where He patiently died;
There in its shadow myself will I hide,
There will I bide His victorious word,
Hear Him exclaim, "It is finished", my Lord
There will I praise for His mercy and grace;
Suffering and dying He stood in my place.

L. Holmes.

64.

7s. 6 lines.

1 GO to dark Gethsemane,
Ye that feel the tempter's power:
Your Redeemer's conflict see;
Watch with Him one bitter hour;
Turn not from His griefs away;
Learn of Jesus Christ to pray.

2 Follow to the judgment-hall,
View the Lord of life arraigned:
Oh, the wormwood and the gall!
Oh, the pangs His soul sustained!
Shun not suffering, shame, or loss;
Learn of Him to bear the cross.

3 Calvary's mournful mountain climb:
There, adoring at His feet.
Mark that miracle of time,
God's own Sacrifice complete:
"It is finished," hear Him cry:
Learn of Jesus Christ to die.

4 Early hasten to the tomb,
Where they laid His breathless clay;
All is solitude and gloom;
Who hath taken Him away?
Christ is risen! He meets our eyes:
Savior, teach us so to rise.

James Montgomery.

65.

L. M.

1 'TIS midnight, and on Olive's brow
The star is dimmed that lately shone:
'Tis midnight, in the garden now
The suffering Savior prays alone.

2 'Tis midnight, and from all removed,
Immanuel wrestles lone, with fears;
E'en the disciple that He loved
Heeds not his Master's grief and tears.

3 'Tis midnight, and for others' guilt
The Man of Sorrows weeps in blood;
Yet He that hath in anguish knelt
Is not forsaken by His God.

4 'Tis midnight, and from ether-plains
Is borne the song that angels know:
Unheard by mortals are the strains
That sweetly soothe the Savior's woe.

W. B. Tappan.

66.

8.7.8.7.7.7.8.8.

1 OVER Kidron Jesus treadeth
To His passion for us all;
Every human eye be weeping,
Tears of bitter grief let fall!
Round His spirit flock the foes,
Place their shafts and bend their bows,
Aiming at the Savior solely,
While the world forsakes Him wholly.

2 David once, with heart afflicted,
Crossed o'er Kidron's narrow strand,
Clouds of gloom and grief about him
When an exile from his land.
But, O Jesus, blacker now
Bends the cloud above Thy brow,
Hasting to death's dreary portals
For the shame and sin of mortals.

3 See Him anguish-stricken falling,
Prostrate, and with struggling breath,
Three times on His Father calling,
Praying that the bitter death

And the cup of doom may go;
Still He cries, in all His woe:
"Not My will, but Thine, O Father",
And the angels round Him gather.

4 See how, in that hour of darkness,
Battling with the evil power,
Agonies untold assail Him,
On His soul the arrows shower;
And the garden flowers are wet
With the drops of bloody sweat,
From His anguished frame distilling—
Our redemption thus fulfilling!

5 But, O flowers, so sadly watered
By this pure and precious dew,
Faith alone can know its power
And your beauty rightly view.
Eden's Garden did not bear
Aught that can with you compare,
For the blood thus freely given
Makes my soul the heir of heaven.

6 When as flowers themselves I wither,
When I droop and fade like grass,
When the life-streams through my pulses
Dull and ever duller pass,
When at last they cease to roll,
Then, to cheer my sinking soul,
Grace of Jesus, be Thou given—
Source of Triumph! Pledge of heaven!

T. Kingo.

67.

11.9.11.9.11.11.9.

1 GOOD Friday, Good Friday, thou beautiful day,
With peace the great battle is ended;
And heaven rejoices in holy array;
Through Jesus the world is befriended!
Though earth may be dark, yet will heaven be light,
And Jesus returns to His glory and might;
The conflict on earth He has finished.

2 Good Friday, Good Friday, thou glorious day,
The heavenly hosts have united
Thy glory to sing, and triumphantly say
By Jesus all wrongs have been righted!
He suffered a shameful and sorrowful death;
His pity compelling, He gave up His breath,
And died in the place of the sinner.

3 O sinners, now come to keep holy the day,
When Jesus for sinners was offered,
And now may we faithfully love and obey
Our Lord, who so patiently suffered!
He offered His life to repay what we owed,
And God, therefore, mercy again has bestowed;
Forever He now will be gracious.

4 Ne'er suffer a day, O my heart, to pass by
On which thou for Jesus not yearnest;

Thy promise renew that in prayer thou will
  try
 More faithful to be and more earnest.
Dear Savior, may Thou cleanse my soul
  every day,
And take Thou my heart; for this only I
  pray,
 Let me at Thy cross ever tarry.

From Hemlandssånger.

68.

8.7.8 7.

1 IN the cross of Christ I glory,
  Towering o'er the wrecks of time;
 All the light of sacred story
  Gathers round its head sublime.

2 When the woes of life o'ertake me,
  Hopes deceive, and fears annoy,
 Never shall the cross forsake me;
  Lo! it glows with peace and joy.

3 When the sun of bliss is beaming
  Light and love upon my way,
 From the cross the radiance streaming
  Adds new lustre to the day.

4 Bane and blessing, pain and pleasure,
  By the cross are sanctified;
 Peace is there that knows no measure,
  Joys that through all time abide

Sir John Bowring.

69.

8.7.8.7.

1 SWEET the moments, rich in blessing,
Which before the cross I spend,
Life, and health, and peace possessing,
From the sinner's dying Friend.

2 Here I'll sit, forever viewing
Mercy's streams, in streams of blood:
Precious drops, my soul bedewing,
Plead and claim my peace with God.

3 Truly blessed is the station,
Low before His cross to lie;
While I see divine compassion
Beaming in His languid eye.

4 Lord, in ceaseless contemplation
Fix my thankful heart on Thee,
Till I taste Thy full salvation
And Thine unveiled glory see

Walter Shirley.

70.

L. M.

1 WHEN I survey the wondrous cross
On which the Prince of glory died,
My richest gain I count but loss,
And pour contempt on all my pride.

2 Forbid it, Lord, that I should boast,
Save in the death of Christ, my God;
All the vain things that charm me most,
I sacrifice them to His blood.

3 See, from His head, His hands, His feet,
Sorrow and love flow mingled down!
Did e'er such love and sorrow meet,
Or thorns compose so rich a crown?

4 Were the whole realm of nature mine,
That were a tribute far too small;
Love so amazing, so divine,
Demands my soul, my life, my all.

Isaac Watts. a.

71.

L. M.

1 'TIS finished! so the Savior cried,
And meekly bowed His head and died:
'Tis finished! yes, the race is run,
The battle fought, the victory won.

2 'Tis finished! all that heaven foretold
By prophets in the days of old;
And truths are opened to our view
That kings and prophets never knew.

3 'Tis finished! Son of God, Thy power
Hath triumphed in this awful hour;
And yet our eyes with sorrow see
That life to us was death to Thee.

4 'Tis finished! let the joyful sound
Be heard through all the nations round;
'Tis finished! let the triumph rise,
And swell the chorus of the skies.

Samuel Stennett.

72.

8.7 8.7 4.4.7.

1 THY cross, O Jesus, Thou didst bear,
Thy path to death extended,
To save the world, which everywhere
With hate and scorn offended.
Oh, love how deep
To bleed and weep
For Thine own persecutors!

2 Thy cross, Redeemer, Thou didst bear,
Our sins away Thou'st taken;
Thine own Thou wilt us still declare,
Though we have Thee forsaken,
And gone astray;
Yea, day by day
Thy love is present with us.

3 Thy cross, O Savior, Thou didst bear,
Thy boundless might and glory,
Forever praised by angels fair,
And told in sacred story,
Thou laidst aside.
Naught shall abide,
Save by the love that bleedeth.

4 Thy cross to victory Thou didst bear.
Oh, grant that I, dear Savior,
May glory in the cross and share
Thy heavenly joy and favor!
Then shall my soul
Have reached its goal
Safe in Thy loving bosom.

E. G. Geijer.

73.

7.6.7.6.D.

1 O SACRED Head, now wounded,
With grief and shame weighed down,
Now scornfully surrounded
With thorns, Thine only crown!
Once reigning in the highest
In light and majesty,
Dishonored now Thou diest,
Yet here I worship Thee.

2 How art Thou pale with anguish,
With sore abuse and scorn!
How does that visage languish,
Which once was bright as morn!
What Thou, my Lord, hast suffered,
Was all for sinners' gain;
Mine, mine was the transgression,
But Thine the deadly pain.

3 Lo, here I fall, my Savior,
'T is I deserve Thy place:
Look on me with Thy favor,
Vouchsafe to me Thy grace.
Receive me, my Redeemer;
My Shepherd, make me Thine,
Of every good the Fountain,
Thy art the Spring of mine!

4 What language shall I borrow
To thank Thee, dearest Friend,
For this Thy dying sorrow,
Thy pity without end!

Oh, make me Thine for ever,
  And should I fainting be,
Lord, let me never, never,
  Outlive my love to Thee.

5 Forbid that I should leave Thee;
  O Jesus, leave not me;
In faith may I receive Thee,
  When death shall set me free.
When strength and comfort languish,
  And I must hence depart,
Release me then from anguish
  By Thine own wounded heart.

Bernard of Clairvaux. Paul Gerhardt.

74.

7s. Iambic. 7 lines.

O LAMB of God, most holy,
  On Calvary an offering;
Despiséd, meek and lowly,
  Thou in Thy death and suffering
Our sins didst bear, our anguish;
The might of death didst vanquish;
  Give us Thy peace, o Jesus!

N. Decius.

75.

8.7. Iambic. 10 lines.

1 A LAMB goes uncomplaining forth,
  The guilt of all men bearing;
'T is laden with the sin of earth;
  None else the burden sharing

It goes its way, grows weak and faint,
To slaughter led without complaint,
Its spotless life to offer;
Bears shame, and stripes, and wounds, and death,
Anguish and mockery, and saith,
"Willing all this I suffer."

2 This spotless Lamb, our soul's great Friend,
And everlasting Savior,
God chooseth sin's dread reign to end
And bring us to His favor.
"Go forth, my Son! redeem to Thee
The children who're exposed by me
To punishment and anger.
The punishment is great, and dread
The wrath, but Thou Thy blood shalt shed,
And free them from this danger."

3 Dilate, shrine of my heart, and swell,
To thee shall now be given
A treasure that doth far excel
The worth of earth and heaven.
Away with silver and with gold,
With treasures of an earthly mold!
I've found a better jewel.
My priceless treasure, Lord my God,
Is Thy most holy, precious blood,
Which flowed from wounds so cruel.

4 And when Thy glory I shall see
And taste Thy kingdom's pleasure,

Thy blood shall then my purple be,
  I'll clothe me in this treasure;
It then shall be my glorious crown;
Thus I'll appear before the throne
  Of God, and need not hide me;
And shall, by Him to Thee bethrothed,
By Thee in bridal garments clothed,
  Stand as a bride beside Thee.

P. Gerhardt.

76.

6.6.7.6.7.6.6.6.

1 WHAT comfort sweet to pause
Close by the holy cross,
  And with the Savior's mother
In silence look upon
  Our dear and dying brother;
For there all fears are gone,
The peace of God abounds,
In His peace-giving wounds.

2 What comfort sweet to own
In His dear blood alone
  All sin and guilt forgiven.
It cheers the weary heart,
  When love divine from heaven
Does life and strength impart;
The soul enjoys the peace
That nevermore shall cease.

3 What comfort to believe
In spite of woe and grief.
  Though worthy of perdition.

Yet to this sinful heart
  Thou givest full remission.
O Lord, Thy grace impart;
I plead, Thy precious blood,
Thou spotless Lamb of God.

4 What comfort sweet to tell
My wants, I know it well—
  And pray for more endurance
When longing to believe,
  But lacking full assurance.
No rest I can receive,
Until I come to Thee,
O Lamb of Calvary!

5 Let all here have access,
Who yearn for happiness.
  Grace to the poor aboundeth.
And peace to troubled hearts;
  For mercy's name here soundeth,
And comfort sweet imparts
To him who comfortless
For help and mercy prays.

L. Linderot.

77.

11s.

1 MY crucified Savior, despised and contemned
Thou innocent Victim for sinners condemned,
Thy garments are blood-stained, Thy spirit doth groan,
In agony prostrate, Thou sufferest alone.

2 Thou weepest and moanest in conflict and prayer,
And writhest in agony, pain, and despair;
In thirty year's anguish our path Thou hast trod,
And diest at last to redeem us to God.

3 For me Thou hast labored salvation to win,
For me tasted death to atone for my sin;
Neglected, forsaken, but mindful of me,
Thou prayest for those who have crucified Thee.

4 Thou consecrate Victim, my Passover slain,
The gall and the wormwood for me Thou dost drain.
That I might be blessed Thou sufferest all woe,
And diest at last on me life to bestow.

5 Our Savior thus finished God's plan with our race,
And laid the foundation for pardon and grace,
And then rose triumphant, the conquering Lord,
Appeased the Creator and mankind restored.

6 Restored to the bliss that was lost in the fall,
Yea, greater, for Jesus prepared for us all

Eternal salvation and mansions above;
Come, poor burdened sinners, rejoice in His love.

7 What is, then, to be reconciled unto God?
It is that He silenced the curse by His blood;
And what the relation to which we're restored?
The right to be counted the friends of the Lord.

8 So come, trembling sinner, come just as thou art,
Thy cares and thy sorrows to Jesus impart;
In Him seek salvation from death and the grave,
For Jesus is willing and mighty to save.

A. C. Rutström.

78.

8.7.8.7.D.

1 STRICKEN, smitten, and afflicted,
See Him dying on the tree!
'T is the Christ by man rejected;
Yes, my soul, 't is He, 't is He!
Many hands were raised to wound Him,
None would interpose to save;
But the deepest stroke that pierced Him
Was the stroke that Justice gave.

2 Ye who think of sin but lightly,
Nor suppose the evil great,
Here may view its nature rightly,
Here its guilt may estimate.

Mark the Sacrifice appointed!
See who bears the awful load,
'T is the Word, the Lord's Anointed,
Son of man, and Son of God.

3 Here we have a firm foundation;
Here the refuge of the lost;
Christ's the Rock of our salvation:
His the Name of which we boast:
Lamb of God for sinners wounded!
Sacrifice to cancel guilt!
None shall ever be confounded
Who on Him their hope have built.

Thomas Kelly. a.

79.

C. M.

1 ALAS! and did my Savior bleed?
And did my Sovereign die?
Would He devote that sacred head
For such a worm as I?

2 Was it for crimes that I had done,
He groaned upon the tree?
Amazing pity! grace unknown!
And love beyond degree!

3 Well might the sun in darkness hide,
And shut his glories in,
When Christ the mighty Maker died
For man, the creature's sin.

4 Thus might I hide my blushing face,
While His dear cross appears;

Dissolve my heart in thankfulness,
And melt my eyes in tears.

5 But drops of grief can ne'er repay
The debt of love I owe;
Here Lord, I give myself away,
'T is all that I can do.

Isaac Watts, a.

EASTER.

80. L. M.

1 BLEST Easter day, what joy is thine!
We praise, dear Lord, Thy Name divine,
For Thou has triumphed o'er the tomb;
No more we need to dread its gloom.

2 That tree, on which Thou offer'dst up
Thy life, now bears the fruit of hope:
Thy precious blood for us is shed,
Now we may feed on heavenly bread.

3 We thank Thee, Jesus, that Thy hand
Has freed us from sin's galling band;
No more its thralldom we need fear;
The year of liberty is here.

4 O Jesus Christ, God's Son elect,
Our Paschal Lamb without defect,
To us Thou givest strength indeed,
In all our conflicts, all our need.

5 Through Thee we always shall prevail,
However hell may us assail,
Thou setst us free, Thy Name to praise.
And leadst us into heavenly ways.

6 Oh, grant, that as Thou didst arise,
I too, with joy, may heavenward rise,
First from my sin, to love Thy way,
Then from the grave, at the last day.

7 All praise to Thee who from death's might,
From carnal lust and sin's dark plight
Redeemest me, and show'st how I
May reach eternal life on high.

O. Petri.

81.

7s.D.

1 CHRIST is risen from the dead!
Darkness now no more shall reign;
Thorns no more shall crown the head
That was bowed with grief and pain:
Christ the Lord, the mighty King,
From our sin hath made us free.
Where, O death, is now thy sting?
Where, O grave, thy victory?

2 Scoffers now no more shall say:
If thou be the Christ, come down
From the cross, and prove to-day
That to Thee belongs the crown!
For our risen Lord and King
From our sin hath made us free.

Where, O death, is now thy sting?
  Where, O grave, thy victory?

3 Faith now knows He is the Lord,
  Gives assent to His decree,
Trusts the promise in His Word,
  And is crowned with victory,
Shouting praises to the King,
  Who from sin hath made us free.
Where, O death, is now thy sting?
  Where, O grave, thy victory?

H. A. Becker.

82.

7s.

1 CHRIST the Lord is risen to-day,
Sons of men and angels say.
Raise your joys and triumphs high;
Sing, ye heavens, and earth reply.

2 Love's redeeming work is done,
Fought the fight, the battle won;
Lo! the sun's eclipse is o'er;
Lo! he sets in blood no more.

3 Vain the stone, the watch, the seal;
Christ hath burst the gates of hell!
Death in vain forbids His rise;
Christ hath opened paradise.

4 Lives again our glorious King;
Where, O death, is now thy sting?
Dying once, He all doth save;
Where thy victory, O grave?

5 Soar we now where Christ has led,
Following our exalted Head;
Made like Him, like Him we rise;
Ours the cross, the grave, the skies!

6 Hail, the Lord of earth and heaven!
Praise to Thee by both be given:
Thee we greet triumphant now;
Hail, the Resurrection Thou!

C. Wesley.

83.

6.5.6.5.6.5.6.5.11.11.10.

1 HE liveth forever!
There's light o'er the grave:
Fulfilled hath the Savior
The promise He gave.
With joy and salvation,
The Victor on earth,
'Mid heaven's adoration,
In glory comes forth.
The seal hath been broken, the stone rolled away,
The watchers have all fled in awe and dismay:
Hell itself is trembling. Hallelujah!

2 The victory was glorious,
Now darkness must flee;
The light was victorious,
And ever shall be.
Now death is o'erpowered,
And faith doth revive;
And hope on us showered,
And hearts made alive.

Ye sorrowing women, whom seek ye now here?
The Savior now liveth! Allay then your fear:
Christ Jesus is risen. Hallelujah!

3 Thus earth was with heaven
Through Christ reconciled;
And joy shall be given
The penitent child.
Ye friends who once bended
Your heads 'neath the cross,
Rejoice! they are ended
Your sorrows and woes!
Thou scattered flock that for guidance dost yearn,
He liveth thy Shepherd, to Him now return:
He guideth thee ever. Hallelujah!

4 'Mid foes that alarm us,
His church stands secure;
No evil can harm us,
His Word shall endure,
Lo! to all the nations,
To friend and to foe,
With courage and patience
His messengers go,
And tell of the Savior who died for our sin,
And rose from the dead, and now liveth again,
The first-fruits of glory. Hallelujah!

5 Believers befriended,
Why do ye lament?
The day is soon ended,

The night is soon spent.
The grave shall embrace you,
And you shall find rest;
The Savior shall raise you,
To live and be blest.
He soweth the grain, and He cometh at last;
And truly the tares from the wheat He shall cast,
And gather the harvest. Hallelujah!

F. M. Franzen.

84.

7s.D

1 CHRIST the Lord is risen to-day,
Christians, haste your vows to pay,
Offer ye your praises meet,
At the Paschal Victim's feet.
For the sheep the Lamb hath bled,
Sinless in the sinner's stead;
Christ is risen, to-day we cry;
Now He lives no more to die.

2 Christ, the Victim undefiled,
Man to God hath reconciled,
Whilst in strange and awful strife
Met together Death and Life.
Christians, on this happy day,
Haste with joy your vows to pay;
Christ is risen, to-day we cry;
Now He lives no more to die.

3 Christ, who once for sinners bled,
Now the first-born from the dead,

Throned in endless might and power
Lives and reigns for evermore.
Hail, eternal Hope on high!
Hail, Thou King of victory!
Hail, Thou Prince of Life adored!
Help and save us, gracious Lord!

From the Latin.

85.

7.6.7.6.D.

1 THE day of Resurrection!
Earth, tell it out abroad!
The Passover of gladness,
The Passover of God!
From death to life eternal,
From earth unto the sky,
Our Christ hath brought us over,
With hymns of victory.

2 Our hearts be pure from evil,
That we may see aright
The Lord in rays eternal
Of resurrection light:
And listening to His accents,
May hear, so calm and plain,
His own "All hail!"—and hearing,
May raise the victor strain.

3 Now let the heavens be joyful!
Let earth her song begin!
Let all the world keep triumph,
And all that is therein!
In grateful exultation

Their notes let all things blend,
For Christ the Lord hath risen,
Our Joy that hath no end.

John of Damascus.

86.

8.7.8.7.D.

1 DAY of wonder, day of gladness,
Hail thy ever glorious light!
Gone is sorrow, gone is sadness,
Ended is the gloomy night!
Listen to the angel's story,—
Cast away all fear and dread;
Give to God the Father glory!
Christ is risen from the dead!

2 In the triumph of this hour,
Jubilant shall swell the song;
Unto Jesus, honor, power,
Blessing, victory belong.
Scattered are the clouds of error,
Sin and hell are captive led:
E'en the grave is free from terror,
Christ is risen from the dead!

3 Every people, every nation,
Soon shall hear the gladsome sound;
Joyous tidings of salvation,
Borne to earth's remotest bound.
Then shall rise, in tones excelling,
Praise for grace so freely shed;
And the Easter hymn be swelling,
Christ is risen from the dead!

W. J. Hall.

87.

7s.

1 MORNING breaks upon the tomb;
Jesus scatters all its gloom;
Day of triumph through the skies,
See the glorious Savior rise.

2 Ye who are of death afraid,
Triumph in the scattered shade,
Drive your anxious cares away,
See the place where Jesus lay!

3 Christian, dry your flowing tears,
Chase your unbelieving fears;
Look on His deserted grave,
Doubt no more His power to save.

W. B. Collyer.

88.

L. M.

1 COME, see the place where Jesus lay,
And hear angelic voices say:
"He rose, He lives, who once was slain;
He said that He would rise again."

2 Oh joyful sound! Oh glorious hour!
When by His own almighty power
Our Savior rose, and left the grave,
And ever liveth now to save.

3 Now let our songs His triumph tell,
Who burst the bands of death and hell;
The First-begotten of the dead,
For us He rose, our glorious Head.

4 No more we tremble at the grave,
For Jesus will our spirits save.
O risen Lord, in Thee we live,
To Thee our ransomed souls we give.

5 All praise be Thine, O risen Lord,
From death to endless life restored;
All praise to God the Father be
And Holy Ghost eternally.

Thomas Kelly.

89.

C. M.

1 WELCOME, Thou Victor in the strife,
Welcome from out the cave!
To-day we triumph in Thy life
Around Thine empty grave.

2 Our enemy is put to shame,
His short-lived triumph o'er;
Our God is with us, we exclaim,
We fear our foe no more.

3 The dwellings of the just resound
With songs of victory;
For in their midst Thou, Lord, art found,
And bringest peace with Thee.

4 Oh, let Thy conquering banner wave
O'er hearts Thou makest free;
And paint the path that from the grave
Leads heavenward up to Thee.

5 We bury all our sin and crime
Deep in our Savior's tomb,

And seek the treasure there, that time
Nor change can e'er consume.

6 Fearless we lay us in the tomb,
And sleep the night away,
If Thou art there to break the gloom,
And call us back to day.

7 Death hurts us not: his power is gone,
And pointless all his darts:
God's favor now on us hath shone,
Joy filleth all our hearts.

Benjamin Schmolk.

90.

4.4.7.4.4.7.4.4.7.

1 PRAISE the Savior
Now and ever!
Praise Him all beneath the skies!
Prostrate lying,
Suffering, dying,
On the cross, a Sacrifice;
Victory gaining,
Life obtaining,
Now in glory he doth rise.

2 All is finished,
And accomplished;
Christ is now our Righteousness
He our Savior,
Hath forever
Set us free from dire distress.
Through His merit,
We inherit
Light and peace and happiness.

3 We're delivered,
Our bonds severed,
Christ hath bruised the serpent's head;
Death no longer
Is the stronger,
Hell itself is captive led.
Christ hath risen
From death's prison,
O'er the tomb He light hath shed.

4 Praise forever
For His favor
Unto God the Father sing;
Praise the Savior,
Praise Him ever,
Son of God, our Lord King;
Praise the Spirit,
Through Christ's merit
He doth us salvation bring.

Fortunatus—J. O. Wallin.

91.

8.7.8.7 8.8.7.

1 IN Death's strong grasp the Savior lay,
For our offenses given:
But now the Lord is risen to-day,
And brings us life from heaven:
And therefore let us all rejoice
And praise our God with cheerful voice,
And sing loud Hallelujahs.

2 No son of man could conquer death,
Such evil sin had wrought us;

For innocence dwelt not on earth,
And therefore death had brought us
Into this thralldom from of old,
And ever grew more strong and bold,
His shadow lay athwart us.

3 But Jesus Christ, God's only Son,
Has come for our salvation.
The cause of death He has undone,
And stopped his devastation;
Christ ruined all his right and claim,
And left him nothing but the name;
His sting is lost forever.

4 It was a strange and dreadful strife,
When life and death contended:
The victory remained with life,
The reign of death was ended:
For Holy Scripture plainly saith,
That death is swallowed up by death,
And put to shame forever.

5 Here the true Paschal Lamb we see,
Whom God so freely gave us;
He died on the accursed tree,
So strong His love! to save us:
The atoning blood now marks our door,
Faith points to it, death passes o'er,
He never more can harm us.

6 So let us keep the festival,
Whereto the Lord invites us;
Christ is Himself the Joy of all,

The Sun which warms and lights us:
And by His grace He doth impart
Eternal sunshine to the heart;
The night of sin is ended.

7 Then let us feast this Easter-day
On the true Bread of heaven;
The Word of grace hath purged away
The old and wicked leaven:
For Christ alone our souls will feed,
He is our meat and drink indeed;
Faith lives upon no other.

Martin Luther.

92.

L. M.

1 I KNOW that my Redeemer lives!
What comfort this sweet sentence gives!
He lives, He lives, who once was dead,
He lives, my ever-living Head.

2 He lives to bless me with His love,
He lives to plead for me above,
He lives my hungry soul to feed,
He lives to help in time of need.

3 He lives to grant me rich supply,
He lives to guide me with His eye,
He lives to comfort me when faint,
He lives to hear my soul's complaint.

4 He lives to silence all my fears,
He lives to wipe away my tears.
He lives to calm my troubled heart,
He lives, all blessings to impart.

5 He lives, and grants me daily breath;
He lives, and I shall conquer death;
He lives, my mansion to prepare;
He lives, to bring me safely there.

6 He lives, all glory to His Name!
He lives, my Jesus, still the same;
Oh, the sweet joy this sentence gives,
I know that my Redeemer lives!

Samuel Medley.

93.

6.6.6.6.8.8.

1 BLOW ye the trumpet, blow
The gladly solemn sound!
Let all the nations know,
To earth's remotest bound,
The year of Jubilee is come;
Return, ye ransomed sinners, home.

2 Exalt the Lamb of God,
The sin-atoning Lamb;
Redemption by His blood
Through all the lands proclaim:
The year of Jubilee is come;
Return, ye ransomed sinners, home.

3 The gospel trumpet hear,
The news of pardoning grace;
Ye happy souls, draw near,
Behold your Savior's face:
The year of Jubilee is come;
Return, ye ransomed sinners, home.

4 Jesus, our great High Priest,
Has full atonement made;
Ye weary spirits, rest;
Ye mournful souls, be glad!
The year of Jubilee is come;
Return, ye ransomed sinners, home.

C. Wesley.

ASCENSION.

94. 8.7.8.7.8.8.

1 TO realms of glory I behold
My risen Lord returning;
While I, a stranger in the earth,
For heaven am ever yearning.
Far from my heavenly Father's home
'Mid toil and sorrow here I roam.

2 Far from my home—how long, dear Lord,
Before my exile endeth?
But far beyond the realms of sense
My fervent prayer ascendeth:
My prayer, unuttered, but a groan,
Shall rend the skies and reach Thy throne.

3 Then visions of the goodly land
By faith my soul obtaineth;
There I shall dwell for evermore
Where Christ in glory reigneth,
In mansions of that blest abode—
The city of the living God.

4 In that blest city is no night,
  Nor any pain or weeping;
There is my treasure and my heart
  Safe in my Savior's keeping:
In heaven, my blessed Lord, with Thee,
May all my conversation be.

5 In glory He shall come again
  To earth as He ascended;
So let me wait and watch and pray,
  Until my day is ended.
That day, O Lord, is hid from me,
But daily do I wait for Thee.

6 And blessed shall that servant be,
  O Lord, at Thy returning,
Whose heart is waiting, Lord, for Thee,
  Whose lamp is trimmed and burning;
Him wilt Thou take to dwell with Thee,
In joy and peace eternally.

J. O. Wallin.

95. C. M.

1 O Jesus, who art gone before
  To Thy blest realms of light,
Oh, thither may our spirits soar,
  And wing their upward flight!

2 Make us to those delights aspire,
  Which spring from love to Thee,
Which pass the carnal heart's desire,
  Which faith alone can see:

3 When to His saints, as their reward,
Himself Jehovah gives,
And thus its all-sufficient Lord
The faithful soul receives.

4 To guide us to Thy glories, Lord,
To lift us to the sky,
Oh, may Thy Holy Ghost be poured
Upon us from on high!

5 Praise to the Father and the Son,
Who dwells aloft in heaven;
And to the Spirit, Three in One,
Let equal praise be given.

From the Latin.

96.

8.7 8.7.D.

1 SEE the Conqueror mounts in triumph;
See the King in royal state,
Riding on the clouds, His chariot,
To His heavenly palace gate!
Hark! the choir of angel voices,
Joyful alleluias sing,
And the portals high are lifted,
To receive their heavenly King.

2 Who is this that comes in glory.
With the trump of jubilee?
Lord of battles, God of armies,
He hath gained the victory!
He who on the cross did suffer,
He who from the grave arose.

He hath vanquished sin and Satan,
He by death hath spoiled His foes.

3 Now our heavenly Aaron enters,
With His blood within the veil;
Joshua now is come to Canaan,
And the kings before Him quail;
Now He plants the tribes of Israel
In their promised resting-place;
Now our great Elijah offers
Double portion of His grace.

4 He hath raised our human nature
On the clouds to God's right hand:
There we sit in heavenly places,
There with Him in glory stand:
Jesus reigns adored by angels:
Man with God is on the throne:
Mighty Lord, in Thine ascension
We by faith behold our own.

Christopher Wordsworth.

97.

7s.

1 HAIL the day that sees Him rise,
To His throne above the skies!
Christ, the Lamb for sinners given,
Re-ascends His native heaven.

2 There the glorious triumph waits;
Lift your heads, eternal gates;
He hath conquered death and sin:
Take the King of glory in!

3 Him though highest heaven receives,
Still He loves the earth He leaves;
Though returning to His throne,
Still He calls mankind His own.

4 See, He lifts His hands above!
See, He shows the prints of love!
Hark, His gracious lips bestow,
Blessings on His church below!

5 Still for us His death He pleads;
Ever for us intercedes;
Near Himself prepares our place,
He the first-fruits of our race.

6 There we shall with Thee remain,
Partners of Thine endless reign;
There Thy face unclouded see,
Find our heaven of heavens in Thee.

C. Wesley. a.

98.

8.7.8.7.D.

1 HAIL, Thou once despiséd Jesus!
  Hail, Thou Galilean King!
Thou didst suffer to release us;
  Thou didst free salvation bring.
Hail, Thou agonizing Savior,
  Bearer of our sin and shame!
By Thy merits we find favor;
  Life is given through Thy Name.

2 Paschal Lamb, by God appointed,
  All our sins on Thee were laid;

By almighty love anointed,
Thou hast full atonement made.
All Thy people are forgiven,
Through the virtue of Thy blood:
Opened is the gate of heaven;
Peace is made 'twixt man and God.

3 Jesus, hail, enthroned in glory,
There forever to abide!
All the heavenly hosts adore Thee,
Seated at Thy Father's side:
There for sinners Thou art pleading,
There Thou dost our place prepare,
Ever for us interceding,
Till in glory we appear.

4 Worship, honor, power, and blessing,
Thou art worthy to receive;
Loudest praises, without ceasing,
Meet it is for us to give.
Help, ye bright angelic spirits,
Bring your sweetest, noblest lays,
Help to sing our Savior's merits,
Help to chant Immanuel's praise.

John Bakewell. a.

99.

C. M

1 THE Head that once was crowned with thorns
Is crowned with glory now;
A royal diadem adorns
The mighty Victor's brow.

2 The highest place that heaven affords
Is His by sovereign right:
The King of kings and Lord of lords,
And heaven's eternal Light.

3 The joy of all who dwell above,
The joy of all below,
To whom He manifests His love,
And grants His Name to know.

4 To them the cross, with all its shame,
With all its grace, is given;
Their name an everlasting name,
Their joy the joy of heaven.

5 They suffer with their Lord below,
They reign with Him above;
Their profit and their joy to know
The mystery of His love.

6 The cross He bore is life and health,
Though shame and death to Him:
His people's hope, His people's wealth,
Their everlasting theme.

Thomas Kelly. a.

100.

8.7.8.7.7.7.

1 HARK, ten thousand harps and voices
Sound the note of praise above!
Jesus reigns, and heaven rejoices;
Jesus reigns, the God of love.
See, He sits on yonder throne;
Jesus rules the world alone.

2 Jesus, hail! whose glory brightens
All above, and makes it fair:
Lord of life, Thy smile enlightens,
Cheers and charms Thy people here.
When we think of love like Thine,
Lord, we own it love divine.

4 King of glory, reign forever;
Thine an everlasting crown:
Nothing from Thy love shall sever
Those whom Thou hast made Thine own;
Happy objects of Thy grace,
Destined to behold Thy face.

4 Savior, hasten Thine appearing;
Bring, oh, bring the glorious day,
When, the awful summons hearing,
Heaven and earth shall pass away.
Then, with golden harps, we'll sing,
"Glory, glory to our King.'

Thomas Kelly. a.

101.

C. M.

1 ALL hail the power of Jesus' Name!
Let angels prostrate fall;
Bring forth the royal diadem,
And crown Him Lord of all.

2 Ye chosen seed of Israel's race,
Ye ransomed from the fall,
Hail Him who saves you by His grace,
And crown Him Lord of all.

3 Hail Him, ye heirs of David's line,
Whom David Lord did call;
The Lord incarnate, Man divine:
And crown Him Lord of all.

4 Ye Gentile sinners, ne'er forget
The wormwood and the gall;
Go, spread your trophies at His feet,
And crown Him Lord of all.

5 Let every kindred, every tribe,
On this terrestrial ball,
To Him all majesty ascribe,
And crown Him Lord of all.

6 Oh, that with yonder sacred throng
We at His feet may fall!
We'll join the everlasting song,
And crown Him Lord of all.

Edward Perronet. a.

PENTECOST.

102. 8s. 9 lines.

1 COME, Holy Spirit, God and Lord!
Be all Thy graces now outpoured
On the believer's mind and soul,
To strengthen, save, and make us whole.
Lord, by the brightness of Thy light,
Thou in the faith dost men unite
Of every land and every tongue:
This to Thy praise, O Lord, be sung.
Hallelujah! Hallelujah!

2 Thou strong Defense, Thou holy Light,
Teach us to know our God aright,
And call him Father from the heart:
The Word of life and truth impart:
That we may love not doctrines strange,
Nor e'er to other teachers range,
But Jesus for our Master own,
And put our trust in Him alone.
Hallelujah! Hallelujah!

3 Thou sacred Ardor, Comfort sweet,
Help us to wait with ready feet
And willing heart, at Thy command,
Nor trial fright us from Thy band.
Lord, make us ready with Thy powers;
Strengthen the flesh in weaker hours.
That as good warriors we may force
Through life and death to Thee our course.
Hallelujah! Hallelujah!

Martin Luther.

103.

8.7.8.7.D.

1 HOLY GHOST, dispel our sadness,
Pierce the clouds of sinful night;
Come, Thou Source of sweetest gladness,
Breathe Thy life and spread Thy light!
Come, Thou best of all donations
God can give, or we implore!
Having Thy sweet consolations,
We need wish for nothing more.

2 From that height that knows no measure,
As a gracious shower descend,
Bringing down the richest treasure
Man can wish, or God can send.
Author of the new creation!
Come with unction and with power;
Make our hearts Thy habitation;
On our souls Thy graces shower.

3 Manifest Thy love forever;
Fence us in on every side;
In distress be our reliever
Guard and teach, support and guide.
Hear, oh, hear our supplication,
Loving Spirit, God of peace!
Rest upon this congregation,
With the fulness of Thy grace,

Paul Gerhardt.

104.

8.7.8.7.7.7.

1 COME, oh, come, Thou quickening Spirit,
Thou forever art divine;
Let thy power never fail me,
Always fill this heart of mine;
Thus shall grace, and truth, and light
Dissipate the gloom of night.

2 Grant my mind and my affections
Wisdom, counsel, purity;
That I may be ever seeking
Naught but that which pleases Thee.

Let Thy knowledge spread and grow,
Working error's overthrow.

3 Lead me to green pastures, lead me
By the true and living way,
Shield me from each strong temptation
That might draw my heart astray;
And if e'er my feet should turn,
For each error let me mourn.

4 Holy Spirit, strong and mighty,
Thou who makest all things new,
Make Thy work within me perfect,
Help me by Thy Word so true,
Arm me with that Sword of Thine,
And the victory shall be mine.

5 In the faith, oh! make me steadfast;
Let not Satan, death or shame
Of my confidence deprive me;
Lord, my refuge is Thy Name.
When the flesh inclines to ill,
Let Thy Word prove stronger still.

6 And when my last hour approaches,
Let my hopes grow yet more bright;
Since I am an heir of heaven,
In Thy glorious courts of light,
Fairer far than voice can tell,
There, redeemed by Christ, to dwell.

H. Held.

105.

C. M.

1 COME, Holy Spirit, heavenly Dove,
With all Thy quickening powers;
Kindle a flame of sacred love
In these cold hearts of ours.

2 Look how we grovel here below,
Fond of these trifling toys;
Our souls, how heavily they go,
To reach eternal joys!

3 Dear Lord, and shall we ever live
At this poor, dying rate?
Our love so cold, so faint to Thee,
And Thine to us so great?

4 Come, Holy Spirit, heavenly Dove,
With all Thy quickening powers,
Come, shed abroad a Savior's love,
And that shall kindle ours.

Isaac Watts.

106.

No. 13, 47.

1 O HOLY Spirit, enter in,
Among these hearts Thy work begin,
Thy temple deign to make us;
Sun of the soul, Thou Light Divine,
Around and in us brightly shine.
To strength and gladness wake us.
Where Thou shinest, life from heaven
There is given.
We before Thee
For that precious gift implore Thee.

2 Left to ourselves we shall but stray;
Oh, lead us on the narrow way,
With wisest counsel guide us,
And give us steadfastness, that we
May henceforth truly follow Thee,
Whatever woes betide us:
Heal Thou gently, hearts now broken,
Give some token
Thou art near us,
Whom we trust to light and cheer us.

3 O mighty Rock! O Source of Life!
Let Thy dear Word, 'mid doubt and strife,
Be so within us burning,
That we be faithful unto death,
In Thy pure love and holy faith,
From Thee true wisdom learning!
Lord, Thy graces on us shower,
By Thy power
Christ confessing,
Let us win His grace and blessing.

4 O gentle Dew, from heaven now fall
With power upon the hearts of all,
Thy tenderness instilling;
That heart to heart more closely bound,
Fruitful in kindly deeds be found,
The law of love fulfilling;
No wrath, no strife, here shall grieve Thee,
We receive Thee,
Where Thou livest
Peace and love and joy Thou givest.

5 Grant that our days, while life shall last,
In purest holiness be past;
Our minds so rule and strengthen
That they may rise o'er things of earth,
The hopes and joys that here have birth;
And if our course Thou lengthen,
Keep Thou pure, Lord, from offences,
Heart and senses;
Blessed Spirit,
Bid us thus true life inherit.

Michael Schirmer.

107.

7s.

1 GRACIOUS Spirit, Dove divine!
Let Thy light within me shine;
All my guilty fears remove,
Fill me with Thy heavenly love.

2 Speak Thy pardoning grace to me,
Set the burdened sinner free;
Lead me to the Lamb of God,
Wash me in His precious blood.

3 Life and peace to me impart;
Seal salvation on my heart;
Breathe Thyself into my breast,
Earnest of immortal rest.

4 Let me never from Thee stray,
Keep me in the narrow way:
Fill my soul with joy divine,
Help me, Lord, forever Thine.

John Stocker. a.

108.

7s.

1 HOLY GHOST, with light divine,
Shine upon this heart of mine!
Chase the shades of night away,
Turn the darkness into day.

2 Let me see my Savior's face,
Let me all his beauties trace;
Show those glorious truths to me,
Which are only known to Thee.

3 Holy Ghost, with power divine,
Cleanse this guilty heart of mine;
In Thy mercy pity me,
From sin's bondage set me free.

4 Holy Ghost, with joy divine,
Cheer this saddened heart of mine;
Yield a sacred, settled peace,
Let it grow and still increase.

5 Holy Spirit, all divine,
Dwell within this heart of mine;
Cast down every idol throne,
Reign supreme, and reign alone.

6 See, to Thee I yield my heart;
Shed Thy life through every part.
A pure temple I would be,
Wholly dedicate to Thee.

Andrew Reed. a.

109.

S. M.

1 LORD God, the Holy Ghost!
In this accepted hour,
As on the day of Pentecost,
Descend in all Thy power.

2 We meet with one accord
In our appointed place,
And wait the promise of our Lord,
The Spirit of all grace.

3 Like mighty rushing wind
Upon the waves beneath,
Move with one impulse every mind,
One soul, one feeling breathe.

4 The young, the old inspire
With wisdom from above;
And give us hearts and tongues of fire,
To pray, and praise, and love,

5 Spirit of light, explore,
And chase our gloom away;
With lustre shining more and more,
Unto the perfect day!

6 Spirit of truth, be Thou
In life and death our Guide;
O Spirit of adoption, now
May we be sanctified!

James Montgomery.

110.

L. M.

1 COME, Holy Spirit, from above,
And kindle in our hearts Thy love;
In all our darkness on us shine,
And fill us with Thy grace divine.

2 The only Comforter Thou art;
Oh, come and dwell within each heart;
And give us power from above
To keep the blessed law of love.

3 Enlighten every darkened heart,
And faith and hope to each impart;
What else we need Thou well dost know,
This let Thy love and grace bestow.

4 In Thy blest gifts on us outpoured,
Thou art the right hand of the Lord;
The Word of Truth Thou sendest forth,
In tongues of fire to all the earth.

5 Defend us from our wily foe,
And upon us Thy peace bestow;
Keep us securely all our days
In Thy blest covenant of grace.

6 Show us the Father's love and care,
And of the Son Thy witness bear;
To Both Thou showest us the way,
Spirit of Both, adored for aye.

7 To God the Father, God the Son,
For precious gifts be honor done;
And for the Spirit's gracious power
Be praise and glory evermore.

Martin Luther. J. O. Wallin.

THE TRINITY.

111.

1 IN all danger be our stay,
O Father, Son, and Spirit;
Cleanse us from our sins we pray,
And let us life inherit.
Keep us from the Evil One,
Firm in the faith abiding,
In Christ our Savior hiding,
And heartily confiding.
Let us put God's armor on,
With all true Christians running
Our heavenly race, and shunning
The Devil's wiles and cunning.
Amen, Amen, be this done.
Hallelujah! Hallelujah!

112.

1 WE all believe in one true God,
Maker of all earth and heaven;
The Father, Who to us in love
Hath the claim of children given.

He in soul and body feeds us,
  All we want His hand provides us,
Through all snares and perils leads us,
    Watches that no harm betides us;
He cares for us by day and night,
All things are governed by His might.

2 And we believe in Jesus Christ,
  His own Son, our Lord, possessing
An equal Godhead, throne and might,
  Through whom comes the Father's blessing;
Conceived of the Holy Spirit,
  Born of Mary, virgin mother!
That lost man might life inherit
  Made true Man, our elder Brother,
Was crucified by sinful men,
And raised by God to life again.

3 Also the Holy Ghost we own,
  Who sweet grace and comfort giveth,
And with the Father and the Son
  In eternal glory liveth;
Who the Christian church doth even
  Keep in unity of spirit;
Sins are verily forgiven
  Through the blest Redeemer's merit;
All flesh shall rise again, and we
Shall live with God eternally.

Martin Luther.

113.

L. M.

1 ALMIGHTY God, eternal Lord,
Grant us Thy grace through Thy dear Word
To praise Thee and to bear in mind
That Thou art ever good and kind.

2 Lord Jesus Christ, incarnate Word,
Thy Name be evermore adored,
For all Thine anguish, death, and pain,
Through which salvation we obtain.

3 O Holy Spirit, grant us grace,
And guide us in Thy righteous ways,
That we may with the heavenly host
Praise Father, Son, and Holy Ghost.

J. O. Wallin.

114.

6.6.4.6.6.6.4.

1 COME, Thou almighty King,
Help us Thy Name to sing,
Help us to praise!
Father all glorious,
O'er all victorious,
Come and reign over us,
Ancient of days.

2 Jesus, our Lord, descend;
From all our foes defend,
Nor let us fall;
Let Thine almighty aid
Our sure defense be made,
Our souls on Thee be stayed;
Lord, hear our call!

3 Come, Thou incarnate Word,
Gird on Thy mighty sword,
Our prayer attend:
Come, and Thy people bless,
And give Thy Word success;
Spirit of holiness,
On us descend.

4 Come, holy Comforter,
Thy sacred witness bear
In this glad hour:
Thou who almighty art,
Now rule in every heart,
And ne'er from us depart,
Spirit of power!

5 To the great One in Three
Eternal praises be,
Hence, evermore!
His sovereign Majesty
May we in glory see,
And to eternity
Love and adore.

C. Wesley.

115.

7s.

1 GLORY to the Father give,
God in whom we move and live;
Children's prayers He deigns to hear,
Children's songs delight His ear.

2 Glory to the Son we bring,
Christ our Prophet, Priest, and King:

Children, raise your sweetest strain
To the Lamb, for He was slain.

3 Glory to the Holy Ghost,
Who reclaims the sinner lost;
Children's minds may He inspire,
Touch their tongues with holy fire.

4 Glory in the highest be
To the blessed Trinity,
For the gospel from above,
For the word that God is love.

James Montgomery.

116.

11.12.11.10.

1 HOLY, Holy, Holy, Lord God Almighty!
Early in the morning our song shall rise to Thee:
Holy, Holy, Holy! merciful and mighty;
God in three Persons, blessed Trinity!

2 Holy, Holy, Holy! all the saints adore Thee,
Casting down their golden crowns upon the glassy sea;
Cherubim and Seraphim falling down before Thee,
Which wert, and art, and evermore shalt be.

3 Holy, Holy, Holy! Though the darkness hide Thee,
Though the eye of sinful man Thy glory may not see,

Only Thou art holy: there is none beside
Thee
Perfect in power, in love, in purity.

4 Holy, Holy, Holy, Lord God Almighty!
All Thy works shall praise Thy Name, in
earth, and sky, and sea:
Holy, Holy, Holy! merciful and mighty;
God in three Persons, blessed Trinity!

117. C. M.

1 HAIL! holy, holy, holy Lord,
Whom One in Three we know;
By all Thy heavenly hosts adored,
By all Thy church below.

2 One undivided Trinity
With triumph we proclaim;
The universe is full of Thee,
And speaks Thy glorious Name.

3 Thee, holy Father, we confess:
Thee, holy Son, adore;
And Thee, the Holy Ghost, we bless,
And worship evermore.

4 Hail! holy, holy, holy Lord,
Our heavenly song shall be;
Supreme, essential one, adored
In co-eternal Three!

C. Wesley. a.

118.

8.7.8.7.8.7.8.7.7

1 OUR Father, merciful and good,
Who dost to Thee invite us,
Oh! cleanse us in our Savior's blood,
And to Thyself unite us.
Send unto us Thy holy Word,
And let it guide us ever;
Then in this world of darkness, Lord,
Shall naught from Thee us sever:
Grant us, O Lord, this favor!

2 We cry to Thee with one accord,
'Tis all that can avail us;
For none doth hear and keep Thy Word,
If Lord, Thy grace doth fail us.
Consider then, we humbly pray,
For our dear Savior's merit,
How Satan soweth tares alway,
And send, O Lord, Thy Spirit,
That we may life inherit.

3 O God and man, Christ Jesus blest!
Our sorrows Thou didst carry.
Our wants and cares Thou knowest best,
For Thou with us didst tarry.
O Jesus Christ, our Brother dear,
To us and every nation
Thy Spirit send, let Him draw near
With truth and consolation,
That we may see salvation.

3 Come, Holy Ghost, Thy grace impart,
Tear Satan's snares asunder.
The Word of God keep in our heart,
And lead us safely yonder;
Then, sanctified, for evermore,
In Christ alone confiding,
We'll sing His praise and Him adore;
His precious Word us guiding
To heavenly joys abiding!

Olaus Petri.

119.

6.6.8.4.D.

1 THE God who reigns on high
The great archangels sing,
And "Holy, holy, holy," cry,
"Almighty King!
Who was and is the same,
And evermore shall be;
Jehovah, Father, great I am,
We worship Thee".

2 Before the Savior's face
The ransomed nations bow,
O'erwhelmed at His almighty grace,
For ever new:
He shows His prints of love;
They kindle to a flame,
And sound, through all the worlds above,
The slaughtered Lamb.

3 The whole triumphant host
Give thanks to God on high;

"Hail, Father, Son, and Holy Ghost!"
  They ever cry:
Hail, Abraham's God, and mine!
  I join the heavenly lays;
All might and majesty are Thine,
  And endless praise.

Thomas Olivers.

II. THE CHRISTIAN LIFE.

WORSHIP.

120. L. M.

1 BEFORE Jehovah's awful throne,
Ye nations, bow with sacred joy;
Know that the Lord is God alone,
He can create, and He destroy.

2 His sovereign power, without our aid,
Made us of clay, and formed us men;
And when like wandering sheep we strayed,
He brought us to His fold again.

3 We are His people, we His care,
Our souls and all our mortal frame:
What lasting honors shall we rear,
Almighty Maker, to Thy Name?

4 We'll crowd Thy gates with thankful songs,
High as the heavens our voices raise;
And earth, with her ten thousand tongues,
Shall fill Thy courts with sounding praise.

5 Wide as the world is Thy command,
Vast as eternity Thy love;
Firm as a rock Thy truth must stand,
When rolling years shall cease to move.

Isaac Watts.

121.

8.7.8.7.8.8.7.

1 All glory be to God on high,
Who hath our race befriended!
To us no harm shall now come nigh,
The strife at last is ended;
God showeth His good will to men,
And peace shall reign on earth again;
Oh! thank Him for His goodness.

2 We praise, we worship Thee, we trust,
And give Thee thanks forever,
O Father, that Thy rule is just,
And wise, and changes never:
Thy boundless power o'er all things reigns,
Thou dost whate'er Thy will ordains;
Well for us that Thou rulest!

3 O Jesus Christ, our God and Lord,
Son of Thy Heavenly Father,
O Thou who hast our peace restored
And the lost sheep dost gather,
Thou Lamb of God, to Thee on high
From out our depths we sinners cry,
Have mercy on us, Jesus!

4 O Holy Ghost, Thou precious gift,
Thou Comforter, unfailing,
O'er Satan's snares our souls uplift,
And let Thy power availing
Avert our woes and calm our dread
For us the Savior's blood was shed;
We trust in Thee to save us!

N. Decius.

122.

8.7.8.7.8.8.7.

1 WITH joyful heart your praises bring
To God the Fount of blessing:
His everlasting goodness sing,
His holy Name confessing:
Our God let all creation bless;
He is our aid in all distress:
Oh, bless His Name forever!

2 Praise God who to the cross and grave
Hath sent His Son from heaven;
His death that did the guilty save,
Eternal life hath given.
He hath redeemed our souls from hell;
Now peace from God with men doth dwell:
Oh, bless His Name forever!

3 Praise God who by His Spirit's light
To faith our souls awaketh:
Our souls with gifts of grace and might,
He strong, He steadfast maketh.
His Word doth light our heavenward way;
His grace inclines us to obey:
Oh, bless His Name forever!

4 Ye mighty Seraphim, your praise
Still to the Lord be bringing,
Let all in heaven their voices raise;
Let earth break forth in singing.
Whate'er hath breath shall Him adore,
Him first, Him last, Him evermore:
Oh, bless His Name forever!

C. Gunther.

123.

8.7.8.7.8.8.7.

1 SING praise to God who reigns above,
The God of all creation,
The God of power, the God of love,
The God of our salvation.
With healing balm my soul He fills,
And every faithless murmur stills;
To God all praise and glory!

2 The angel host, O King of kings,
Thy praise forever telling,
In earth and sky all living things
Beneath Thy shadow dwelling,
Adore the wisdom that could span,
And power which formed creation's plan;
To God all praise and glory!

3 I cried to God in my distress,
His mercy heard me calling;
My Savior saw my helplessness,
And kept my feet from falling;
For this, Lord, praise and thanks to Thee!
Praise God Most High, praise God with me!
To God all praise and glory!

4 Thus all my gladsome way along,
I'll sing aloud Thy praises,
That men may hear the grateful song
My voice unwearied raises:
Be joyful in the Lord, my heart!
Both soul and body, bear your part!
To God all praise and glory!

John Jacob Schuetz.

124.

S. M.

1 OH, bless the Lord, my soul!
Let all within me join,
And aid my tongue to bless His Name,
Whose favors are divine.

2 Oh, bless the Lord, my soul!
Nor let His mercies lie
Forgotten in unthankfulness,
And without praises die.

3 'Tis He forgives thy sins;
'Tis he relieves thy pain;
'Tis he that heals thy sicknesses,
And gives thee strength again.

4 He crowns thy life with love,
When ransomed from the grave;
He that redeemed my soul from death
Hath sovereign power to save.

5 He fills the poor with good;
He gives the sufferers rest:
The Lord hath judgments for the proud,
And justice for the opprest.

6 His wondrous works and ways
He made by Moses known;
But sent the world his truth and grace
By His beloved Son.

Isaac Watts. a.

125. S. M.

1 MY soul, repeat His praise,
Whose mercies are so great;
Whose anger is so slow to rise,
So ready to abate.

2 God will not always chide;
And, when His wrath is felt,
His strokes are fewer than our crimes,
And lighter than our guilt.

3 High as the heavens are raised
Above the ground we tread,
So far the riches of His grace
Our highest thoughts exceed.

4 His power subdues our sins;
And His forgiving love,
Far as the east is from the west,
Doth all our guilt remove.

5 Our days are as the grass,
Or like the morning flower;
If one sharp blast sweep o'er the field,
It withers in an hour.

6 But Thy compassions, Lord,
To endless years endure;
And children's children ever find
Thy words of promise sure.

Isaac Watts.

126.

S. M.

1 COME, sound His praise abroad,
And hymns of glory sing:
Jehovah is the sovereign God,
The universal King.

2 He formed the deeps unknown;
He gave the seas their bound;
The watery worlds are all His own,
And all the solid ground.

3 Come, worship at His throne;
Come, bow before the Lord.
We are His work, and not our own:
He formed us by His word.

4 To-day attend His voice,
Nor dare provoke His rod;
Come, like the people of His choice,
And own your gracious God.

Isaac Watts.

127.

8.7.8.7.

1 PRAISE the Lord, ye heavens, adore Him,
Praise Him, angels in the height;
Sun and moon, rejoice before Him;
Praise Him, all ye stars of light.

2 Praise the Lord, for He hath spoken;
Worlds His mighty voice obeyed;
Laws which never shall be broken,
For their guidance He hath made.

3 Praise the Lord, for he is glorious;
Never shall His promise fail;
God hath made His saints victorious,
Sin and death shall not prevail.

4 Praise the God of our salvation,
Hosts on high His power proclaim;
Heaven and earth, and all creation,
Laud and magnify His Name.

Anon.

128.

8.7.8.7.D.

1 LORD, with glowing heart I'd praise Thee
For the bliss Thy love bestows,
For the pardoning grace that saves me,
And the peace that from it flows.
Help, O God, my weak endeavor;
This dull soul to rapture raise:
Thou must light the flame, or never
Can my love be warmed to praise.

2 Praise, my soul, the God that sought thee,
Wretched wanderer, far astray;
Found thee lost, and kindly brought thee
From the paths of death away.
Praise, with love's devoutest feeling,
Him who saw thy guilt-born fear,
And the light of hope revealing,
Bade the blood-stained cross appear.

2 Lord, this bosom's ardent feeling
Vainly would my lips express:

Low before Thy footstool kneeling,
  Deign Thy suppliant's prayer to bless.
Let Thy grace, my soul's chief treasure,
  Love's pure flame within me raise:
And, since words can never measure,
  Let my life show forth Thy praise.

Francis Scott Key.

129.

8.7.8.7.D.

1 OH, what praises shall we render
  To the Lord, who reigns above,
For His mercies, constant, tender,
  For His condescending love!
Though we often have offended,
  And transgressed His holy will,
Still has He our souls befriended;
  We may call Him Father still.

2 Heavenly Father, Thou hast taught us
  Thus to seek Thee in our youth;
Hitherto Thy grace hath brought us,
  Lead us onward in Thy truth.
We are weak, do Thou uphold us,
  And from every snare defend;
Let Thy mighty arms enfold us,
  Save us, keep us, to the end.

3 Oh, our Father, great and glorious!
  Draw our youthful hearts to Thee;
Let Thy grace be there victorious,
  Let Thy love our portion be.

May we know Thy great salvation,
Serve and love Thee all our days;
Then in heaven, Thy habitation,
Join to sing Thine endless praise.

John Burton, Jr.

130.

8.7.8.7.

1 GOD is Love: His mercy brightens
All the path in which we rove;
Bliss He wakes, and woe He lightens:
God is Wisdom, God is Love.

2 Time and change are busy ever;
Man decays, and ages move:
But His mercy waneth never;
God is Wisdom, God is Love.

3 E'en the hour that darkest seemeth
Will His changeless goodness prove;
From the gloom His brightness streameth:
God is Wisdom, God is Love.

4 He with earthly cares entwineth
Hope and comfort from above:
Everywhere His glory shineth;
God is Wisdom, God is Love.

Sir John Bowring. a.

131.

8.7.8.7.D.

1 LOVE divine, all love excelling,
Joy of heaven, to earth come down!
Fix in us Thy humble dwelling,
All Thy faithful mercies crown.

Jesus, Thou art all compassion,
Pure, unbounded love Thou art;
Visit us with Thy salvation,
Enter every trembling heart.

2 Breathe, oh! breathe Thy loving spirit
Into every troubled breast.
Let us all in Thee inherit,
Let us find Thy promised rest.
Take away the love of sinning,
Alpha and Omega be;
End of faith, as its beginning,
Set our hearts at liberty.

3 Come, Almighty to deliver,
Let us all Thy life receive;
Graciously return, and never,
Never more Thy temples leave.
Thee we would be always blessing,
Serve Thee as Thy hosts above,
Pray and praise Thee without ceasing,
Glory in Thy precious love.

5 Finish then Thy new creation,
Pure and spotless let us be;
Let us see our whole salvation
Perfectly secured by Thee.
Changed from glory into glory,
Till in heaven we take our place,
Till we cast our crowns before Thee,
Lost in wonder, love, and praise.

C. Wesley.

132.

8.7.8.7.7.7.

1 PRAISE the Lord, each tribe and nation,
Praise Him with a joyous heart;
Ye who know His full salvation,
Gather now from every part;
Let your voices glorify,
In His temple, God on high.

2 He's our God and our Creator,
We, His flock and chosen seed:
He, our Lord and Liberator,
Us from sin and peril freed;
And at last His flock shall rest
In the mansions of the blest.

3 Give Him thanks in all His portals;
In the courts his deeds proclaim;
Hither come, ye ransomed mortals,
Glorify our Savior's Name.
Ever kind and loving, He
Keeps His faith eternally.

J. Franck.—J. Svedberg.

133.

6.7.6.7.6.6.6 6.

1 NOW thank we all our God,
With heart and hands and voices,
Who wondrous things hath done,
In whom His earth rejoices;
Who from our mother's arms
Hath blessed us on our way
With countless gifts of love,
And still is ours to-day.

2 Oh! may this bounteous God,
Through all our life be near us,
With ever joyful hearts,
And blessed peace to cheer us;
And keep us in His grace,
And guide us when perplexed,
And free us from all ills,
In this world and the next.

3 All praise and thanks to God
The Father, now be given,
The Son and Him who reigns
With them in highest heaven;
The One eternal God,
Whom earth and heaven adore;
For thus it was, is now,
And shall be evermore.

Martin Rinkart.

134.

11s.

1 WE gather, we gather, dear Jesus, to bring
The breathings of love 'mid the blossoms of spring;
Our Maker, Redeemer, we gratefully raise
Our hearts and our voices in hymning Thy praise.

2 When stooping to earth from the brightness of heaven,
Thy blood for our ransom so freely was given,

Thou deignedst to listen while children adored,
With joyful hosannas, the blest of the Lord.

3 Those arms, which embraced little children of old,
Still love to encircle the lambs of the fold;
That grace which inviteth the wandering home,
Hath never forbidden the youngest to come.

4 Hosanna! Hosanna! Great Teacher we raise
Our hearts and our voices in hymning Thy praise
For precept and promise so graciously given,
For blessings of earth, and for glories of heaven.

J. N. Van Harlingen.

135.

7.6.7.6.D.

1 COME, let us sing of Jesus,
While hearts and accents blend;
Come, let us sing of Jesus,
The sinner's only Friend;
His holy soul rejoices
Amid the choirs above,
To hear our youthful voices
Exulting in His love.

2 We love to sing of Jesus,
Who wept our path along;
We love to sing of Jesus,
The tempted and the strong;

None who besought His healing,
He passed unheeded by;
And still retains His feeling
For us above the sky.

3 We love to sing of Jesus,
Who died our souls to save;
We love to sing of Jesus,
Triumphant o'er the grave;
And in our hour of danger,
We'll trust His love alone,
Who once slept in a manger,
And now sits on a throne.

4 Then let us sing of Jesus,
While yet on earth we stay,
And hope to sing of Jesus
Throughout eternal day.
For those who here confess Him
He will in heaven confess,
And faithful hearts that bless Him,
He will forever bless.

G. W. Bethune.

136.

6.5.6.5.3.

1 SEE the shining dew-drops
On the flowers strewed,
Proving as they sparkle
"God is ever good.
Ever good."

2 See the morning sunbeams
Lighting up the wood,

Silently proclaiming
"God is ever good.
Ever good."

3 Hear the mountain streamlet
In its solitude,
With its ripple saying
"God is ever good.
Ever good."

4 In the leafy tree-tops,
Where no fears intrude,
Merry birds are singing
"God is ever good.
Ever good."

5 He who came to save us
Shed His precious blood;
Better things it speaketh:
"God is ever good.
Ever good."

6 Bring, my heart, thy tribute,
Songs of gratitude;
All things join to tell us
"God is ever good.
Ever good."

137.

7s.

1 CHILDREN of the heavenly King,
As ye journey, sweetly sing;
Sing your Savior's worthy praise,
Glorious in His works and ways.

2 Ye are traveling home to God,
In the way the fathers trod;
They are happy now, and ye
Soon their happiness shall see.

3 O ye banished seed, be glad!
Christ our Advocate is made;
Us to save, our flesh assumes,
Brother to our souls becomes.

4 Shout, ye little flock, and blest;
You on Jesus' throne shall rest:
There your seat is now prepared;
There your kingdom and reward.

5 Lord, submissive make us go,
Gladly leaving all below;
Only Thou our leader be,
And we still will follow Thee.

J. Cennick.

138.

6.5.6.5.

1 JESUS, high in glory,
Lend a listening ear,
When we bow before Thee,
Children's praises hear.

2 Though Thou art so holy,
Heaven's Almighty King,
Thou wilt stoop to listen,
When Thy praise we sing.

3 We are little children,
Weak and apt to stray;
Savior, guide and keep us
In the heavenly way.

4 Save us, Lord, from sinning;
Watch us day by day;
Help us now to love Thee;
Take our sins away.

5 Then, when Thou dost call us
To our heavenly home.
We would gladly answer,
Savior, Lord, we come.

J. E. Clarke.

139.

8.7.8.7. and Chorus.

1 HUMBLE praises, holy Jesus,
Infant voices raise to Thee:
In Thy mercy, oh, receive us!
Suffer us Thy lambs to be.
Chorus—Hallelujah, sweetly singing,
Joyful tribute now we bring.
Hallelujah, Hallelujah!
Hallelujah, to our King!

2 Gracious Savior, be Thou with us;
Let Thy mercy richly flow:
Give Thy Spirit, blessed Jesus,
Light and life on us bestow.
Chorus—Hallelujah, sweetly singing, etc.

Composite.

140.

8.7.8.7.

1 SAVIOR, who Thy flock art feeding,
With the Shepherd's kindest care,
All the feeble gently leading,
While the lambs Thy bosom share.

2 Now, these little ones receiving,
Fold them in Thy gracious arm;
There, we know, Thy Word believing,
Only there, secure from harm.

3 Never, from Thy pasture roving,
Let them be the lion's prey;
Let Thy tenderness, so loving,
Keep them through life's dangerous way.

4 Then within Thy fold eternal
Let them find a resting-place:
Feed in pastures ever vernal,
Drink the rivers of Thy grace.

William Augustus Muhlenberg.

141.

H. M.

1 WHEN little Samuel woke,
And heard His Maker's voice,
At every word He spoke,
How much did he rejoice!
Oh, blessed, happy child! to find
The God of heaven so near and kind.

2 If God would speak to me,
And say He was my Friend,

How happy I should be!
  Oh, how I would attend!
The smallest sin I then would fear,
If God Almighty were so near.

3 And does He never speak?
  Oh, yes, for in His Word
He bids me come to seek
  The God that Samuel heard.
And every sin I well may fear,
Since God Almighty is so near.

4 Like Samuel let us say,
  Whene'er we read His Word,
"Speak, Lord, I would obey
  The voice that Samuel heard;
And when I in Thy house appear,
Speak, for Thy servant waits to hear."

Mrs. Ann Gilbert.

142. C. M.

1 O THOU, whose infant feet were found
  Within Thy Father's shrine,
Whose years, with changeless virtue crowned,
  Were all alike divine.

2 Dependent on Thy bounteous breath,
  We seek Thy grace alone,
In childhood, manhood, age, and death,
  To keep us still Thine own.

Reginald Heber.

143.

8.7. 6 lines.

1 SAVIOR, like a shepheard lead us,
Much we need Thy tenderest care;
In Thy pleasant pastures feed us,
For our use Thy fold prepare.
Blessed Jesus, blessed Jesus,
Thou hast bought us, Thine we are.

2 Thou hast promised to receive us,
Poor and sinful though we be;
Thou hast mercy to relieve us,
Grace to cleanse, and power to free.
Blessed Jesus, blessed Jesus,
Let us early turn to Thee.

3 Early let us seek Thy favor,
Early let us do Thy will;
Blessed Lord and only Savior,
With Thy love our bosom fill.
Blessed Jesus, blessed Jesus,
Thou hast loved us, love us still.

Dorothy A. Thrupp.

144.

8.7 8.7.D.

1 WHAT a friend we have in Jesus,
All our sins and griefs to bear!
What a privilege to carry
Every thing to God in prayer.
Oh, what peace we often forfeit!
Oh, what needless pain we bear!
All because we do not carry
Everything to God in prayer.

2 Have we trials and temptations?
Is there trouble anywhere?
We should never be discouraged,
Take it to the Lord in prayer.
Can we find a friend so faithful,
Who will our sorrows share?
Jesus knows our every weakness,
Take it to the Lord in prayer.

3 Are we weak and heavy laden,
Cumbered with a load of care?
Precious Savior, still our refuge,—
Take it to the Lord in prayer.
Do thy friends despise, forsake thee?
Take it to the Lord in prayer;
In His arms He'll take and shield thee,
Thou wilt find a solace there.

H. Bonar.

145.

7s.

1 COME, my soul, thy suit prepare,
Jesus loves to answer prayer:
He Himself has bid thee pray,
Therefore will not say thee nay.

2 Thou art coming to a King;
Large petitions with thee bring;
For His grace and power are such
None can ever ask too much.

3 With my burden I begin;
Lord, remove this load of sin:

Let Thy blood for sinners spilt,
Set my conscience free from guilt.

4 Lord, I come to Thee for rest,
Take possession of my breast;
There Thy blood-bought right maintain,
And without a rival reign.

5 While I am a pilgrim here,
Let Thy love my spirit cheer:
As my Guide, my Guard, my Friend,
Lead me to my journey's end.

6 Show me what I have to do,
Every hour my strength renew:
Let me live a life of faith,
Let me die Thy people's death.

John Newton.

146. L. M. D.

1 SWEET hour of prayer, sweet hour of prayer,
That calls me from a world of care,
And bids me at my Father's throne
Make all my wants and wishes known;
In seasons of distress and grief,
My soul has often found relief,
And oft escaped the tempter's snare
By thy return, sweet hour of prayer.

2 Sweet hour of prayer, sweet hour of prayer,
Thy wings shall my petition bear

To Him whose truth and faithfulness
Engage the waiting soul to bless;
And since He bids me seek His face,
Believe His Word, and trust His grace,
I'll cast on Him my every care,
And wait for thee, sweet hour of prayer.

3 Sweet hour of prayer, sweet hour of prayer,
May I thy consolation share;
Till from Mount Pisgah's lofty height
I view my home, and take my flight;
This robe of flesh I'll drop, and rise
To seize the everlasting prize;
And shout, while passing through the air,
Farewell, farewell, sweet hour of prayer.

Fanny J. Crosby.

147.

7.6.7.6.D.

1 O FOUNT of truth and mercy,
Thy promise can not fail;
What Thou hast said must ever,
In heaven and earth prevail:
"Call upon Me in trouble,
And I will help afford."
Yea, to my latest moment,
I'll call upon Thee, Lord.

2 What comfort in affliction
To rest upon Thy grace,
And in Thy wise direction
My fainting heart to place!

When Thou, O Lord, didst teach me
In Thine own Name to pray,
Thou to my hope affordedst
A refuge and a stay.

3 The yearnings of my bosom
Thou hearest, Lord, I know;
What to my weal pertaineth
I know Thou wilt bestow.
In times of deepest anguish
Thy helping hand is near;
And on Thy loving bosom
My sorrows Thou wilt bear.

4 And to this blest assurance
I'll cling for evermore;
And never shall I weary
A Father to implore.
Depart, despair and anguish,
That oft my soul oppress;
I'll cling unto my Savior
Till He my soul shall bless.

P. O. Nyström.

148. C. M.

1 LORD, teach us how to pray aright,
With reverence and with fear:
Though dust and ashes in Thy sight,
We may, we must, draw near.

2 Burdened with guilt, convinced of sin,
In weakness, want, and woe,

Fightings without and fears within,
Lord, whither shall we go?

3 God of all grace, we come to Thee
With broken, contrite hearts;
Give, what Thine eye delights to see,
Truth in the inward parts.

4 Give deep humility; the sense
Of godly sorrow give;
A strong desire, with confidence,
To hear Thy voice and live:

5 Faith in the only Sacrifice
That can for sin atone;
To cast our hopes, to fix our eyes,
On Christ, on Christ alone.

6 Give these, and then Thy will be done,
Thus strengthened with all might,
We, through Thy Spirit and Thy Son,
Shall pray, and pray aright.

James Montgomery.

149.

8.7.8.7.8.8.7.

1 COME, Savior dear, with us abide,
We need Thy kind compassion;
Thy flock to living waters guide,
Which are Thy wounds and passion;
And lead us into pastures green
Where faithful souls are ever seen
In peace and blissful union.

2 O Sea of love, pour out Thy flood
O'er all in blessed showers;
The fiery darts quench with Thy blood
And crush hell's evil powers.
Thou, of the world the Mercy Seat,
Let of Thy love the gentle heat
Set all our hearts a glowing.

A. C. Rutström.

150. L. M.

1 O JESUS Christ, Thy grace us lend,
Thy Holy Spirit to us send,
Lift up our hearts, hear us, we pray,
And lead us in life's narrow way!

2 Help us, O Lord, Thy Name to praise,
On us bestow Thy power and grace,
Increase our faith, give us Thy light
To hear and keep Thy Word aright!

3 Till we in heaven with one accord
Sing, "Holy, holy, holy Lord,"
And there in glory Thee behold,
Revealed 'mid angel hosts untold.

4 Praise to the Father and the Son,
And to the Spirit, Three in One.
Yea, to the Holy Trinity
Be praise throughout eternity!

William August II.—J. Gezelius.

151.

7.8.7.8.8.8.

1 BLESSED Jesus, at Thy word
We are gathered all to hear Thee;
Let our hearts and souls be stirred
Now to seek and love and fear Thee;
By Thy teachings sweet and holy,
Drawn from earth to love Thee solely.

2 All our knowledge, sense, and sight
Lie in deepest darkness shrouded,
Till Thy Spirit breaks our night
With the beams of truth unclouded.
Thou alone to God canst win us,
Thou must work all good within us.

3 Glorious Lord, Thyself impart!
Light of light, from God proceeding,
Open Thou our ears and heart,
Help us by Thy Spirit's pleading,
Hear the cry Thy people raises,
Hear, and bless our prayers and praises.

Tobias Clausnitzer.

152.

8.7.8.7.7.7.

1 OPEN now thy gates of beauty,
Zion, let me enter there,
Where my soul, in joyful duty,
Waits for Him who answers prayer;
Oh, how blessed is this place,
Filled with solace, light, and grace!

2 Yes, my God, I come before Thee,
Come Thou also down to me;
Where we find Thee and adore Thee
There a heaven on earth must be.
To my heart oh! enter Thou,
Let it be Thy temple now.

3 Here Thy praise is gladly chanted,
Here Thy seed is duly sown:
Let my soul, where it is planted,
Bring forth precious sheaves alone.
So that all I hear may be
Fruitful unto life in me.

4 Thou my faith increase and quicken,
Let me keep Thy gift divine,
Howsoe'er temptations thicken,
May Thy Word still o'er me shine;
As my pole-star through my life,
As my comfort in my strife.

5 Speak, O God, and I will hear Thee,
Let Thy will be done indeed;
May I undisturbed draw near Thee
While Thou dost Thy people feed;
Here of life the fountain flows,
Here is balm for all our woes.

Benjamin Schmolk.

153.

8.7.8.7.4.7.

1 IN Thy Name, O Lord, assembling,
We, Thy people, now draw near:
Teach us to rejoice with trembling;

Speak, and let Thy servants hear;
Hear with meekness,
Hear Thy Word with godly fear.

2 While our days on earth are lengthened,
May we give them, Lord, to Thee;
Cheered by hope, and daily strengthened,
May we run, nor weary be,
Till Thy glory
Without cloud in heaven we see.

3 There, in worship purer, sweeter,
All Thy people shall adore;
Tasting of enjoyment greater
Than they could conceive before;
Full enjoyment,
Full and pure for evermore.

Thomas Kelly.

154.

7.6.7.6.D.

1 OH! enter, Lord, Thy temple,
Be Thou my spirit's Guest,
Who at my birth didst give me
A second birth more blest.
Though here to dwell Thou deignest,
Thou in the Godhead, Lord,
Forever equal reignest,
Art equally adored.

2 Oh! enter, let me know Thee,
And feel Thy power within,
The power that breaks our fetters,
And rescues us from sin.

That I may serve Thee truly,
Oh! wash and cleanse Thou me,
To render honor duly
With perfect heart to Thee.

3 'Tis Thou, O Spirit, teachest
The soul to pray aright;
Thy songs have sweetest music,
Thy prayers have wondrous might.
They pierce the highest heaven,
Unheard they cannot fall,
Till He His help hath given
Who surely helpeth all.

4 The whole wide world, O Spirit,
Upon Thy hands doth rest;
Our wayward hearts Thou turnest
As it may seem Thee best.
As Thou hast done so often,
Once more Thy power make known,
Convert the wicked, soften
To tears the heart of stone.

5 Order our path in all things
According to Thy mind,
And when this life is over,
And all must be resigned,
With calm and fearless spirit
Oh! grant us then to die,
And after death inherit
Eternal life on high.

Paul Gerhardt.

155.

8.7.8.7.

1 COME, Thou Fount of every blessing,
Tune my heart to sing Thy grace;
Streams of mercy, never ceasing,
Call for songs of loudest praise.

2 Here I raise mine Ebenezer,
Hither by Thy help I'm come;
And I hope, by Thy good pleasure,
Safely to arrive at home.

3 Jesus sought me when a stranger,
Wandering from the fold of God;
He, to rescue me from danger,
Interposed His precious blood.

4 Oh, to grace how great a debtor
Daily I'm constrained to be!
Let that grace, Lord, like a fetter,
Bind my wandering heart to Thee.

5 Prone to wander, Lord, I feel it,
Prone to leave the God I love,
Here's my heart; oh! take and seal it,
Seal it from Thy courts above.

Robert Robinson? a.

156.

7s. 6 lines.

1 SAFELY through another week,
God has brought us on our way;
Let us now a blessing seek,
Waiting in His courts to-day:

Day of all the week the best,
Emblem of eternal rest.

2 Mercies multiplied each hour
Through the week, our praise demand;
Guarded by Thy mighty power,
Fed and guided by Thy hand;
Though ungrateful we have been,
Only made returns of sin.

3 While we pray for pardoning grace,
Through the dear Redeemer's Name,
Show Thy reconciling face,
Take away our sin and shame:
From our wordly cares set free,
May we rest this day in Thee.

4 Here we come, Thy Name to praise;
Let us feel Thy presence near;
May Thy glory meet our eyes,
While we in Thy house appear:
Here afford us, Lord, a taste
Of our everlasting feast.

5 May the gospel's joyful sound
Conquer sinners, comfort saints;
Make the fruits of grace abound,
Bring relief for all complaints:
Thus may all our sabbaths prove,
Till we join the church above.

John Newton. a.

157.

7.6.7.6.D.

1 O DAY of rest and gladness!
  O day of joy and light!
O balm of care and sadness,
  Most beautiful and bright!
On thee the high and lowly,
  Through ages joined in tune,
Sing, holy, holy, holy,
  To God the great Triune.

2 On thee, at the creation,
  The light first had its birth;
On thee, for our salvation,
  Christ rose from depths of earth;
On thee, our Lord, victorious,
  The Spirit sent from heaven;
And thus on thee, most glorious,
  A triple light was given.

3 To-day, on weary nations,
  The heavenly manna falls;
To holy convocations
  The silver trumpet calls,
Where gospel light is glowing
  With pure and radiant beams,
And living water flowing
  With soul-refreshing streams.

4 New graces ever gaining
  From this one day of rest,
We reach the rest remaining
  To spirits of the blest;

To Holy Ghost be praises,
  To Father and to Son,
The church her voice upraises
  To Thee, blest Three in One.

C. Wordsworth.

158.

8.7.8.7.7.7.8.8.

1 GUARDIAN of pure hearts, and Hearer,
  Lord, of every faithful prayer,
In Thy courts one day is dearer,
  Than a thousand days elsewhere.
Worn with earth's unrest, how sweet
In Thy temple fair to meet!
There to sing away each sorrow
That from life and toil we borrow!

2 With the righteous oft it fareth
  Here, as if his deeds were ill;
Blight fair virtue's flowers impaireth,
  Weeds of vice do flourish still;
Joy and fortune haste away,
Friends with friends—how short their stay!
Rachel still her children mourneth,
And her soul from comfort turneth.

3 But when here devoutly soareth
  High the temple-anthem sweet,
Grief grows calm, no plaint outpoureth—
  Hearts with holy rapture beat:
Free from earthly clouds the soul
Presses toward a higher goal,

Takes from hope the comfort given,
Speaks e'en now the tongue of heaven.

4 O my soul, thy wing ascending
Yet on Salem's mount shall rest;
There where cherub-harps are blending
With the singing of the blest;
Let thy note of praise and prayer
To thy God precede thee there,
While e'en yet a care-worn mortal,
Still without thy Father's portal.

5 Days are dawning, days are flying!
Hold thou fast the Word of God:
"Lamp unto my feet", still crying,
"Light unto my dreary road!"
Joy thou in that Holy Word
Which of old on earth was heard,
For man's peace and comfort given,
Only guide from earth to heaven.

6 Let us, Christians, here that wander,
As our fathers in their day,
Piously together ponder,
Gladly sing and meekly pray;
Be the children's voices raised
To the God their fathers praised.
Let Thy bounty failing never
Be on us and all forever.

7 Bless us, Father, and protect us,
Be our souls' sure hiding place,

Let Thy wisdom still direct us,
  Light our darkness with Thy grace!
Let Thy countenance on us shine,
Fill us all with peace divine.
Praise the Father, Son, and Spirit,
Praise Him all that life inherit!

J. O. Wallin and J. Svedberg.

159.

8.7.8.7.4.7.

1 LORD, dismiss us with Thy blessing,
    Fill our hearts with joy and peace!
  Let us each, Thy love possessing,
    Triumph in redeeming grace.
        Oh! refresh us,
    Traveling through this wilderness.

2 Thanks we give and adoration
    For Thy gospel's joyful sound.
  May the fruits of Thy salvation
    In our hearts and lives abound:
        May Thy presence
    With us evermore be found.

3 So, whene'er the signal's given
    Us from earth to call away,
  Borne on angels' wings to heaven,
    Glad the summons to obey,
        May we, ready,
    Rise and reign in endless day.

John Fawcett?

160.

7.6.7.6.

1 ABIDE with us, our Savior,
Nor let Thy mercy cease;
From Satan's might defend us,
And grant our souls release.

2 Abide with us, our Savior,
Sustain us by Thy Word;
That we with all Thy people
To life may be restored.

3 Abide with us, our Savior,
Thou Light of endless light;
Increase to us Thy blessings,
And save us by Thy might.

4 To Father, Son, and Spirit,
Eternal One in Three,
As was, and is forever,
All praise and glory be.

Joshua Stegmann.

161.

C. M.

1 ALMIGHTY God, Thy Word is cast
Like seed into the ground;
Now let the dew of heaven descend,
And righteous fruits abound.

2 Let not the foe of Christ and man
This holy seed remove;
But give it root in every heart,
To bring forth fruits of love.

3 Let not the world's deceitful cares
The rising plant destroy;
But let it yield a hundred fold
The fruits of peace and joy.

4 Oft as the precious seed is sown,
Thy quickening grace bestow,
That all whose souls the truth receive,
Its saving power may know.

John Cawood.

162.

7s.

1 FOR a season called to part,
Let us now ourselves commend
To the gracious eye and heart
Of our ever-present Friend.

2 Jesus, hear our humble prayer:
Tender Shepherd of Thy sheep,
Let Thy mercy and Thy care
All our souls in safety keep.

3 What we each have now been taught,
Let our memories retain:
May we, if we live, be brought
Here to meet in peace again.

4 Then, if Thou instruction bless,
Songs of praises shall be given;
We'll our thankfulness express,
Here on earth, and when in heaven.

J. Newton.

163.

H.M.

1 ON what has now been sown,
Thy blessing, Lord, bestow;
The power is Thine alone
To make it spring and grow:
Do Thou the gracious harvest raise,
And Thou alone shalt have the praise.

2 To Thee our wants are known,
From Thee are all our powers,
Accept what is Thine own,
And pardon what is ours:
Our praises, Lord, and prayers receive,
And to Thy Word a blessing give.

3 Oh! grant that each of us,
Who meet before Thee here,
May meet together thus,
When Thou and Thine appear,
And follow Thee to heaven our home;
E'en so, Amen, Lord Jesus, come!

John Newton.

164.

7.8.7.8.8.8.

1 NOW our worship sweet is o'er—
Singing, praying, teaching, hearing:
Let us gladly God adore,
For his gracious strength and cheering:
Bless His Name, who fain would save us,
For the rich repast he gave us.

2 Now the blessing cheers our heart,
And the service all is ended,
Let us joyfully depart,
Be our souls to God commended:
His good Spirit e'ver guide us,
And with all things well provide us.

3 Let our going out be blest,
Bless our entrance in like measure;
Bless, O Lord, our toil and rest,
Bless our bread, our grief, and pleasure;
Be in death Thy blessing given;
And make us blest heirs of heaven!

H. Schenk.

165.

S. M.

1 BLEST be the tie that binds
Our hearts in Christian love:
The fellowship of kindred minds
Is like to that above.

2 Before our Father's throne
We pour our ardent prayers;
Our fears, our hopes, our aims are one,
Our comforts and our cares.

3 We share our mutual woes,
Our mutual burdens bear;
And often for each other flows
The sympathizing tear.

4 When we asunder part,
It gives us inward pain;

But we shall still be joined in heart,
And hope to meet again.

5 From sorrow, toil, and pain,
And sin, we shall be free;
And perfect love and friendship reign
Through all eternity.

John Fawcett.

166.

L. M.

1 AWAKE, my soul, and with the sun
Thy daily stage of duty run;
Shake off dull sloth, and joyful rise
To pay thy morning sacrifice.

2 Wake and lift up thyself, my heart,
And with the angels bear thy part,
Who all night long unwearied sing
High praise to the eternal King.

3 All praise to Thee, who safe hast kept,
And hast refreshed me while I slept:
Grant, Lord, when I from death shall wake,
I may of endless life partake.

4 Lord, I my vows to Thee renew;
Disperse my sins as morning dew;
Guard my first springs of thought and will,
And with Thyself my spirit fill.

5 Direct, control, suggest, this day,
All I design, or do, or say;
That all my powers, with all their might,
In Thy sole glory may unite.

6 Praise God, from whom all blessings flow;
Praise Him, all creatures here below;
Praise Him, above, ye heavenly host,
Praise Father, Son, and Holy Ghost.

Thomas Ken. a.

167.

C. M.

1 NOW that the sun is beaming bright,
Once more to God we pray,
That He, the uncreated Light,
May guide our souls this day.

2 No sinful word, no deed of wrong,
Nor thoughts that idly rove;
But simple truth be on our tongue,
And in our hearts be love.

3 And while the hours in order flow,
O Christ, securely fence
Our gates beleaguered by the foe,
The gate of every sense.

4 And grant that to Thine honor, Lord,
Our daily toil may tend:
That we begin it at Thy word,
And in Thy favor end.

From the Latin.

168.

7.6.7.6.D.

1 WHILE yet the morn is breaking,
I thank my God once more,
Beneath whose care awaking
I find the night is o'er;

I thank Him that He calls me
  To life and health anew,
I know, whate'er befalls me,
  His care will still be true.

2 Guardian of Israel, hear me,
  Watch o'er me through the day,
In all I do be near me:
  For others too I pray;
To Thee I would commend them,
  Our church, our youth, our land,
Direct them and defend them,
  When dangers are at hand.

3 Oh! gently grant Thy blessing,
  That we may do Thy will,
No more Thy ways transgressing,
  Our proper task fulfill;
With Peter's full affiance
  Let down our nets again,
If Thou art our reliance,
  Our toil will not be vain.

4 Thou art the Vine—oh! nourish
  The branches graft in Thee,
And let them grow and flourish
  A fair and fruitful tree;
Thy Spirit put within us,
  And let His gifts of grace
To all good actions win us,
  That best may show His praise,

J. Muhlmann.

169.

7.6.7.6.6.7 7.6.

1 MY inmost heart now raises,
In this fair morning hour,
A song of thankful praises
To Thine almighty power,
O God, upon Thy throne!
To honor and adore Thee,
I bring my praise before Thee,
Through Christ, Thine only Son.

2 For Thou from me hast warded
All perils of the night;
From every harm hast guarded
My soul till morning's light.
Humbly to Thee I cry:
O Savior, have compassion,
And pardon my transgression:
Have mercy, Lord most high!

3 And shield me from all evil,
O gracious God, this day,
From sin, and from the Devil,
From shame and from dismay,
From fire's consuming breath,
From water's devastation,
From need and consternation,
From evil, sudden death.

4 God shall do my advising,
Whose might with wisdom blends;
May He bless rest and rising,
My efforts, means and ends!

To God, forever blessed,
Will I with mine confide me,
And suffer Him to guide me
As seemeth to Him best.

5 Amen! I say, not fearing
That God rejects my prayer;
I doubt not He is hearing
And granting me His care.
So I put forth my hands,
And look not long behind me,
But ply the task assigned me
By God, as He commands.

M. I. Matthesius.

170.

C. M.

1 AGAIN Thy glorious sun doth rise,
I praise Thee, O my Lord;
With courage, strength, and hope renewed,
I touch the joyful chord.

2 On good and evil, Lord, Thy sun
Is rising as on me;
Let me in patience and in love,
Seek thus to be like Thee.

3 May I in virtue and in faith,
And with Thy gifts content,
Rejoice beneath Thy covering wings,
Each day in mercy sent,

4 Safe with Thy counsel in my work
Thee, Lord, I'll keep in view,
And feel that still Thy saving grace
Is every morning new.

J. O. Wallin.

171.

L. M.

1 ALL praise to Thee, my God, this night,
For all the blessings of the light:
Keep me, oh! keep me, King of kings,
Beneath Thine own Almighty wings!

2 Forgive me, Lord, for Thy dear Son,
The ill that I this day have done:
That with the world, myself, and Thee,
I, ere I sleep, at peace may be.

3 Teach me to live, that I may dread
The grave as little as my bed;
To die, that this vile body may
Rise glorious at the awful day.

4 Oh! when shall I, in endless day,
Forever chase dark sleep away,
And hymns divine with angels sing
In endless praise to Thee, my King?

5 Praise God, from whom all blessings flow;
Praise Him, all creatures here below;
Praise Him above, ye heavenly host;
Praise Father, Son, and Holy Ghost.

Thomas Ken. a.

172.

10s.

1 ABIDE with me! fast falls the eventide;
The darkness deepens: Lord, with me abide!
When other helpers fail, and comforts flee,
Help of the helpless, oh, abide with me!

2 Swift to its close ebbs out life's little day;
Earth's joys grow dim, its glories pass away;
Change and decay in all around I see;
O Thou who changest not, abide with me!

3 Not a brief glance I beg, a passing word,
But as Thou dwell'st with Thy disciples, Lord,
Familiar, condescending, patient, free,
Come, not to sojourn, but abide with me!

4 Come not in terrors as the King of kings,
But kind and good, with healing on Thy wings;
Tears for all woes, a heart for every plea;
O Friend of sinners, thus abide with me!

5 Thou on my head in early youth didst smile,
And, though rebellious and perverse meanwhile,
Thou hast not left me, oft as I left Thee:
On to the close, O Lord, abide with me!

6 I need Thy presence every passing hour:
What but Thy grace can foil the tempter's power?

Who like Thyself my guide and stay can be?
Through cloud and sunshine, oh, abide with me!

7 I fear no foe, with Thee at hand to bless:
Ills have no weight, and tears no bitterness.
Where is death's sting? where, grave, thy victory?
I triumph still, if Thou abide with me!

8 Hold Thou Thy cross before my closing eyes,
Shine through the gloom, and point me to the skies:
Heaven's morning breaks, and earth's vain shadows flee;
In life, in death, O Lord, abide with me!

Henry Francis Lyte.

173.

L. M.

1 SUN of my soul, Thou Savior dear,
It is not night if Thou be near:
Oh, may no earth-born cloud arise
To hide Thee from Thy servant's eyes,

2 When the soft dews of kindly sleep
My wearied eyelids gently steep,
Be my last thought, how sweet to rest
Forever on my Savior's breast.

3 Abide with me from morn till eve,
For without Thee I cannot live,
Abide with me when night is nigh,
For without Thee I dare not die.

4 If some poor wandering child of Thine
Have spurned to-day the voice divine,
Now, Lord, the gracious work begin;
Let him no more lie down in sin,

5 Watch by the sick; enrich the poor
With blessings from Thy boundless store;
Be every mourner's sleep to-night,
Like infant's slumber, pure and light.

6 Come near and bless us when we wake,
Ere through the world our way we take;
Till in the ocean of Thy love
We lose ourselves in heaven above.

John Keble.

174. 7s.

1 SOFTLY now the light of day
Fades upon my sight away;
Free from care, from labor free,
Lord, I would commune with Thee.

2 Thou whose all-pervading eye
Naught escapes, without, within,
Pardon each infirmity,
Open fault, and secret sin.

3 Soon for me the light of day
Shall forever pass away:
Then, from sin and sorrow free,
Take me, Lord, to dwell with Thee.

4 Thou who, sinless, yet hast known
All of man's infirmity;
Then, from Thine eternal throne,
Jesus, look with pitying eye.

George Washington Doane.

175.

L. M.

1 SUNK is the sun's last beam of light,
And now the world is wrapt in night;
Christ! light us with Thy heavenly ray,
Nor let our feet in darkness stray.

2 Thanks Lord, that Thou throughout the day
Hast kept all grief and harm away;
That angels tarried round about
Our coming in and going out.

3 Whate'er of wrong we've done or said,
Let not the charge on us be laid;
That through Thy free forgiveness blest,
In peaceful slumber we may rest.

4 Thy guardian angels round us place,
All evil from our couch to chase;
Our soul and body, while we sleep,
In safety, gracious Father keep.

Nicholas Hermann. a.

176.

8.7.8.7.

1 JESUS, tender Shepherd, hear me;
Bless thy little lamb to-night;
Through the darkness be Thou near me;
Keep me safe till morning light.

2 All this day Thy hand has led me,
And I thank Thee for Thy care;
Thou hast clothed me, warmed, and fed me,
Listen to my evening prayer.

3 May my sins be all forgiven;
Bless the friends I love so well:
Take me, Lord, at last to heaven,
Happy there with Thee to dwell.

Mrs. Mary Duncan.

177.

8.7.8.7.D.

1 SAVIOR, breathe an evening blessing,
Ere repose our spirits seal;
Sin and want we come confessing,
Thou canst save, and Thou canst heal;
Though destruction walk around us,
Though the arrow near us fly,
Angel-guards from Thee surround us,
We are safe if Thou art nigh.

2 Though the night be dark and dreary,
Darkness cannot hide from Thee;
Thou art He, who never weary,
Watchest where Thy people be;
Should swift death this night o'ertake us,
And our couch become our tomb,
May the morn in heaven awake us,
Clad in light and deathless bloom.

James Edmeston.

178.

8.7.8.7.

1 HEAR my prayer, O Heavenly Father,
Ere I lay me down to sleep;
Bid Thy angels, pure and holy,
Round my bed their vigil keep.

2 Great my sins are, but Thy mercy
Far outweighs them every one;
Down before Thy cross I cast them,
Trusting in Thy help alone.

3 Keep me, through this night of peril,
Underneath its boundless shade:
Take me to Thy rest, I pray Thee,
When my pilgrimage is made.

4 None shall measure out Thy patience
By the span of human thought;
None shall bound the tender mercies
Which Thy Holy Son hath wrought.

5 Pardon all my past transgressions;
Give me strength for days to come;
Guide and guard me with Thy blessing,
Till Thine angels bid me home.

Harriet Parr.

179.

6.5 6.5.

1 NOW the day is over,
Night is drawing nigh,
Shadows of the evening
Steal across the sky.

2 Now the darkness gathers,
Stars begin to peep.
Birds, and beasts, and flowers
Soon will be asleep.

3 Jesus, give the weary
Calm and sweet repose,
With Thy tenderest blessing
May my eyelids close.

4 Through the long night-watches
May Thine angels spread
Their white wings above me,
Watching round my bed.

5 When the morning wakens,
Then may I arise
Pure and fresh and sinless
In Thy holy eyes.

6 Glory to the Father,
Glory to the Son,
And to Thee, blest Spirit,
Whilst all ages run.

S. Baring-Gould.

180. C. M.

1 I LOVE to steal awhile away
From every cumbering care,
And spend the hours of setting day
In humble, grateful prayer.

2 I love in solitude to shed
The penitential tear,

And all His promises to plead
Where none but God can hear.

3 I love to think of mercies past,
And future good implore,
And all my cares and sorrows cast
On Him whom I adore.

4 I love by faith to take a view
Of brighter scenes in heaven;
The prospect doth my strength renew,
While here by tempests driven.

5 Thus when life's toilsome day is o'er,
May its departing ray
Be calm as this impressive hour,
And lead to endless day.

Phœbe H. Brown.

181.

8.7.8.7.7.7.8.8.

1 FATHER, merciful and holy,
Thee to-night I praise and bless,
Who to labor true and lowly,
Grantest ever meet success;
Many a sin and many a woe,
Many a fierce and subtle foe
Hast Thou checked that once alarmed me,
So that naught to-day has harmed me.

2 Now the light, that nature gladdens,
And the pomp of day is gone,
And my heart is tired and saddens,
As the gloomy night comes on;

Ah, then with Thy changeless light
Warm and cheer my heart to-night;
As the shadows round me gather,
Keep me close to Thee, my Father.

3 Though I have from Thee departed,
Now I seek Thy face again,
For Thy Son, the loving-hearted,
Made our peace through bitter pain.
Yes, far greater than our sin,
Though it still be strong within,
Is Thy love that fails us never,
Mercy that endures forever.

4 Though my weary eyes are closing,
And my senses fall asleep,
Still my soul, on Thee reposing,
Ever must it vigils keep.
Let my spirit longingly
Always dream, my God, of Thee,
Firmly unto Thee e'er cleaving,
E'en in sleep Thy grace receiving.

5 Lord, the twilight now hath vanished,
Send Thy blessing on my sleep,
Every sin and terror banished,
Let my rest be calm and deep.
Soul and body, mind and health,
Wife and children, house and wealth,
Friend and foe, the sick, the stranger,
Keep Thou safe from harm and danger.

6 O Thou mighty God, now hearken
To the prayer Thy child hath made;
Jesus, while the night-hours darken,
Be Thou still my Hope, my Aid;
Holy Ghost, on Thee I call,
Friend and Comforter of all,
Hear my earnest prayer, oh, hear me!
Lord, Thou hearest, Thou art near me.

J. Rist.

182. C. M.

1 ONCE more a day is at its close,
Its joys and sorrows spent;
Another night with sweet repose
Unto the earth is sent.

2 In Thee, O Lord, my trust I place,
No change can Thee befall;
My days and nights, in Thy rich grace,
By Thee are numbered all.

3 Safe to Thy care committing me,
When down the sun is gone,
I'll gladly wake to worship Thee,
When day again shall dawn.

4 If death should summon me this night,
O Jesus, be Thou nigh;
Give me the comfort by Thy might
That Thine I live and die!

F. J. Herzog. J. O. Wallin.

183.

6.6.4.6.6.6.4.

1 GOD bless our native land,
Firm may she ever stand,
Through storm and night,
When the wild tempests rave,
Ruler of wind and wave,
Do Thou our country save
By Thy great might!

2 For her our prayer shall rise
To God above the skies;
On Him we wait:
Thou who art ever nigh,
Guarding with watchful eye,
To Thee alone we cry,
God save the State!

John S. Dwight.

184.

6.6.4.6.6.6 4.

1 MY country 'tis of thee,
Sweet land of liberty,
Of thee I sing;
Land where my fathers died,
Land of the pilgrim's pride,
From every mountain side
Let freedom ring.

2 My native country, thee—
Land of the noble, free—
Thy name I love.
I love thy rocks and rills,

Thy woods and templed hills;
My heart with rapture thrills
  Like that above.

3 Let music swell the breeze,
And ring from all the trees
  Sweet freedom's song:
Let mortal tongues awake;
Let all that breathe partake;
Let rocks their silence break—
  The sound prolong.

4 Our fathers' God, to Thee,
Author of liberty,
  To Thee we sing:
Long may our land be bright,
With freedom's holy light;
Protect us by Thy might,
  Great God, our King.

F. S. Smith.

THE CHURCH.

185. 8.7.8.7.4.7.

1 ZION stands with hills surrounded;
  Zion kept by power divine:
All her foes shall be confounded,
  Though the world in arms combine.
    Happy Zion,
  What a favored lot is thine!

2 Every human tie may perish;
Friend to friend unfaithful prove;
Mothers cease their own to cherish;
Heaven and earth at last remove:
But no changes
Can attend Jehovah's love,

3 In the furnace God may prove thee,
Thence to bring thee forth more bright,
But can never cease to love thee;
Thou art precious in His sight:
God is with thee,
God, thine everlasting Light.

Thomas Kelly.

186.

8.7.8.7.D.

1 GLORIOUS things of thee are spoken,
Zion, city of our God;
He, whose Word can not be broken,
Formed thee for His own abode.
On the Rock of Ages founded,
What can shake thy sure repose?
With salvation's walls surrounded,
Thou may'st smile at all thy foes,

2 See the streams of living waters,
Springing from eternal love,
Well supply thy sons and daughters,
And all fear of want remove.
Who can faint while such a river
Ever flows their thirst to assuage?
Grace, which, like the Lord, the Giver,
Never fails from age to age.

3 Savior, if of Zion's city
I, through grace, a member am,
Let the world deride or pity,
I will glory in Thy Name.
Fading is the worldling's pleasure,
All his boasted pomp and show;
Solid joys and lasting treasure
None but Zion's children know.

John Newton.

187.

7.6.7.6.D.

1 THE church's one foundation
Is Jesus Christ her Lord;
She is His new creation
By water and the Word;
From heaven He came and sought her
To be His holy bride,
With His own blood He bought her,
And for her life He died.

2 Elect from every nation,
Yet one o'er all the earth,
Her charter of salvation
One Lord, one Faith, one Birth,
One holy Name she blesses,
Partakes one holy Food,
And to one Hope she presses,
With every grace endued.

3 Though with a scornful wonder
Men see her sore opprest,
By schisms rent asunder,

By heresies distrest,
Yet saints their watch are keeping,
Their cry goes up, "How long?"
And soon the night of weeping
Shall be the morn of song.

4 'Mid toil, and tribulation,
And tumult of her war,
She waits the consummation
Of peace for evermore;
Till with the vision glorious
Her longing eyes are blest,
And the great church victorious
Shall be the church at rest.

Samuel J. Stone.

188.

S. M.

1 I LOVE Thy Zion, Lord,
The house of Thine abode;
The church our blest Redeemer saved
With His own precious blood.

2 I love Thy church, O God;
Her walls before Thee stand,
Dear as the apple of Thine eye,
And graven on Thy hand.

3 For her my tears shall fall;
For her my prayers ascend:
To her my cares and toils be given,
Till toils and cares shall end.

4 Beyond my highest joy
  I prize her heavenly ways,
Her sweet communion, solemn vows,
  Her hymns of love and praise.

5 Jesus, Thou Friend divine,
  Our Savior and our King,
Thy hand from every snare and foe,
  Shall great deliverance bring.

6 Sure as Thy truth shall last,
  To Zion shall be given
The brightest glories earth can yield,
  And brighter bliss of heaven.

Timothy Dwight.

189.

C. M. D.

1 MY church! my church! my dear old church!
  My fathers' and my own!
On Prophets and Apostles built,
  And Christ the corner-stone!
All else beside, by storm or tide,
  May yet be overthrown;
But not my church—my dear old church—
  My fathers' and my own!

2 My church! my church! my dear old church!
  My glory and my pride!
Firm in the faith Immanuel taught,
  She holds no faith beside.
Upon this rock, 'gainst every shock,
  Though gates of hell assail,

She stands secure, with promise sure,
"They never shall prevail."

3 My church! my church! my dear old church!
I love her ancient name;
And God forbid, a child of hers
Should ever do her shame!
Her mother-care, I'll ever share;
Her child I am alone,
Till He who gave me to her arms
Shall call me to His own.

4 My church! my church! my dear old church!
I've heard the tale of blood,
Of hearts that loved her to the death—
The great, the wise, the good.
Our martyred sires defied the fires
For Christ the crucified;
The one delivered faith to keep,
They burned, they bled, they died.

5 My church! my church! I love my church,
For she exalts my Lord!
She speaks, she breathes, she teaches not,
But from His written Word,
And if her voice bids me rejoice,
From all my sins released;
'Tis through the atoning sacrifice,
And Jesus is the Priest.

6 My church! my church! I love my church,
For she doth lead me on

To Zion's Palace Beautiful,
  Where Christ my Lord hath gone.
From all below, she bids me go,
  To Him, the Life, the Way,
The Truth to guide my erring feet
  From darkness into day.

7 Then here, my church! my dear old church!
  Thy child would add a vow,
To that whose token once was signed
  Upon his infant brow :—
Assault who may, kiss and betray,
  Dishonor and disown,
My church shall yet be dear to me,
  My fathers' and my own!

Anon.

190.

8.8.7.8.8.7.

1 BE not dismayed, thou little flock,
Although the foe's fierce battle shock,
  Loud on all sides, assail thee.
Though o'er thy fall they laugh secure,
Their triumph cannot long endure,
  Let not thy courage fail thee.

2 Thy cause is God's—go at His call,
And to His hand commit thine all;
  Fear thou no ill impending:
His Gideon shall arise for thee,
God's Word and people manfully,
  In God's own time defending.

3 Our hope is sure in Jesus' might;
Against themselves the godless fight,
Themselves, not us, distressing;
Shame and contempt their lot shall be;
God is with us, with Him are we;
To us belongs His blessing.

Gustavus Adolphus. J. O. Wallin.

191.

L. M.

1 JESUS shall reign where'er the sun
Does his successive journeys run;
His kingdom stretch from shore to shore
Till moons shall wax and wane no more.

2 For Him shall endless prayer be made,
And endless praises crown His head;
His Name, like sweet perfume, shall rise
With every morning sacrifice.

3 People and realms of every tongue
Dwell on His love with sweetest song;
And infant voices shall proclaim
Their early blessings on His Name.

4 Blessings abound where'er He reigns;
The prisoner leaps to lose his chains;
The weary find eternal rest,
And all the sons of want are blest.

5 Where He displays His healing power,
Death and the curse are known no more;
In Him the tribes of Adam boast
More blessings than their father lost.

6 Let every creature rise and bring
Peculiar honors to our King;
Angels descend with songs again,
And earth repeat the loud Amen.

Isaac Watts.

192.

8.7.8.7.8.8.7.

1 THY scepter, Jesus, shall extend
As far as day prevaileth;
Thy glorious kingdom, without end,
Shall stand when all else faileth.
Thy blessed Name shall be confessed,
And round Thy cross forever blest,
Shall kings and people gather.

2 The child that's born to Thee we take,
To Thee in death we hasten;
In joy we often Thee forsake,
But not when sorrows chasten.
Where truth and virtue are oppressed,
Where sorrow dwells, pain and unrest,
Thy help alone availeth.

3 Come, Jesus, then, in weal and woe,
In life and death be near us;
Thy grace upon our hearts bestow,
And let Thy Spirit cheer us.
For every conflict strength afford,
And gather us in peace, O Lord,
When all the world Thou judgest.

F. M. Franzen.

193.

8.7.8.7.6.6.6.6.7.

1 A MIGHTY Fortress is our God,
A trusty Shield and Weapon;
He helps us in our every need
That hath us now o'ertaken.
The old malignant foe
Means us deadly woe:
Deep guile and cruel might
Are his dread arms in fight,
On earth is not his equal.

2 With might of ours can naught be done,
Soon were our loss effected;
But for us fights the Valiant One
Whom God Himself elected.
Ask ye who this may be?
Jesus Christ, 'tis He,
As Lord of Hosts adored,
Our only King and Lord,
He holds the field forever.

3 Though devils all the world should fill,
All watching to devour us,
We tremble not, we fear no ill,
They cannot overpower us.
For this world's prince may still
Scowl fierce as he will,
We need not be alarmed,
For he is now disarmed;
One little word o'erthrows him.

4 The Word they still shall let remain,
Nor any thanks have for it;
He's by our side upon the plain,
With His good gifts and Spirit,
Take they, then, what they will,
Life, goods, all; and still,
E'en when their worst is done,
They yet have nothing won,
The kingdom ours remaineth.

Martin Luther.

194.

L. M.

1 ABIDE with us, O Savior dear,
For dark and lowering clouds appear;
And let Thy light, Thy Word divine,
Continue in Thy church to shine.

2 This is a dark and evil day,
Forsake us not, O Lord, we pray;
And let us in our grief and pain
Thy Word and Sacraments retain.

3 Lord Jesus, help, Thy church uphold,
For we are weak, indifferent, cold;
Give us Thy Spirit and Thy grace,
And spread Thy truth in every place.

4 And keep us steadfast in Thy Word,
Stay Satan's fatal wiles, O Lord;
To us Thy grace and power reveal,
And let Thy church Thy presence feel.

5 And, gracious Lord, consider too
How many teachers are untrue;

By wisdom they would know the Lord,
And set at naught His holy Word.

6 Those haughty spirits, Lord, restrain,
Who do Thy holy Word disdain,
And ever seek for something new,
Contrived to change Thy doctrines true.

7 And since the cause is Thine we pray,
Do Thou the arm of evil stay;
And grace and power and wisdom lend
To those who would Thy Word defend.

8 Thy Word is in distress and need
Our comfort and defence indeed;
By it Thy church keep pure within
And free from error, shame, and sin.

9 Grant that Thy Word may light our way
That we in darkness may not stray,
But through this vale of sin and woe,
May to the heavenly mansions go.

N. Selnecker. J. Svedberg.

195.

8.7.8.7.D.

1 CHOSEN seed and Zion's children,
Ransomed from eternal wrath,
Traveling to the heavenly Canaan
On a rough and thorny path;
Church of God in Christ elected,
Thou to God art reconciled,
But on earth thou art a stranger,
Persecuted and reviled.

2 Still rejoice amid thy trials,
Nor regard thy lot amiss;
For the kind and loving Savior
Is the source of all thy bliss.
May He ever be thy portion,
He who gave thee life and breath;
In His keeping fear no evil
Now or in the hour of death.

3 Pleasantly thy lines have fallen
Underneath the tree of life;
For the Lord is thy salvation
And thy shield in all thy strife:
Here the timid bird finds shelter,
Here the swallow finds a nest,
Trembling fugitive a refuge,
And the weary pilgrim rest.

4 Faith and love are the conditions;
All on faith and love depends;
Love of law is the fulfilment,
Faith God's mercy apprehends;
Who hath faith shall see salvation,
Who hath love shall life obtain.
May, O Lord, Thy love possess us,
And Thy Spirit in us reign.

5 And upon this blest foundation,
Lord, our Lord, and Savior King,
May Thy Spirit e'er unite us,
To it may we ever cling.
May we, members of one body,

Grow into a perfect whole;
Grant, O Lord, that in Thy people
There may be one heart and soul.

A. C. Rutström.

196.

11.11.11.6.6.11.

1 WITH God and His mercy, His Spirit and Word
And loving communion at altar and board,
We meet with assurance the dawn of each day:
The Shepherd is with us,
The Shepherd is with us,
To lead and protect us and teach us the way.

2 In perilous times, amid tempests and night,
A band presses on, through the gloom toward light,
Though humble, and meek, and disowned by the world,
They follow the Savior,
They follow the Savior,
And march on to glory, with banners unfurled.

3 While groveling worldlings with dross are content,
And ever on sin and transgression are bent,
I follow, victorious hosts, at your word,
And march on to glory,
And march on to glory,
We march on to glory, our captain, the Lord.

4 The sign of the cross I triumphantly bear,
Though none of my kindred that emblem may wear,
I joyfully follow the champions of right,
Who march on to glory,
Who march on to glory,
Who march on to glory, with weapons of might.

5 The Pillar that guides us through peril and strife,
The Rock that is cleft, giving waters of life,
Is Christ, and His cross. By His Spirit and Word,
The heart He refreshes,
The heart He refreshes,
The heart He refreshes, our Savior and Lord.

6 Though Satan may sift me, and sinning brings death,
Yet will I hold fast, till my last dying breath,
The glorious truth of the consecrate Son,
Who died for the many,
Who died for the many,
And suffering death, our atonement has won.

7 I know that in spite of transgression and sin
God's heart bears for sinners but mercy within,
For Christ for mankind has full righteousness won,

The One for the many,
The One for the many,
The One for the world standing righteous alone.

8 Yea, this is the ground for my comfort and joy,
In moments when doubt seeks my faith to destroy;
Whenever my body and soul be oppressed
I flee to Thy presence,
I flee to Thy presence,
And find in Thy presence protection and rest.

9 O Shepherd, abide with us, care for us still,
And feed us and lead us and teach us Thy will;
And when in Thy heavenly fold we shall be,
Our thanks and our praises,
Our thanks and our praises,
Our thanks and our praises we'll render to Thee.

C. O. Rosenius.

197.

8.7.8.7.4.7.

1 ON the mountain's top appearing,
Lo! the sacred herald stands,
Welcome news to Zion bearing,
Zion long in hostile lands:
Mourning captive,
God himself will loose thy bands.

2 Has the night been long and mournful?
Have thy friends unfaithful proved?

Have thy foes been proud and scornful,
By thy sighs and tears unmoved?
Cease thy mourning;
Zion still is well beloved.

3 God, thy God, will now restore thee;
He Himself appears thy Friend;
All thy foes shall flee before thee;
Here their boasts and triumphs end:
Great deliverance
Zion's King vouchsafes to send.

4 Enemies no more shall trouble;
All thy wrongs shall be redressed;
For thy shame thou shalt have double,
In thy Maker's favor blest:
All thy conflicts
End in everlasting rest.

Thomas Kelly.

198.

8.7. 6 lines.

1 CHRIST, Thou art the sure Foundation,
Thou the Head and Corner-stone;
Chosen of the Lord, and precious,
Binding all the church in one;
Thou Thy Zion's help forever,
And her confidence alone.

2 To this temple, where we call Thee,
Come, O Lord of Hosts, to-day!
With Thy wonted loving-kindness
Hear Thy servants as they pray;

And Thy fullest benediction
Shed within these walls alway.

3 Here vouchsafe to all Thy servants
What they ask of Thee to gain,
What they gain from Thee forever
With the blessed to retain,
And hereafter in Thy glory
Evermore with Thee to reign.

4 Praise and honor to the Father,
Praise and honor to the Son,
Praise and honor to the Spirit,
Ever Three and ever One;
One in might, and one in glory,
While eternal ages run.

John Mason Neale. a.

199.

S. M.

1 How beauteous are their feet,
Who stand on Zion's hill!
Who bring salvation on their tongues,
And words of peace reveal.

2 How charming is their voice!
How sweet their tidings are!
Zion behold thy Savior King;
He reigns and triumphs here.

3 How happy are our ears,
That hear this joyful sound,
Which kings and prophets waited for,
And sought, but never found!

4 How blessed are our eyes,
That see this heavenly light!
Prophets and kings desired it long,
But died without the sight.

5 The watchmen join their voice,
And tuneful notes employ;
Jerusalem breaks forth in songs,
And deserts learn the joy.

6 The Lord makes bare His arm
Through all the earth abroad;
Let all the nations now behold
Their Savior and their God.

Isaac Watts. a.

200.

8.7.8.7.D.

1 SAVIOR, sprinkle many nations,
Fruitful let Thy sorrows be;
By Thy pains and consolations
Draw the Gentiles unto Thee.
Of Thy cross the wondrous story
Be it to the nations told;
Let them see Thee in Thy glory,
And Thy mercy manifold.

2 Far and wide, though all unknowing,
Pants for Thee each mortal breast:
Human tears for Thee are flowing,
Human hearts in Thee would rest.
Thirsting as for dews of even,
As the new-mown grass for rain,

Thee they seek, as God of heaven,
  Thee as Man, for sinners slain.

3 Savior, lo, the isles are waiting,
  Streched the hand, and strained the sight,
For Thy Spirit, new-creating,
  Love's pure flame, and wisdom's light.
Give the Word, and of the preacher
  Speed the foot, and touch the tongue,
Till on earth, by every creature,
  Glory to the Lamb be sung.

Arthur Cleveland Coxe.

201.

6 6.4.6.6.6.4.

1 THOU, whose almighty word
Chaos and darkness heard,
  And took their flight;
Hear us, we humbly pray;
And where the gospel day
Sheds not its glorious ray,
  Let there be light!

2 Thou, who didst come to bring,
On Thy redeeming wing,
  Healing and sight,
Health to the sick in mind,
Sight to the inly blind,
Oh, now to all mankind
  Let there be light!

3 Spirit of truth and love,
Life-giving, holy Dove,

Speed forth Thy flight;
Move on the waters' face,
Bearing the lamp of grace,
And in earth's darkest place
Let there be light!

4 Holy and blessed Three,
Glorious Trinity,
Wisdom, Love, Might!
Boundless as ocean's tide,
Rolling in fullest pride,
Through the earth, far and wide,
Let there be light!

John Marriott.

202.

7.6.7.6.D.

1 THE morning light is breaking;
The darkness disappears;
The sons of earth are waking
To penitential tears;
Each breeze that sweeps the ocean
Brings tidings from afar,
Of nations in commotion,
Prepared for Zion's war.

2 See heathen nations bending
Before the God we love,
And thousand hearts ascending
In gratitude above;
While sinners, now confessing,
The gospel call obey,

And seek the Savior's blessing—
A nation in a day.

3 Blest river of salvation,
Pursue thine onward way;
Flow thou to every nation,
Nor in thy richness stay;
Stay not till all the lowly
Triumphant reach their home:
Stay not till all the holy
Proclaim—"The Lord is come!"

S. F. Smith.

203.

7.6.7.6.D.

1 FROM Greenland's icy mountains,
From India's coral strand;
Where Afric's sunny fountains
Roll down their golden sand;
From many an ancient river,
From many a palmy plain,
They call us to deliver
Their land from error's chain.

2 What though the spicy breezes
Blow soft o'er Ceylon's isle;
Though every prospect pleases,
And only man is vile:
In vain with lavish kindness
The gifts of God are strown:
The heathen, in his blindness,
Bows down to wood and stone.

3 Shall we, whose souls are lighted
With wisdom from on high,
Shall we to men benighted
The lamp of life deny?
Salvation, oh, salvation!
The joyful sound proclaim,
Till each remotest nation
Has learned Messiah's Name.

4 Waft, waft, ye winds, His story,
And you, ye waters, roll,
Till, like a sea of glory,
It spreads from pole to pole;
Till o'er our ransomed nature
The Lamb for sinners slain,
Redeemer, King, Creator,
In bliss returns to reign.

Reginald Heber.

204.

7.6.7.6.D.

1 NOW be the gospel banner
In every land unfurled;
And be the shout—Hosanna!
Re-echoed through the world;
Till every isle and nation,
Till every tribe and tongue,
Receive the great salvation,
And join the happy throng.

2 Yes, Thou shalt reign forever,
O Jesus, King of kings!

Thy light, Thy love, Thy favor,
  Each ransomed captive sings:
The isles for Thee are waiting,
  The deserts learn Thy praise,
The hills and valleys greeting,
  The song responsive raise.

Thomas Hastings.

205.

8.7.8.7.4.7.

1 MIGHTY Lord, extend Thy kingdom,
  Be the truth with triumph crowned;
Let the lands that sit in darkness
  Hear the glorious gospel sound,
    From our borders
To the world's remotest bound.

2 By Thine arm, eternal Father,
  Scatter far the shades of night;
Let the great Immanuel's kingdom
  Open like the morning light:
    Let all barriers
  Yield before Thy heavenly might.

3 Come, in all Thy Spirit's power;
  Come, Thy reign on earth restore;
In Thy strength, ride forth and conquer,
  Still advancing more and more,
    Till all people,
  Shall Thy holy Name adore.

Joseph Cottle. a.

206.

S. M.

1 O LORD our God, arise,
The cause of truth maintain;
And wide o'er all the peopled world
Extend her blessed reign.

2 Thou Prince of Life, arise,
Nor let Thy conquests cease:
Far spread the glory of Thy Name,
And bless the earth with peace.

3 Thou, Holy Ghost, arise,
Exert Thy quickening power,
And o'er a dark and ruined world
Thy light and peace outpour.

4 All on the earth, arise,
To God the Savior sing;
From shore to shore, from earth to heaven,
Let His High praises ring.

Ralph Wardlaw.

207.

6.5.5.5.6.5.6.5.

1 HOW wondrous and great
Thy works, God of praise!
How just, King of saints,
And true are Thy ways!
Oh, who shall not fear Thee,
And honor Thy Name?
Thou only art holy,
Thou only supreme.

2 To nations long dark
Thy light shall be shown;
Their worship and vows
Shall come to Thy throne:
Thy truth and Thy judgments
Shall spread all abroad,
Till earth's every people
Confess Thee their God.

H. U. Onderdonk.

208.

6.5. 16 lines.

1 WHO is on the Lord's side?
Who will serve the King?
Who will be His helpers,
Other lives to bring?
Who will leave the world's side?
Who will face the foe?
Who is on the Lord's side?
Who for Him will go?
Who is on the Lord's side?
Who will serve the King?
Who will be His helpers,
Other lives to bring?
By Thy grand redemption,
By Thy grace divine,
We are on the Lord's side;
Savior, we are Thine.

2 Not for weight of glory,
Not for crown and palm,
Enter we the army,
Raise the warrior-psalm;

But for love that claimeth
 Lives for whom He died,
He whom Jesus nameth
 Must be on His side.
Who is on the Lord's side?
 Who will serve the King?
Who will be His helpers,
 Other lives to bring?
By Thy grand redemption,
 By Thy grace divine,
We are on the Lord's side;
 Savior, we are Thine.

3 Jesus, Thou hast bought us,
 Not with gold or gem,
But with Thine own life-blood,
 For Thy diadem;
With Thy blessing filling
 All who come to Thee,
Thou hast made us willing,
 Thou hast made us free.
Who is on the Lord's side?
 Who will serve the King?
Who will be His helpers,
 Other lives to bring?
By Thy grand redemption
 By Thy grace divine,
We are on the Lord's side;
 Savior we are Thine.

Frances R. Havergal.

THE WORD.

209. 7.6.7.6.D.

1 O WORD of God Incarnate,
O Wisdom from on high,
O Truth unchanged, unchanging,
O Light of our dark sky;
We praise Thee for the radiance
That from the hallowed page,
A lantern to our footsteps,
Shines on from age to age.

2 The church from her dear Master
Received the gift divine,
And still that light she lifteth
O'er all the earth to shine.
It is the golden casket
Where gems of truth are stored;
It is the heaven-drawn picture
Of Christ, the living Word.

3 It floateth like a banner
Before God's hosts unfurled;
It shineth like a beacon
Above the darkling world:
It is the chart and compass,
That o'er life's surging sea,
Mid mists, and rocks, and quicksands,
Still guides, O Christ, to Thee.

4 Oh make Thy church, dear Savior,
A lamp of burnished gold,
To bear before the nations
Thy true light as of old:
Oh, teach Thy wandering pilgrims
By this their path to trace,
Till, clouds and darkness ended,
They see Thee face to face.

Wm. W. How.

210.

C. M.

1 HOW precious is the Book divine,
By inspiration given!
Bright as a lamp its doctrines shine,
To guide our souls to heaven.

2 It sweetly cheers our drooping hearts
In this dark vale of tears,
Life, light, and joy it still imparts,
And quells our rising fears.

3 This lamp, through all the tedious night
Of life, shall guide our way,
Till we behold the clearer light
Of an eternal day.

John Fawcett.

211.

C. M.

1 FATHER of mercies, in Thy Word
What endless glory shines!
Forever be Thy Name adored
For these celestial lines.

2 Here the Redeemer's welcome voice
Spreads heavenly peace around;
And life and everlasting joys
Attend the blissful sound.

3 Oh, may these heavenly pages be
My ever dear delight;
And still new beauties may I see,
And still increasing light!

4 Divine Instructor, gracious Lord!
Be Thou forever near;
Teach me to love Thy sacred Word,
And view my Savior there.

Anne Steele.

212.

L. M.

1 LORD, keep us steadfast in Thy Word:
Curb those who fain by craft or sword
Would wrest the kingdom from Thy Son,
And set at naught all He hath done.

2 Lord Jesus Christ, Thy power make known;
For Thou art Lord of lords alone:
Defend Thy Christendom, that we
May evermore sing praise to Thee.

3 O Comforter, of priceless worth,
Send peace and unity on earth,
Support us in our final strife,
And lead us out of death to life.

Martin Luther.

213.

C. M.

1 HOW shall the young secure their hearts,
And guard their lives from sin?
Thy Word the choicest rules imparts
To keep the conscience clean.

2 'Tis like the sun, a heavenly light,
That guides us all the day;
And through the dangers of the night
A lamp to lead our way.

3 The starry heavens Thy rule obey,
The earth maintains her place;
And these Thy servants, night and day,
Thy skill and power express.

4 But still Thy law and gospel, Lord,
Have lessons more divine;
Not earth stands firmer than Thy Word,
No stars so nobly shine.

5 Thy Word is everlasting truth:
How pure is every page!
That holy Book shall guide our youth,
And well support our age.

Isaac Watts.

214.

8.8.9.9.8.8.

1 WHAT gives the power, what gives the might
And courage to the Christian knight?
What is the best fortification?

What sword can conquer every nation,
And never once did break or bend?
It is the Word that God did send.

2 What arrow fleet doth never yield?
Doth break and puncture every shield?
What two-edged sword through heart and feeling
Doth pierce and soon the wound is healing;
And makes the enemy a friend?
It is the Word that God did send.

3 What, like a whirlwind in its might,
With power of thunder to affright,
Speaks to the sinner's heart and feeling,
And causes to come o'er him stealing
Thoughts of the awful judgment hour?
It is God's holy Word of power.

4 What, whispering like the zephyrs low,
Doth peace and happiness bestow;
Doth wipe the tears and stop the sighing,
And bringeth comfort to the dying;
And light'neth sorrow's heavy load?
It is the Word, the Word of God.

5 O Word of power, Thou Word of life!
For sinners gavest Thou Thy life,
That all our sins might be forgiven,
And we might find a way to heaven.
In Thee both life and truth begun,
O Word of God, God's only Son!

6 Oh, come with life, oh, come with might!
Be armor to the Christian knight.
Lead on Thy little flock from sorrow,
Who here do toil that they to-morrow
May go to peace from war and strife!
Come lead us home; O Word of Life!

Ernst M. Arndt.

215.

6.6.4.6.6.6.4.

1 LORD of all power and might,
Father of love and light,
Speed on the Word!
Oh, let the gospel sound
All the wide world around,
Wherever man is found!
God speed His Word!

2 Lo! what embattled foes,
Stern in their hate, oppose
God's holy Word;
One for His truth we stand,
Strong in His own right hand,
Firm as a martyr band.
God shield His Word!

3 Onward shall be our course,
Despite of fraud and force;
God is before:
His Word ere long shall run
Free as the noon-day sun;
His purpose must be done:
God bless His Word.

Hugh Stowell.

216.

11s.

1 THE Bible! the Bible! more precious than gold,
The hopes and the glories its pages unfold!
It speaks of a Savior, and tells of His love;
It shows us the way to the mansions above.

2 The Bible! the Bible! blest volume of truth,
How sweetly it smiles on the season of youth!
It bids us seek early the pearl of great price,
Ere the heart is enslaved in the bondage of vice.

3 The Bible! the Bible! we hail it with joy,
Its truths and its glories our tongues shall employ;
We'll sing of its triumphs, we'll tell of its worth,
And send its glad tidings afar o'er the earth.

Anon.

217.

7.6.7.6.D. and Chorus.

1 Tell me the old, old story,
Of unseen things above;
Of Jesus and His glory,
Of Jesus and His love.
Tell me the story simply,
As to a little child;
For I am weak and weary,
And helpless and defiled.

Chorus—Tell me the old, old story,
Tell me the old, old story;
Tell me the old, old story,
of Jesus and His love.

2 Tell me the story slowly,
That I may take it in—
That wonderful redemption,
God's remedy for sin;
Tell me the story often,
For I forget so soon;
The early dew of morning
Has passed away at noon.

Chorus—Tell me the old, etc.

3 Tell me the story softly,
With earnest tones and grave;
Remember, I'm the sinner
Whom Jesus came to save.
Tell me that story always,
If you would really be,
In any time of trouble,
A comforter to me.

Chorus—Tell me the old, etc.

4 Tell me the same old story,
When you have cause to fear
That this world's empty glory,
Is costing me too dear.

Yes, and when that world's glory
Is dawning on my soul,
Tell me the old, old story:
"Christ Jesus makes thee whole."
Chorus—Tell me the old, etc.

Catherine Hankey.

BAPTISM.

218.

7.8.7.8.8.8.

1 BLESSED Jesus, here we stand,
Met to do as Thou hast spoken;
And this child, at Thy command,
Now we bring to Thee, in token
That to Thee it here is given;
For of such shall be Thy heaven.

2 Yes, Thy warning voice is plain,
And we fain would keep it duly;
"He who is not born again,
Heart and life renewing truly,
Born of water and the Spirit,
Can My kingdom not inherit."

3 Therefore hasten we to Thee;
Take the pledge we bring, oh, take it!
Let us here Thy glory see,
And in tender pity make it
Now Thy child, and leave it never,
Thine on earth and Thine forever.

4 Make it, Lord, Thy member now;
Shepherd, take Thy lamb, and feed it,
Prince of peace, its peace be Thou;
Way of life, to heaven lead it,
Vine, this branch may nothing sever,
Be it graft in Thee forever.

5 Now upon Thy heart it lies,
What our heart so dearly treasure:
Heavenward lead our burdened sighs,
Pour Thy blessing without measure;
Write the name we now have given,
Write it in the book of heaven.

Benjamin Schmolk.

219.

8.7.8.7.D.

1 GOD, in human flesh appearing,
Took the children to His breast,
Lambs with His green pastures cheering,
Fitting for His heavenly rest;
This is gentleness unbounded,
This is lowliness of heart;
All are by His love surrounded,
None are ever bid depart.

2 Lord! I bless Thy mercy endless,
For Thy pleasure is to bless;
Me too, when my soul was friendless,
Thou didst to Thy bosom press:
For I, too, to Thee was given
In the pure baptismal wave,
There Thou mad'st me heir of heaven,
Who hast died my soul to save.

3 Feeble is the love of mother,
Father's blessings are as naught,
When compared, my King and Brother,
With the wonders Thou hast wrought;
Thus it pleased Thy heavenly meekness;
Pleasing also be my praise,
Till my songs of earthly weakness
Burst into celestial lays.

P. F. Hiller.

220.

C. H. M.

1 FATHER, who hast created all
In wisest love, we pray,
Look on this babe, who at Thy call
Is entering on life's way.
Bend o'er it now with blessing fraught,
And make Thou something out of naught.

2 O Son, who diedst for us, behold,
We bring our child to Thee!
Great Shepherd, take it to Thy fold,
Thine own for aye to be:
Defend it through this earthly strife,
And lead it in the path of life.

3 Spirit, who broodest o'er the wave,
Descend upon this child:
Give endless life, its spirit lave
With waters undefiled:
Grant it, while yet a babe, to be
A child of God, a home for Thee!

4 O God, what Thou command'st is done:
We speak, but Thine the might:
This child, which scarce hath seen the sun,
Oh, pour on it Thy light,
In faith and hope, in joy and love,
Thou Sun of all below, above!

Albert Knapp.

221.

9.8.9.8.8.8.

1 BAPTIZED into Thy Name most holy,
O Father, Son, and Holy Ghost,
I claim a place, though weak and lowly,
Among Thy seed, Thy chosen host;
Buried with Christ, and dead to sin,
Thy Spirit now shall live within.

2 My loving Father, Thou dost take me
To be henceforth Thy child and heir;
My faithful Savior, Thou dost make me
The fruit of all Thy sorrows share,
Thou, Holy Ghost, wilt comfort me,
When darkest clouds around I see.

3 And I have vowed to fear and love Thee,
And to obey Thee, Lord, alone;
I felt Thy Holy Spirit move me,
And freely pledged myself Thine own,
Renouncing sin to keep the faith,
And war with evil unto death.

4 My faithful God, Thou failest never,
Thy covenant will e'er abide;

Oh, cast me not away forever.
  Should I transgress it on my side;
If I have sore my soul defiled,
Yet still forgive, restore Thy child.

5 Yea, all I am, and love most dearly,—
  To Thee anew I give the whole;
Oh, let me make my vows sincerely,
  Take full possession of my soul,
Let naught within me, naught I own,
Serve any will but Thine alone.

6 And never let my purpose falter,
  O Father, Son, and Holy Ghost,
But keep me faithful to Thine altar,
  Till Thou shalt call me from my post;
So unto Thee I live and die,
And praise Thee evermore on high.

J. J. Ramback.

THE LORD'S SUPPER.

222.

L. M.

1 THE death of Jesus Christ, our Lord,
We celebrate with one accord;
It is our comfort in distress,
Our heart's sweet joy and happiness.

2 He blotted out with His own blood
The judgment that against us stood;

He full atonement for us made,
And all our debt He fully paid.

3 That this is so and ever true
He gives an earnest ever new,
In this His holy Supper, here
We taste His love so sweet, so near.

4 For His true body, as He said,
And His true blood, for sinners shed,
In this communion we receive,
His sacred Word we do believe.

5 A precious food this is indeed,
It never faileth, such we need,
A heavenly manna for our soul,
That we may safely reach our goal.

6 Then blessed is each worthy guest
Who in this promise finds his rest,
For Jesus will in love abide
With those who do in Him confide:

7 The guest that comes with true intent
To turn to God and to repent,
To live for Christ, to die to sin,
And thus a holy life begin.

8 Who does unworthy here appear,
Does not believe, nor is sincere,
Salvation here he can not find.
May we this warning bear in mind.

9 O Jesus Christ, our Brother dear,
Unto Thy cross we now draw near;
Thy sacred wounds indeed make whole
A wounded and afflicted soul.

10 Help us sincerely to believe
That we Thy mercy do receive,
And in Thy grace do find our rest,
Amen. He who believes is blest.

H. Spegel. J. O. Wallin.

223.

7.6.7.6.8.7.6.

1 THINE own, O loving Savior,
Thou bidst come near to Thee,
Thy passion's fruits, Thy favor,
Thy grace, Thou givest free
To them who by Thy grace and love
Are members of Thy kingdom
Now here and there above.

2 To us on earth yet dwelling
Thou dost descend to give,
In love all love excelling,
Thyself that we may live,
And sayest ever kind and good:
"Take, eat, this is My body,
Take, drink, this is My blood."

3 We hear Thine invitation;
We hear, O Lord, Thy call,
The word of consolation,
It is for us, for all;

It draws us to Thy loving heart,
It brings to us Thy blessing,
It does Thy peace impart.

4 Thy heart is in all anguish,
A refuge to the poor,
Thy heart for us did languish,
And bitter death endure.
Thy heart yet filled with peace and rest,
With comfort and salvation
Draws near to every breast.

5 Thou still in loving favor
To us, Thine own, art near,
To lead us as our Savior
Unto a Father dear,
A Father willing to forgive
The children Thou didst ransom,
Those who through Thee shall live.

6 Thine own we are, and ever,
Until our latest breath,
Will we remain, and never
In joy, in grief, in death,
Depart from Thee; and all our days
Thou art with us here present
As Thine own promise says.

F. M. Franzen.

224.

8s.D.

1 DECK thyself, my soul, with gladness,
Leave the gloomy haunts of sadness,
Come into the daylight's splendor,

There with joy thy praises render
Unto Him whose grace unbounded
Hath this wondrous banquet founded;
High o'er all the heavens He reigneth,
Yet to dwell with thee He deigneth.

2 Hasten as a bride to meet Him,
And with loving reverence greet Him,
For with words of life immortal
Now He knocketh at thy portal;
Haste to ope the gates before Him,
Saying, while thou dost adore Him,
"Suffer, Lord, that I receive Thee,
And I never more will leave Thee."

3 He who costly goods desireth
To obtain, much gold requireth;
But to freely give the treasure
Of Thy love is Thy good pleasure,
For on earth there is no coffer
Which as payment we might offer
For this cup Thy blood containing,
And this manna in us raining.

4 Ah! how hungers all my spirit
For the love I do not merit!
Oft have I, with sighs fast thronging,
Thought upon this food with longing,
In the battle well-nigh worsted,
For this cup of life have thirsted,
For the Friend, who here invites us,
And to God Himself unites us.

5 Sun, who all my life dost brighten,
Light, who dost my soul enlighten,
Joy, the sweetest man e'er knoweth,
Fount, whence all my being floweth,
At Thy feet I cry, my Maker,
Let me be a fit partaker
Of this blessed food from heaven,
For our good, Thy glory, given.

6 Lord, Thy fervent love hath driven
Thee to leave Thy throne in heaven,
For us on the cross to languish,
And to die in bitter anguish,
To forego all joy and gladness,
And to shed Thy blood in sadness,
Which we drink now; grant that never
We forget Thy love, dear Savior!

7 Jesus, Bread of life, I pray Thee,
Let me gladly here obey Thee,
Never to my hurt invited,
Be Thy love with love requited;
From this banquet let me measure,
Lord, how vast and deep love's treasure;
Through the gifts Thou here dost give me
As Thy guest in heaven receive me.

J. Franck.

225.

7.6.7.6.D.

1 O LIVING Bread from heaven,
How hast Thou fed Thy guest!
The gifts Thou now hast given

Have filled my heart with rest.
Oh, wondrous food of blessing,
Oh, cup that heals our woes!
My heart this gift possessing,
In thankful song o'erflows.

2 My Lord, Thou here hast led me
Within Thy holiest place,
And there Thyself hast fed me
With treasures of Thy grace:
And Thou hast freely given
What earth could never buy,
The Bread of Life from heaven,
That now I shall not die!

3 Thou givest all I wanted,
The food can death destroy;
And Thou hast freely granted
The cup of endless joy.
Ah, Lord, I do not merit
The favor Thou hast shown,
And all my soul and spirit
Bow down before Thy throne!

4 Lord, grant me that, thus strengthened
With heavenly food, while here
My course on earth is lengthened,
I serve with holy fear:
And when Thou call'st my spirit
To leave this world below,
I enter, through Thy merit,
Where joys unmingled flow.

J. Rist.

226.

L. M.

1 LORD Jesus Christ! To Thee we pray,
From us God's wrath Thou turn'st away,
Thine agony and bitter death
Redeem us from eternal wrath.

2 That we may never this forget
Thy body for our food is set;
And in the wine Thou giv'st Thy blood
To cleanse our souls, a sacred flood.

3 Then praise the Father, by whose love
The Son descended from above,
Became the Bread of Life to thee,
And bore thy sins upon the tree.

4 Firmly on this thou must believe;
That here the sick their food receive,
Which heals them from the wounds of sin,
Creating heavenly health within.

5 Our Savior saith: Come unto Me,
Ye who now feel your poverty:
My mercy I will freely give,
Your anguished conscience I'll relieve.

6 If in thy heart this faith doth rest,
Which thou hast here in words confessed,
A welcome guest thou here shalt be,
And Christ Himself shall banquet thee.

7 But fruits must still thy faith approve;
Thy neighbor thou must truly love;
That love let him from thee receive,
Which here to thee thy God doth give.

Martin Luther.

227.

L. M.

1 WITH holy joy my heart doth beat,
I go my blessed Lord to meet;
Thy mercy and Thy grace afford
That I may taste Thy goodness, Lord.

2 O Lord, forgive my sin I pray,
Turn not from my distress away;
Thou barest all our sin and woe,
On me Thy saving grace bestow.

3 Though I have done this evil, Lord,
And sinned against Thy holy Word,
Yet do I now draw near to Thee,
Extend Thy mercy, Lord, to me.

4 And let me all my sorrows see
Turned into joy and peace by Thee.
When at Thy table, Lord, I kneel,
Let me Thy loving presence feel.

5 A heavenly food I there receive,
Which doth my hungry soul relieve;
What care I now for want or need?
Thy precious love is wealth indeed.

6 Oh, come, dear Savior, then to me,
Deign to prepare a place for Thee
Within my heart, and there remain,
And faith, and hope, and love maintain.

7 Thine let me be whate'er befall,
Thou art my life, my joy, my all;
Thou, light and comfort of my heart,
In life, in death, my hope Thou art.

S. J. Hedborn.

228.

8.7.8.7.8.8.7.

1 CRUSHED by my sin, O Lord, to Thee
I come in my affliction:
Oh, full of pity, look on me,
Impart Thy benediction.
My sins are great, where shall I flee?
The blood of Jesus speaks for me;
For all our sins He carried.

2 Repentant at Thy feet I fall,
To Thy cross humbly clinging,
O Jesus, hear me when I call,
My wants before Thee bringing.
My trust is in Thy grace and power;
For all was finished in that hour,
When Thou didst make atonement.

3 When I approach Thine altar, Lord,
May I this comfort cherish,
That on the cross, Thy blood was poured
For me, lest I should perish.

Thou didst for me God's law fulfill,
That holy joy my heart might thrill
When on Thy love I'm feasting.

4 Be Thou my shield 'gainst Satan's power,
Whene'er he would assail me;
The victor's crown, when comes death's -hour,
Oh, let it never fail me!
Lord Jesus, Thou who savedst me,
My life I would devote to Thee,
To praise Thy Name forever.

C. F. Gellert.

229.

L. M.

1 JESUS, Thou Joy of loving hearts!
Thou Fount of life! Thou light of men!
From the best bliss that earth imparts,
We turn unfilled to Thee again.

2 Thy truth unchanged hath ever stood,
Thou savest those that on Thee call;
To them that seek Thee, Thou art good,
To them that find Thee, All in all.

3 We taste Thee, O Thou living Bread,
And long to feast upon Thee still;
We drink of Thee, the Fountain Head,
And thirst our souls from Thee to fill.

4 Our restless spirits yearn for Thee,
Where'er our changeful lot is cast;

Glad that Thy gracious smile we see,
Blest, that our faith can hold Thee fast.

5 O Jesus, ever with us stay!
Make all our moments calm and bright;
Chase the dark night of sin away,
Shed o'er the world Thy holy light.

Bernard of Clairvaux.

230.

C. M.

1 ACCORDING to Thy gracious word,
In meek humility,
This will I do, my dying Lord,
I will remember Thee.

2 Thy body, broken for my sake,
My bread from heaven shall be;
Thy testamental cup I take,
And thus remember Thee.

3 Gethsemane can I forget,
Or there Thy conflict see,
Thine agony and bloody sweat,
And not remember Thee?

4 When to the cross I turn mine eyes,
And rest on Calvary,
O Lamb of God, my Sacrifice!
I must remember Thee.

5 Remember Thee and all Thy pains,
And all Thy love to me;
Yes, while a breath, a pulse remains,
Will I remember Thee.

6 And when these failing lips grow dumb,
And mind and memory flee,
When Thou shalt in Thy kingdom come,
Jesus, remember me.

James Montgomery.

231. C. M.

1 HERE at Thy Table, Lord, we meet
To feed on food divine:
Thy body is the bread we eat,
Thy precious blood the wine.

2 He that prepares this rich repast,
Himself comes down and dies;
And then invites us thus to feast
Upon the sacrifice.

3 Sure, there was never love so free,
Dear Savior, so divine!
Well Thou may'st claim that heart of me,
Which owes so much to Thine.

4 Yes, Thon shalt surely have my heart,
My soul, my strength, my all;
With life itself I'll freely part,
My Jesus, at Thy call.

Samuel Stennett.

REPENTANCE.

232.

L. M.

1 GOD calling yet! shall I not hear?
Earth's pleasures shall I still hold dear?
Shall life's swift passing years all fly,
And still my soul in slumbers lie?

2 God calling yet! shall I not rise?
Can I His loving voice despise,
And basely His kind care repay?
He calls me still: can I delay?

3 God calling yet! and shall He knock,
And I my heart the closer lock?
He still is waiting to receive,
And shall I dare His Spirit grieve?

4. God calling yet! and shall I give
No heed, but still in bondage live?
I wait, but He does not forsake;
He calls me still: my heart, awake!

5 Ah, yield Him all: in Him confide:
Where but with Him doth peace abide?
Break loose, let earthly bonds be riven,
And let the spirit rise to heaven!

6 God calling yet! I cannot stay;
My heart I yield without delay:
Vain world, farewell! from thee I part;
The voice of God hath reached my heart!

Gerhard Tersteegen.

233.

7.6.7.6.D.

1 AWAKE! the watchman crieth
On Zion's ramparts still!
The Lord His grace supplieth,
Repent, and heed His will.
Life's journey fast is nearing
The ever-boundless shore:
The hour of death appearing,
When time shall be no more.

2 Too late the sinners waken
Where morn hath ceased to dawn;
Where grace, in time forsaken,
Is evermore withdrawn;
Where's heard no praying sentence,
Nor mercy to implore;
For there is no repentance,
When time shall be no more.

3 O soul! beyond salvation,
See this eternity
Of darkness, desolation,
And constant agony.
The torments none shall banish,
Nor aught can peace restore;
And hope itself shall vanish,
When time shall be no more!

4 Awake! the voice still soundeth,
'Tis now the accepted hour;
The grace of God aboundeth,
To save from sin's dread power.

Make haste, implore Christ's favor,
  Thy sins confess, and bow
Before thy Lord and Savior;
  The accepted time is now.

F. M. Franzen.

234.

S. M. and Chorus.

1 I HEAR Thy welcome voice
  That calls me, Lord, to Thee;
For cleansing in Thy precious blood
  That flowed on Calvary.
Chorus—I am coming Lord;
    Coming now to Thee;
   Wash me, cleanse me in the blood
    That flowed on Calvary.

2 Though coming weak and vile,
  Thou dost my strength assure;
Thou dost my vileness fully cleanse,
  Till spotless all, and pure.
Chorus—I am coming, Lord; etc.

3 'T is Jesus calls me on
  To perfect faith and love,
To perfect hope, and peace, and trust,
  For earth and heaven above.
Chorus—I am coming, Lord; etc.

4 And He the witness gives
  To loyal hearts and free,
That every promise is fulfilled,
  If faith but brings the plea.
Chorus—I am coming, Lord; etc.

5 All hail the, atoning blood;
All hail, redeeming grace;
All hail, the gift of Christ, our Lord,
Our Strength and Righteousness.
Chorus—I am coming Lord; etc.

L. Hartsough.

235.

9 9.9.6. and Chorus.

1 COME to the Savior, make no delay;
Here in His Word He's shown us the way;
Here in our midst He's standing to-day,
Tenderly saying, "Come!"
Chorus—Joyful, joyful will the meeting be,
When from sin our hearts are pure and free.
And we shall gather, Savior, with Thee
In our eternal home.

2 "Suffer the children!" Oh, hear His voice,
Let every heart leap forth and rejoice,
And let us freely make Him our choice;
Do not delay, but come!
Chorus—Joyful, joyful, etc.

3 Think once again, He's with us to-day;
Heed now His blest commands, and obey;
Here now His accents tenderly say,
"Will you, my children, come?"
Chorus—Joyful, joyful, etc.

G. F. Root.

236.

L. M.

1 JUST as thou art—without one trace
Of love, or joy, or inward grace,
Or meetness for the heavenly place,
O guilty sinner! come, oh, come!

2 Thy sins I bore on Calvary's tree;
The stripes, thy due, were laid on Me,
That peace and pardon might be free;
O wretched sinner! come, oh, come!

3 Burdened with guilt, would'st thou be blessed?
Trust not the world; it gives no rest;
I bring relief to hearts oppressed;
O weary sinner! come, oh, come!

4 Come, leave thy burden at the cross,
Count all thy gains but empty dross:
My grace repays all earthly loss;
O needy sinner! come, oh, come!

5 Come, hither bring thy boding fears,
Thine aching heart, thy bursting tears;
'T is mercy's voice salutes thine ears;
O trembling sinner! come, oh, come!

6 "The Spirit and the bride say, come!"
Rejoicing saints re-echo, "come!"
Who faints, who thirsts, who will, may come;
Thy Savior bids thee come, oh come!

R. S. Cook.

237.

L. M.

1 BEHOLD a Stranger at the door!
He gently knocks—has knocked before,
Has waited long—is waiting still:
You treat no other friend so ill.

2 Oh lovely attitude, He stands
With melting heart and loaded hands!
Oh, matchless kindness! and He shows
This matchless kindness to His foes!

3 But will He prove a friend indeed?
He will; the very friend you need;
The Friend of sinners—yes, 't is He,
With garments dyed on Calvary.

4 Admit Him, lest His anger burn,
And He, departing, ne'er return;
Admit Him, or the hour's at hand
You'll at His door rejected stand.

Joseph Grigg.

238.

8.7.8.7.4.7.

2. COME, ye sinners, poor and needy,
Weak and wounded, sick and sore,
Jesus ready stands to save you,
Full of pity, love, and power:
He is able,
He is willing: doubt no more.

2 Come, ye thirsty, come and welcome,
God's free bounty glorify:

True belief, and true repentance,
  Every grace that brings us nigh.
      Without money,
  Come to Jesus Christ, and buy.

3 Let not conscience make you linger,
  Nor of fitness fondly dream;
All the fitness He requireth,
  Is to feel your need of Him;
      This He gives you;
  'T is His Spirit's rising beam.

4 Agonizing in the garden,
  Lo! your Maker prostrate lies;
On the blood-stained tree behold Him;
  Hear Him cry, before He dies,
      "It is finished!"
  Sinner, will not this suffice?

5 Lo! the incarnate God, ascended,
  Pleads the merit of His blood:
Venture to Him, venture wholly,
  Let no other trust intrude;
      None but Jesus
  Can do helpless sinners good.

Joseph Hart. a.

239.

8.7.8.7.8.8.7

1 OUT of the depths I cry to Thee,
  Lord, hear me, I implore Thee!
Bend down Thy gracious ear to me,
  Let my prayer come before Thee!

If Thou remember each misdeed,
If each should have its rightful meed,
Who may abide Thy presence?

2 Our pardon is Thy gift; Thy love
And grace alone avail us.
Our works could ne'er our guilt remove,
The strictest life must fail us.
That none may boast himself of aught,
But own in fear Thy grace hath wrought
What in him seemeth righteous.

3 And thus my hope is in the Lord,
And not in mine own merit;
I rest upon His faithful word
To them of contrite spirit.
That He is merciful and just,
Here is my comfort and my trust,
His help I wait with patience.

4 And though it tarry till the night,
And round till morning waken,
My heart shall ne'er mistrust Thy might,
Nor count itself forsaken.
Do thus, O ye of Israel's seed,
Ye of the Spirit born indeed,
Wait for your God's appearing.

5 Though great our sins and sore our woes,
His grace much more aboundeth;
His helping love no limit knows,
Our utmost need it soundeth.

Our kind and faithful Shepherd, He,
Who shall at last set Israel free
From all their sin and sorrow.

Martin Luther.

240.

8.7.8.7.8.8. Trochaic.

1 LORD, to Thee I make confession,
I have sinned and gone astray,
I have multiplied transgression,
Chosen for myself my way,
Forced at last to see my errors,
Lord, I tremble at Thy terrors.

2 Yet though conscience' voice appalls me,
Father, I will seek Thy face;
Though Thy child I dare not call me,
Yet receive me to Thy grace;
Do not for my sins forsake me,
Let not yet Thy wrath o'ertake me.

3 For Thy Son hath suffered for me,
And the blood He shed for sin,
That can heal me and restore me,
Quench this burning fire within;
'Tis alone His cross can vanquish
These dark fears and soothe this anguish.

4 Then on Him I cast my burden,
Sink it in the depths below:
Let me feel Thy gracious pardon,
Wash me, make me white as snow.
Let Thy Spirit leave me never,
Make me only Thine forever!

J. Franck.

241.

C. M.

1 LORD, we confess our numerous faults,
How great our guilt has been:
Foolish and vain were all our thoughts,
And all our lives were sin.

2 But, O my soul, forever praise,
Forever love His Name,
Who turns thy feet from dangerous ways
Of folly, sin, and shame.

3 'Tis not by works of righteousness
Which our own hands have done;
But we are saved by sovereign grace
Abounding through His Son.

4 'Tis from the mercy of our God
That all our hopes begin;
'Tis by the water and the blood
Our souls are washed from sin.

5 'Tis through the purchase of His death
Who hung upon the tree,
The Spirit is sent down to breathe
On such dry bones as we.

6 Raised from the dead we live anew;
And justified by grace,
We shall appear in glory too,
And see our Father's face.

Isaac Watts.

242.

C. M.

1 APPROACH, my soul, the mercy seat,
Where Jesus answers prayer;
There humbly fall before His feet,
For none can perish there.

2 Thy promise is my only plea,
With this I venture nigh:
Thou callest burdened souls to Thee,
And such, O Lord, am I.

3 Bowed down beneath a load of sin,
By Satan sorely pressed,
By wars without and fears within,
I come to Thee for rest.

4 Be Thou my Shield and Hiding-place,
That, sheltered near Thy side,
I may my fierce accuser face
And tell Him, Thou hast died.

5 O wondrous love, to bleed and die,
To bear the cross and shame,
That guilty sinners such as I,
Might plead Thy gracious Name.

J. Newton.

243.

C. M.

1 HOW helpless guilty nature lies,
Unconscious of its load!
The heart unchanged can never rise
To happiness and God,

2 Can aught beneath a power divine
The stubborn will subdue?
'Tis Thine, Almighty Savior, Thine
To form the heart anew.

3 'Tis Thine the passions to recall,
And upwards bid them rise;
And make the scales of error fall
From reason's darkened eyes.

4 To chase the shades of death away,
And bid the sinner live,
A beam of heaven, a vital ray,
'Tis Thine alone to give.

5 Oh, change these wretched hearts of ours,
And give them life divine!
Then shall our passions and our powers,
Almighty Lord, be Thine.

Anne Steele.

244. L. M.

1 SHOW pity, Lord; O Lord! forgive;
Let a repentant rebel live.
Are not Thy mercies large and free?
May not a sinner trust in Thee?

2 Great God, Thy nature hath no bound,
So let Thy pardoning love be found.
Oh, wash my soul from every sin,
And make my guilty conscience clean!

3 My lips with shame my sins confess
Against Thy law, against Thy grace:
Lord, should Thy judgment grow severe,
I am condemned, but Thou art clear.

4 Yet save a trembling sinner, Lord,
Whose hope, still hovering round Thy Word,
Would light on some sweet promise there,
Some sure support against despair.

Isaac Watts. a.

245.

8.8.8.8.8.8.8:4.8.

1 LORD Jesus Christ, in Thee alone
My only hope on earth I place,
For other comforter is none,
No help have I but in Thy grace.
There is no man nor creature here,
No angel in the heavenly sphere,
Who at my need can succor me.
I cry to Thee,
For Thee I trust implicitly.

2 My sin is very sore and great,
I mourn beneath its dreadful load;
Oh, free me from this heavy weight,
My Savior, through Thy precious blood;
And with Thy Father for me plead
That Thou hast suffered in my stead;
From me the burden then is rolled.
Lord, I lay hold
On Thy dear promises of old.

3 And in Thy mercy now bestow
True Christian faith on me, O Lord!
That all the sweetness I may know
Which in Thy holy cross is stored,
Love Thee o'er earthly pride or pelf,
And love my neighbor as myself;
And when, at last, is come my end,
Be Thou my Friend,
From Satan's wiles my soul defend.

4 Glory to God in highest heaven,
The Father of eternal love;
For His dear Son, for sinners given,
Whose watchful grace we daily prove;
To God the Holy Ghost on high;
Oh, ever be His comfort nigh,
And teach us, in His love and fear
To please Him here,
And serve Him in the heavenly sphere!

J. Schneeseng.

246.

7s.

1 GOD of mercy! God of grace!
Hear our sad repentant songs.
Oh, restore Thy suppliant race,
Thou to whom our praise belongs!

2 Deep regret for follies past,
Talents wasted, time misspent;
Hearts debased by worldly cares,
Thankless for the blessings lent:

3 Foolish fears and fond desires,
Vain regret for things as vain:
Lips too seldom taught to praise,
Oft to murmur and complain;

4 These, and every secret fault,
Filled with grief and shame, we own.
Humbled at Thy feet we lie,
Seeking pardon from Thy throne.

John Taylor.

247.

8.5.8.5.9.8.5.

1 PASS me not, O gentle Savior,
Hear my humble cry;
While on others Thou art smiling,
Do not pass me by.
Savior, Savior, hear my humble cry,
While on others Thou art calling,
Do not pass me by.

2 Let me at the throne of mercy
Find a sweet relief,
Kneeling there in deep contrition,
Help my unbelief.
Savior, Savior, etc.

3 Trusting only in Thy merit,
Would I seek Thy face:
Heal my wounded, broken spirit,
Save me by Thy grace.
Savior, Savior, etc.

4 Thou the spring of all my comfort,
  More than life to me,
Whom have I on earth beside Thee?
  Whom in heaven but Thee?
Savior, Savior, etc.

Fanny J. Crosby (Mrs. Van Alstyne.)

248.

8.7.8.7.7.7.8.8.

1 SHUN, my heart, such thought forever
  As that Thou art cast away,
Rest upon God's Word and favor,
  Never cease to watch and pray.
E'en though thou unrighteous art,
True and faithful is God's heart;
Hast thou death deserved forever?
God's appeased, despond thou never!

2 Thou art, as is every other,
  Tainted with the poison sin,
That the serpent and our father
  Adam, by the fall, brought in.
But if thou God's voice doth hear,
With a contrite heart draw near
Unto God, He will receive thee,
All thy sins he will forgive thee.

3 Thou wilt find in Him a Father
  Who is patient, kind, and true,
He doth love thee as no brother
  And no other friend can do.
E'en our smallest cares He knows,

He is touched by all our woes;
Well our inmost prayer He heareth,
And our saddened hearts He cheereth.

4 Hear His word "As I am living
I the death of none would see,
But that every sinner giving
Up his heart would turn to Me.
How my heart with rapture burns
When a prodigal returns!
As My own I love to call him.
And no evil shall befall him."

5 Never shepherd's heart so yearneth
For the sheep that go astray
As God's loving bosom burneth
For His erring child alway.
How He thirsts, and longs, and yearns
For the soul that from Him turns!
Couldst thou see His love so tender
Joyful praise thou wouldst Him render.

6 O my soul, so sad and dreary,
Rest now and contented be!
Why wilt thou thyself so weary
When there is no need for thee?
Though thy sins appear to thee
Like a vast and shoreless sea,
In God's mercy they will vanish;
Thy despair and fear, then, banish.

7 Were there thousand worlds created,
Lost in sin and misery,

Had their sins both small and greater,
Every one been done by thee;
Still God's love and mercy are
Greater than these sins by far;
Naught His mercy can diminish,
Nor His love and grace extinguish.

8 Of such wondrous love and favor
Open wide the door to me;
And Thy goodness, precious Savior,
Let me ever taste and see.
Love me, Lord, and let me be
Ever nearer drawn to Thee;
Let Thy Spirit lead and guide me,
In Thy loving bosom hide me.

P. Gerhardt. J. O. Wallin.

249.

8.7.8.7. Iambic.

1 ALAS, my God! my sins are great,
My conscience doth upbraid me;
And now I find that in my strait
No man hath power to aid me.

2 And fled I hence, in my despair,
In some lone spot to hide me,
My griefs would still be with me there,
And peace still be denied me.

3 Lord, Thee I seek; I merit naught,
Yet pity and restore me;
Be not Thy wrath, just God, my lot,
Thy Son hath suffered for me.

4 If pain and woe must follow sin,
Then be my path still rougher,
Here spare me not: if heaven I win,
On earth I gladly suffer.

5 But curb my heart, forgive my guilt,
Make Thou my patience firmer,
For they must miss the good Thou wilt,
Who at Thy chastenings murmur.

6 Then deal with me as pleaseth Thee,
Thy grace will help me bear it,
If but at last I see Thy rest,
And with my Savior share it.

7 The Father, Son, upon one throne,
And Holy Ghost together,
Receive my prayer, and let me share
Thy grace and truth forever.

M. Rutilius.

FAITH AND JUSTIFICATION.

250. L. M.

1 JUST as I am, without one plea,
But that Thy blood was shed for me,
And that Thou bidst me come to Thee,
O Lamb of God, I come, I come!

2 Just as I am, and waiting not
To rid my soul of one dark blot,

To Thee, whose blood can cleanse each spot,
O Lamb of God, I come, I come!

3 Just as I am, though tossed about
With many a conflict, many a doubt,
Fightings and fears within, without,
O Lamb of God, I come, I come!

4 Just as I am, poor, wretched, blind;
Sight, riches, healing of the mind,
Yea, all I need, in Thee to find,
O Lamb of God, I come, I come!

5 Just as I am; Thou wilt receive,
Wilt welcome, pardon, cleanse, relieve,
Because Thy promise I believe;
O Lamb of God, I come, I come!

6 Just as I am; Thy love unknown
Has broken every barrier down;
Now to be Thine, yea, Thine alone,
O Lamb of God, I come, I come!

Charlotte Elliott.

251. C. M.

1 IN vain we seek for peace with God
By methods of our own:
Jesus, there's nothing but Thy blood
Can bring us near the throne.

2 'Tis Thine atoning sacrifice
Hath answered all demands;

And peace and pardon from the skies
Are blessings from Thy hands.

3 'Tis by Thy death we live, O Lord;
'Tis on Thy cross we rest:
Forever be Thy love adored,
Thy Name forever blest.

Isaac Watts.

252.

L. M. 6 lines.

1 MY hope is built on nothing less
Than Jesus' blood and righteousness:
I dare not trust the sweetest frame,
But wholly lean on Jesus' Name.
On Christ, the solid Rock, I stand,
All other ground is sinking sand.

2 When darkness veils His lovely face,
I rest on His unchanging grace;
In every high and stormy gale,
My anchor holds within the veil.
On Christ, the solid Rock, I stand,
All other ground is sinking sand.

3 His oath, His covenant and blood,
Support me in the sinking flood;
When every earthly prop gives way,
He then is all my hope and stay.
On Christ, the solid Rock, I stand,
All other ground is sinking sand.

4 When I shall launch to worlds unseen,
Oh, may I then be found in Him!

Dressed in His righteousness alone,
Faultless to stand before the throne.
On Christ, the solid Rock, I stand,
All other ground is sinking sand.

Edward Mote.

253.

S. M.

1 NOT all the blood of beasts,
On Jewish altars slain,
Could give the guilty conscience peace
Or wash away the stain.

2 But Christ, the heavenly Lamb,
Takes all our stains away;
A Sacrifice of nobler name,
And richer blood than they.

3 My faith would lay her hand
On that dear head of Thine,
While like a penitent I stand,
And there confess my sin.

4 My soul looks back to see
The burden Thou didst bear,
When hanging on the curséd tree,
And knows her guilt was there.

5 Believing, we rejoice
To see the curse remove;
We bless the Lamb with cheerful voice,
And sing His bleeding love.

Isaac Watts.

254.

7.6.7.6. D.

1 I LAY my sins on Jesus,
The spotless Lamb of God;
He bears them all, and frees us,
From the accurséd load.
I bring my guilt to Jesus,
To wash my crimson stains
White, in His blood most precious,
Till not a spot remains.

2 I lay my wants on Jesus;
All fulness dwells in Him;
He heals all my diseases,
He doth my soul redeem.
I lay my griefs on Jesus,
My burdens and my cares;
He from them all releases,
He all my sorrows shares.

3 I long to be like Jesus,
Meek, loving, lowly, mild;
I long to be like Jesus,
The Father's holy child.
I long to be with Jesus,
Amid the heavenly throng,
To sing with saints His praises,
To learn the angels' song.

Horatius Bonar. a.

255.

7s. D.

1 JESUS, Lover of my soul,
Let me to Thy bosom fly,

While the nearer waters roll,
  While the tempest still is high!
Hide me, O my Savior, hide,
  Till the storm of life is past;
Safe into the haven guide;
  Oh, receive my soul at last!

2 Other refuge have I none;
  Hangs my helpless soul on Thee:
Leave, ah, leave me not alone,
  Still support and comfort me!
All my trust on Thee is stayed,
  All my help from Thee I bring:
Cover my defenceless head
  With the shadow of Thy wing.

3 Thou, O Christ, art all I want;
  More than all in Thee I find:
Raise the fallen, cheer the faint,
  Heal the sick, and lead the blind.
Just and holy is Thy Name;
  I am all unrighteousness:
False and full of sin I am;
  Thou art full of truth and grace.

4 Plenteous grace with Thee is found,
  Grace to cover all my sin;
Let the healing streams abound;
  Make and keep me pure within.
Thou of life the Fountain art,
  Freely let me take of Thee:
Spring Thou up within my heart,
  Rise to all eternity.

C. Wesley.

256.

7s. 6 lines.

1 ROCK of Ages, cleft for me,
Let me hide myself in Thee!
Let the water and the blood,
From Thy riven side which flowed,
Be of sin the perfect cure,
Save me, Lord, and make me pure.

2 Not the labors of my hands
Can fulfill Thy Law's demands:
Could my zeal no respite know,
Could my tears forever flow,
All for sin could not atone:
Thou must save and Thou alone!

3 Nothing in my hand I bring,
Simply to Thy cross I cling;
Naked, come to Thee for dress;
Helpless, look to Thee for grace;
Foul, I to the Fountain fly;
Wash me, Savior, or I die!

4 While I draw this fleeting breath,
When my eyelids close in death,
When I soar to worlds unknown,
See Thee on Thy judgment throne,
Rock of Ages, cleft for me,
Let me hide myself in Thee!

Augustus M. Toplady. a.

257.

7s.

1 CHIEF of sinners, though I be,
Jesus shed His blood for me;

Died, that I might live on high;
Lives, that I may never die.

2 Oh, the height of Jesus' love!
Higher than the heavens above,
Deeper than the depths of sea,
Lasting as eternity.

3 Jesus only can impart
Balm to heal the smitten heart;
Peace that flows from sins forgiven,
Joy that lifts the soul to heaven.

4 Chief of sinners though I be,
Christ is all in all to me;
All my wants to Him are known,
All my sorrows are His own.

William McComb. a.

258.

C. M.

1 'TIS not by works of righteousness
Which our own hands have done,
But we are saved by sovereign grace
Abounding through His Son,

2 'Tis from the mercy of our God
That all our hopes begin;
'Tis by the water and the blood
Our souls are washed from sin.

3 'Tis through the purchase of His death
Who hung upon the tree,
The Spirit is sent down to breathe
On such dry bones as we.

4 Raised from the dead we live anew,
And, justified by grace,
We shall appear in glory too,
And see our Father's face,

Isaac Watts.

259.

L. M.

1 JESUS, Thy blood and righteousness
My beauty are, my glorious dress;
'Midst flaming worlds, in these arrayed,
With joy shall I lift up my head.

2 Bold shall I stand in Thy great day,
For who aught to my charge shall lay?
Fully through these absolved I am
From sin and fear, from guilt and shame.

3 This spotless robe the same appears,
When ruined nature sinks in years:
No age can change its constant hue;
Thy blood preserves it ever new.

4 Oh, let the dead now hear Thy voice;
Now bid Thy banished ones rejoice!
Their beauty this, their glorious dress,
Jesus, Thy blood and righteousness!

5 When from the dust of death I rise,
To claim my mansion in the skies,
E'en then this shall be all my plea,
"Jesus hath lived and died for me."

Nicholas Louis, Count Zinzendorf.

260. C. M.

1 THOU art the way: to Thee alone
From sin and death we flee:
And he who would the Father seek,
Must seek Him, Lord, by Thee.

2 Thou art the Truth: Thy Word alone
Sound wisdom can impart:
Thou only canst inform the mind,
And purify the heart.

3 Thou art the Life: the rending tomb
Proclaims Thy conquering arm:
And those who put their trust in Thee,
Nor death nor hell shall harm.

4 Thou art the Way, the Truth, the Life:
Grant us that Way to know,
That Truth to keep, that Life to win,
Whose joys eternal flow.

George W. Doane.

261. S. M. D.

1 I WAS a wandering sheep,
I did not love the fold;
I did not love my Shepherd's voice,
I would not be controlled.
I was a wayward child,
I did not love my home;
I did not love my Father's voice,
I loved afar to roam.

2 The Shepherd sought His sheep,
The Father sought His child;
They followed me o'er vale and hill,
O'er deserts waste and wild;
They found me nigh to death,
Famished, and faint, and lone;
They bound me with the bands of love,
They found the wandering one.

3 Jesus my Shepherd is,
'Twas He that loved my soul,
'Twas He that washed me in His blood,
'Twas He that made me whole.
'Twas He that sought the lost,
That found the wandering sheep;
'Twas He that brought me to the fold,
'Tis He that still doth keep.

4 I was a wandering sheep,
I would not be controlled;
But now I love my Shepherd's voice,
I love, I love the fold!
I was a wayward child,
I once preferred to roam;
But now I love my Father's voice,
I love, I love His home.

Horatius Bonar.

262.

8.7.8.7.7.7.

1 ONE there is above all others,
Well deserves the name of Friend.
His is love beyond a brother's,

Costly, free, and knows no end.
They who once His kindness prove,
Find it everlasting love.

2 Which of all our friends, to save us
Could or would have shed his blood?
But this Savior died to have us
Reconciled in Him to God:
This was boundless love indeed:
Jesus is a Friend in need.

3 When He lived on earth abaséd,
Friend of sinners was His Name:
Now, above all glory raiséd,
He rejoices in the same:
Still He calls them brethren, friends,
And to all their wants attends.

4 Oh, for grace our hearts to soften!
Teach us, Lord, at length to love.
We, alas! forget too often
What a Friend we have above:
But when home our souls are brought,
We will love Thee as we ought.

John Newton.

263.

L. M.

1 FROM every stormy wind that blows,
From every swelling tide of woes,
There is a calm, a sure retreat,
'Tis found beneath the mercy-seat.

2 There is a place where Jesus sheds
The oil of gladness on our heads;
A place than all besides more sweet;
It is the blood-bought mercy-seat.

3 There is a scene where spirits blend,
Where friend holds fellowship with friend,
Though sundered far, by faith they meet
Around one common mercy-seat.

4 Ah! whither could we flee for aid,
When tempted, desolate, dismayed;
Or how the host of hell defeat,
Had suffering saints no mercy-seat?

5 There, there, on eagle wing we soar,
And sin and sense seem all no more,
And heaven comes down our souls to greet,
And glory crowns the mercy-seat!

Hugh Stowell.

264.

C. M.

1 ALL that I was, my sin, my guilt,
My death, was all my own;
All that I am, I owe to Thee,
My gracious God, alone.

2 The evil of my former state
Was mine, and only mine;
The good in which I now rejoice
Is Thine, and only Thine.

3 The darkness of my former state,
The bondage, all was mine;
The light of life in which I walk,
The liberty, is Thine.

4 Thy grace first made me feel my sin,
It taught me to believe;
Then in believing, peace I found,
And now I live, I live.

5 All that I am, e'en here on earth,
All that I hope to be
When Jesus comes and glory dawns,
I owe it, Lord, to Thee.

Horatius Bonar.

265.

11.9.11.9.9.

1 PRAY, tell me, how cam'st thou so easily in
Through yonder bright portals of heaven,
Since not to a soul here polluted by sin
Admission there ever was given?
Wast thou not akin to the fallen?

2 By grace did I live, and in grace did I die,
By grace did I enter these portals;
Lo, this is the ground and the reason why I
Am one of the blessed immortals,
Who sing hallelujah forever.

3 Oh, blessed art thou who in life and in death
Hadst grace for thine only foundation!
For sinners condemned, so His holy Word
saith,

Can plead nothing else for salvation.
For grace, then, give thanks everlasting.

A. C. Rutström.

266.

L. M.

1 OUR God so loved the world that He
Gave His own Son, and did decree
That all who would in Him believe
Should everlasting life receive.

2 Christ Jesus is the ground of faith,
Who was made flesh and suffered death;
All that confide in Him alone
Have built on this chief Corner-stone.

3 God would not have the sinner die,
His Son with saving grace is nigh,
His Spirit in the Word doth teach
How man the blessèd goal may reach.

4 Be of good cheer, for God's own Son
Forgives all sins which thou hast done;
Thou'rt justified by Jesus' blood,
Thy baptism grants the highest good.

5 If thou be sick, if death draw near,
This truth thy troubled heart can cheer;
Christ Jesus saves my soul from death,
That is the firmest ground of faith.

6 Glory to God the Father, Son,
And Holy Spirit, Three in One!
To Thee, O blessed Trinity,
Be praise now and eternally!

J. Olearius.

267.

8.7.8.7.8.8.7.

1 DEAR Christians one and all rejoice,
With exultation springing,
And, with united heart and voice
And holy rapture singing,
Proclaim the wonders God hath done,
How His right arm the victory won;
Right dearly it hath cost Him.

2 Fast bound in Satan's chains I lay,
Death brooded darkly o'er me,
Sin was my torment night and day,
In sin my mother bore me;
Deeper and deeper still I fell,
Life had become a living hell,
So firmly sin possessed me.

3 My good works so imperfect were,
They had no power to aid me;
My will God's judgments could not bear,
Yea, prone to evil made me:
Grief drove me to despair, and I
Had nothing left me but to die;
To hell I fast was sinking.

4 Then God beheld my wretched state
With deep commiseration;
He thought upon His mercy great,
And willed my soul's salvation;
He turned to me a Father's heart;
Not small the cost! to heal my smart,
He gave His best and dearest.

5 He spoke to His beloved Son:
"Tis time to take compassion:
Then go, bright Jewel of my crown,
And bring to man salvation;
From sin and sorrow set him free,
Slay bitter death for him, that he
May live with Thee forever."

6 The Son obeyed Him cheerfully,
And born of virgin mother,
Came down upon the earth to me,
That He might be my brother:
His mighty power doth work unseen,
He came in fashion poor and mean,
And took the devil captive.

7 He sweetly said, "Hold fast by Me,
I am thy Rock and Castle,
Thy Ransom I myself will be,
For thee I strive and wrestle:
For I am with thee, I am thine
And evermore thou shalt be mine,
The foe shall not devide us.

8 "The foe shall shed my precious blood,
Me of my life bereaving:
All this I suffer for thy good,
Be steadfast and believing:
Life shall from death the victory win,
My innocence shall bear thy sin,
So art thou blest forever.

9 Now to my Father I depart,
From earth to heaven ascending,
Thence heavenly wisdom to impart,
The Holy Spirit sending:
He shall in trouble comfort thee,
Teach thee to know and follow me,
And to the truth conduct thee.

10 What I have done and taught, teach thou,
My ways forsake thou never,
So shall my kingdom flourish now,
And God be praised, forever:
Take heed lest men with base alloy
The heavenly treasure should destroy;
This counsel I bequeath thee."

Martin Luther.

268.

8.7.8.7.8.7.5.6.7.

1 OH, joy of joys! God so did love
This world and show compassion,
That He sent down from heaven above
His Son for our salvation.
So deep in sin this world was bound,
Had God His Son not given,
Our bonds thus riven,
No help had e'er been found,
However man had striven.

2 This doth our hearts now satisfy,
And quiets all our terrors,
That Jesus Christ our Lord did die
To save us from our errors.

O God, Thy love to us is great!
Thy mercies are most tender!
Our sole defender,
None in this earthly state
Thee ample praise can render.

3 He who on Jesus Christ doth trust
Shall happy be in heaven;
The happiness which once was lost
Through Jesus Christ is given.
For God His Son did never send
Here for our condemnation;
His incarnation
Had for its gracious end
Our joy and our salvation.

4 But all who turn from Christ away
Shall be condemned forever;
Their doom is sealed this very day
And death awaits them ever.
For since they willfully refused
Salvation to inherit
Through Jesus' merit,
They stand of sin accused,
And so must suffer for it.

5 All who are faithful unto death
Are given life forever,
The life which is the fruit of faith
In Jesus Christ our Savior.
Give us, O Lord, the faith to come
And ever cling to Jesus!

When death releases
Our souls, oh, take them home,
To dwell in heavenly places.

J. Kolmodin.

269.

C. M. D.

1 I HEARD the voice of Jesus say,
Come unto me and rest;
Lay down, thou weary one, lay down
Thy head upon my breast.
I came to Jesus as I was,
Weary, and worn, and sad;
I found in Him a resting-place.
And He has made me glad.

2 I heard the voice of Jesus say,
Behold, I freely give
The living water; thirsty one,
Stoop down, and drink, and live.
I came to Jesus and I drank
Of that life-giving stream;
My thirst was quenched, my soul revived,
And now I live in Him.

3 I heard the voice of Jesus say,
I am this dark world's Light;
Look unto Me, thy morn shall rise,
And all thy day be bright.
I looked to Jesus, and I found
In Him, my Star, my Sun;
And in that Light of life I'll walk
Till traveling days are done.

Horatius Bonar.

270.

11s

1 HOW firm a foundation, ye saints of the Lord,
Is laid for your faith in His excellent Word!
What more can He say than to you He has said,
Who unto the Savior for refuge have fled?

2 "In every condition—in sickness, in health,
In poverty's vale, or abounding in wealth,
At home and abroad, on the land, on the sea,
As thy days may demand, so thy succor shall be.

3 "Fear not, I am with thee; oh, be not dismayed;
For I am thy God, and will still give thee aid;
I'll strengthen thee, help thee, and cause thee to stand
Upheld by My righteous, omnipotent hand.

4 "When through the deep waters I call thee to go,
The rivers of sorrow shall not overflow;
For I will be with thee, thy troubles to bless,
And sanctify to thee thy deepest distress.

5 "When through fiery trials thy pathway shall lie,
My grace, all-sufficient, shall be thy supply;

The flame shall not hurt thee; I only design
Thy dross to consume, and thy gold to refine.

6 "E'en down to old age, all My people shall prove
My sovereign eternal, unchangeable love;
And then, when gray hairs shall their temples adorn
Like lambs they shall still in My bosom be borne.

7 "The soul that on Jesus hath leaned for repose,
I will not, I cannot desert to his foes:
That soul, though all hell should endeavor to shake,
I'll never—no, never—no, never forsake!"

Keen?

271.

6 6.4.6.6.6.4.

1 MY faith looks up to Thee,
Thou Lamb of Calvary,
Savior divine!
Now hear me while I pray;
Take all my guilt away;
Oh, let me from this day
Be wholly Thine.

2 May Thy rich grace impart
Strength to my fainting heart,
My zeal inspire;
As Thou hast died for me,

Oh, may my love to Thee
Pure, warm, and changeless be,
A living fire.

3 While life's dark maze I tread,
And griefs around me spread,
Be Thou my Guide;
Bid darkness turn to day,
Wipe sorrow's tears away,
Nor let me ever stray
From Thee aside.

4 When ends life's transient dream,
When death's cold sullen stream
Shall o'er me roll;
Blest Savior, then, in love,
Fear and distrust remove;
Oh, bear me safe above,
A ransomed soul.

Ray Palmer.

272. C. M.

1 OH, for a faith that will not shrink,
Though prest by many a foe;
That will not tremble on the brink
Of poverty or woe;

2 That will not murmur nor complain
Beneath the chastening rod:
But in the hour of grief or pain
Can lean upon its God.

3 A faith that shines more bright and clear
When tempests rage without;
That when in danger knows no fear,
In darkness feels no doubt:

4 That bears unmoved the world's dread frown,
Nor heeds its scornful smile;
That sin's wild ocean cannot drown,
Nor Satan's arts beguile:

5 A faith that keeps the narrow way
Till life's last hour is fled,
And with a pure and heavenly ray
Lights up a dying bed.

6 Lord, give us such a faith as this,
And then whate'er may come,
We'll taste e'en here the hallowed bliss
Of an eternal home.

William H. Bathurst. a.

SANCTIFICATION.

273.

8.7.8.7.D.

1 JESUS, I my cross have taken,
All to leave and follow Thee;
Destitute, despised, forsaken,
Thou, from hence, my all shalt be.

Perish every fond ambition,
  All I've sought, or hoped, or known;
Yet how rich is my condition!
  God and heaven are still my own.

2 Man may trouble and distress me,
  'Twill but drive me to Thy breast;
Life with trials hard may press me,
  Heaven will bring me sweeter rest.
Oh, 'tis not in grief to harm me,
  While Thy love is left to me;
Oh, 'twere not in joy to charm me,
  Were that joy unmixed with Thee.

3 Take, my soul, thy full salvation;
  Rise o'er sin, and fear, and care;
Joy to find in every station
  Something still to do or bear.
Think what Spirit dwells within thee;
  What a Father's smile is thine;
What a Savior died to win thee:
  Child of heaven, shouldst thou repine?

4 Haste thee on from grace to glory,
  Armed by faith and winged by prayer;
Heaven's eternal day's before thee,
  God's own hand shall guide thee there.
Soon shall close thine earthly mission,
  Swift shall pass thy pilgrim days;
Hope shall change to glad fruition,
  Faith to sight, and prayer to praise.

Henry Francis Lyte.

274. C. M.

1 AM I a soldier of the cross,
A follower of the Lamb?
And shall I fear to own His cause,
Or blush to speak His Name?

2 Must I be carried to the skies
On flowery beds of ease,
While others fought to win the prize,
And sailed through bloody seas?

3 Are there no foes for me to face?
Must I not stem the flood?
Is this vain world a friend to grace,
To help me on to God?

4 Sure I must fight, if I would reign:
Increase my courage, Lord;
I'll bear the toil, endure the pain,
Supported by Thy Word.

5 Thy saints, in all this glorious war,
Shall conquer, though they die;
They see the triumph from afar,
By faith they bring it nigh.

6 When that illustrious day shall rise
And all Thine armies shine
In robes of victory through the skies,
The glory shall be Thine.

Isaac Watts. a

275.

S. M.

1 MY soul, be on Thy guard;
Ten thousand foes arise,
And hosts of sin are pressing hard
To draw thee from the skies.

2 Oh, watch, and fight, and pray,
The battle ne'er give o'er;
Renew it boldly every day,
And help divine implore.

3 Ne'er think the victory won,
Nor once at ease sit down;
Thine arduous work will not be done,
Till thou receive thy crown.

4 Fight on, my soul, till death
Shall bring thee to thy God;
He'll take thee at thy parting breath,
To His divine abode.

George Heath.

276.

7.6.7.6.D.

1 STAND up, stand up for Jesus!
Ye soldiers of the cross,
Lift high His royal banner,
It must not suffer loss;
From victory unto victory
His army shall be led,
Till every foe is vanquished,
And Christ is Lord indeed.

2 Stand up, stand up for Jesus!
The trumpet call obey;
Forth to the mighty conflict
In this His glorious day;
Ye that are men, now serve him
Against unnumbered foes;
Your courage rise with danger,
And strength to strength oppose.

3 Stand up, stand up for Jesus!
Stand in His strength alone;
The arm of flesh will fail you,
Ye dare not trust your own;
Put on the gospel armor,
And, watching unto prayer,
Where duty calls or danger,
Be never wanting there.

4 Stand up, stand up for Jesus!
The strife will not be long;
This day the noise of battle,
The next the victor's song:
To him that overcometh,
A crown of life shall be;
He with the King of glory
Shall reign eternally. *George Duffield.*

277. L. M.

1 So let our lips and lives express
The holy gospel we profess:
So let our works and virtues shine,
To prove the doctrine all divine.

2 Thus shall we best proclaim abroad
The honors of our Savior God;
When His salvation reigns within,
And grace subdues the power of sin.

3 Our flesh and sense must be denied,
Passion and envy, lust and pride;
While justice, temperance, truth, and love
Our inward piety approve.

4 His promise bears our spirits up,
While we expect that blessed hope,
The bright appearance of the Lord,
And faith stands leaning on His Word.

Isaac Watts. a.

278.

C. M.

1 OH, for a closer walk with God,
A calm and heavenly frame;
A light to shine upon the road
That leads me to the Lamb!

2 Return, O holy Dove, return,
Sweet Messenger of rest!
I hate the sins that made Thee mourn,
And drove Thee from my breast.

3 The dearest idol I have known,
Whate'er that idol be,
Help me to tear it from Thy throne,
And worship only Thee.

4 So shall my walk be close with God,
Calm and serene my frame;
So purer light shall mark the road
That leads me to the Lamb.

William Cowper.

279.

C. M.

1 OH, for a heart to praise my God,
A heart from sin set free!
A heart that always feels Thy blood,
So freely shed for me!

2 A heart resigned, submissive, meek,
My great Redeemer's throne;
Where only Christ is heard to speak,
Where Jesus reigns alone.

3 An humble, lowly, contrite heart,
Believing, true, and clean;
Which neither life nor death can part
From Him that dwells within.

4 A heart in every thought renewed,
And full of love divine;
Perfect, and right, and pure, and good,
A copy, Lord, of Thine!

5 Thy nature, gracious Lord, impart,
Come quickly, from above;
Write Thy new Name upon my heart,
Thy new, best Name of Love.

C. Wesley. a.

280.

C. M.

1 MUST Jesus bear the cross alone,
And all the world go free?
No, there's a cross for every one,
And there's a cross for me.

2 How happy are the saints above,
Who once were sorrowing here!
But now they taste unmingled love,
And joy without a tear.

3 The consecrated cross I'll bear,
Till death shall set me free;
And then go home, my crown to wear,
For there's a crown for me.

G. N. Allen.

281.

7.6.7.6. Trochaic, and Chorus.

1 JESUS keep me near the cross,
There a precious fountain
Free to all, a healing stream,
Flows from Calvary's mountain.
Chorus—In the cross, in the cross,
Be my glory ever;
Till my raptured soul shall find
Rest beyond the river.

2 Near the cross, a trembling soul,
Love and mercy found me;
There the bright and morning star
Shed its beams around me.
Chorus—In the cross, etc.

3 Near the cross! O Lamb of God,
Bring its scenes before me;
Help me walk from day to day,
With its shadows o'er me.
Chorus—In the cross, etc.

4 Near the cross I'll watch and wait,
Hoping, trusting ever,
Till I reach the golden strand,
Just beyond the river.
Chorus—In the cross, etc.

Fanny J. Crosby (Mrs. Van Alstyne.)

282.

6.4.6.4.6.6.4.

1 Nearer, my God, to Thee!
Nearer to Thee!
Through Word and Sacrament,
Thou com'st to me.
Thy grace is ever near,
Thy Spirit ever here,
Drawing to Thee.

2 Ages on ages rolled,
Ere earth appeared,
Yet Thine unmeasured love
The way prepared;
E'en then Thou yearnedst for me
That I might nearer be,
Nearer to Thee!

3 Thy Son has come to earth,
My sin to bear,

My every wound to heal,
  My pain to share.
God in the flesh for me,
Brings me now nearer Thee.
  Nearer to Thee!

4 Lo! all my debt is paid,
  My guilt is gone.
See! He has risen for me,
  My throne is won.
Thanks, O my God, to Thee!
None now can nearer,
  Nearer to Thee!

5 Welcome, then, to Thy home,
  Blest One in Three!
As Thou hast promised, come!
  Come Lord to me!
Work, Thou, O God, through me,
Live Thou, O God, in me,
  Ever in me!

6 By the baptismal stream,
  Which made me Thine,
By the dear flesh and blood
  Thy love made mine,
Purge Thou all sin from me,
That I may nearer be,
  Nearer to Thee!

7 Surely it matters not
  What earth may bring;
Death is of no account,

Grace will I sing.
Nothing remains for me
Save to be near Thee,
Nearer to Thee!

H. E. Jacobs.

283.

6.4.6.4.6.6.4.

1 NEARER, my God, to Thee!
Nearer to Thee!
E'en though it be a cross
That raiseth me;
Still all my song shall be,
Nearer, my God, to Thee,
Nearer to Thee!

2 Though, like the wanderer,
The sun gone down,
Darkness be over me,
My rest a stone,
Yet in my dreams I'd be
Nearer, my God, to Thee,
Nearer to Thee!

3 There let my way appear
Steps unto heaven;
All that Thou sendest me
In mercy given;
Angels to beckon me
Nearer, my God, to Thee,
Nearer to Thee!

4 Then with my waking thoughts
Bright with Thy praise,

Out of my stony griefs
  Bethel I'll raise;
So by my woes to be
Nearer, My God, to Thee,
  Nearer to Thee!

5 Or if on joyful wing
  Cleaving the sky,
Sun, moon, and stars forgot,
  Upwards I fly;
Still all my song shall be,
Nearer, my God, to Thee,
  Nearer to Thee!

Mrs. Sarah Flower Adams.

284.

7.6.7.6.D.

1 I NEED Thee, precious Jesus,
  For I am full of sin;
My soul is dark and guilty,
  My heart is dead within:
I need the cleansing fountain,
  Where I can always flee,
The blood of Christ, most precious,
  The sinner's perfect plea.

2 I need Thee, blesséd Jesus,
  For I am very poor;
A stranger and a pilgrim,
  I have no earthly store:
I need the love of Jesus
  To cheer me on my way,

To guide my doubting footsteps,
  To be my strength and stay.

3 I need Thee, blesséd Jesus,
  I need a friend like Thee,
A friend to soothe and pity,
  A friend to care for me:
I need the heart of Jesus
  To feel each anxious care,
To tell my every trouble,
  And all my sorrows share.

5 I need Thee, blesséd Jesus,
  I need Thee day by day,
To fill me with Thy fulness,
  To lead me on my way:
I need Thy Holy Spirit
  To teach me what I am,
To show me more of Jesus,
  To point me to the Lamb.

Frederick Whitfield.

285.

6.4.6.4. and Chorus.

1 I NEED Thee every hour,
  Most gracious Lord,
No tender voice like Thine
  Can peace afford.
Chorus—I need Thee, oh! I need Thee,
  Every hour I need Thee:
Oh bless me now, my Savior,
  I come to Thee.

2 I need Thee every hour,
Stay Thou near by;
Temptations lose their power
When Thou art nigh.
Chorus—I need Thee, etc.

3 I need Thee every hour,
In joy or pain;
Come quickly and abide,
Or life is vain.
Chorus—I need Thee, etc.

4 I need Thee every hour:
Teach me Thy will;
And Thy rich promises
In me fulfill.
Chorus—I need Thee, etc.

5 I need Thee every hour,
Most Holy One,
Oh, make me Thine indeed,
Thou blessed Son.
Chorus—I need Thee, etc.

Mrs. Annie S. Hawks.

286.

8.7.8.7.4.7.

1 GUIDE me, O Thou great Jehovah,
Pilgrim through this barren land;
I am weak, but Thou art mighty,
Hold me with Thy powerful hand;
Bread of heaven,
Feed me till I want no more!

2 Open now the crystal fountain,
Whence the healing streams do flow;
Let the fiery, cloudy pillar,
Lead me all my journey through;
Strong Deliverer,
Be Thou still my strength and shield!

3 When I tread the verge of Jordan,
Bid my anxious fears subside:
Death of death and hell's Destruction,
Land me safe on Canaan's side:
Songs of praises
I will ever give to Thee.

William Williams.

287.

5.5.8.8.5.5.

1 JESUS, still lead on,
Till our rest be won,
And although the way be cheerless,
We will follow, calm and fearless.
Guide us by Thy hand
To our Fatherland!

2 If the way be drear,
If the foe be near,
Let not faithless fears o'ertake us,
Let not faith and hope forsake us;
For through many a foe
To our home we go!

3 When we seek relief
From a long-felt grief;

When temptations come alluring,
Make us patient and enduring;
Show us that bright shore
Where we weep no more!

4 Jesus, still lead on,
Till our rest be won;
Heavenly Leader, still direct us,
Still support, console, protect us,
Till we safely stand
In our Fatherland!

Nicholas Louis, Count Zinzendorf.

288.

6.5. 12 lines.

1 ONWARD, Christian soldiers,
Marching as to war,
With the cross of Jesus
Going on before.
Christ, the royal Master,
Leads against the foe:
Forward into battle,
See His banners go,
Onward, Christian soldiers,
Marching as to war,
With the cross of Jesus
Going on before.

2 At the sign of triumph,
Satan's armies flee:
On, then, Christian soldiers,
On to victory.
Hell's foundations quiver,

At the shout of praise:
Brothers, lift your voices,
Loud your anthems raise.
Onward, Christian soldiers, etc,

3 Like a mighty army,
Moves the church of God:
Brothers, we are treading
Where the saints have trod.
We are not divided,
All one body we,
One in hope, in doctrine,
One in charity.
Onward, Christian soldiers, etc.

4 Crowns and thrones may perish,
Kingdoms rise and wane,
But the church of Jesus
Constant will remain.
Gates of hell can never
'Gainst that church prevail:
We have Christ's own promise,
And that cannot fail.
Onward, Christian soldiers, etc.

5 Onward, then, ye faithful,
Join our happy throng,
Blend with ours your voices,
In the triumph-song:
Glory, laud, and honor,
Unto Christ the King:

This, through countless ages,
Men and angels sing.
Onward, Christian soldiers, etc.

S. Baring-Gould.

289.

6.5. 12 lines.

1 JESUS, King of glory,
Throned above the sky,
Jesus, tender Savior,
Hear Thy children cry.
Pardon our transgressions,
Cleanse us from our sin,
By Thy Spirit help us
Heavenly life to win.
Jesus, King of glory,
Throned above the sky,
Jesus, tender Savior,
Hear Thy children cry.

2 Help us ever steadfast
In the faith to be:
In Thy church's conflicts
Fighting valiantly.
Loving Savior, strengthen
These weak hearts of ours,
Through Thy cross to conquer
Crafty evil powers.
Jesus, King of glory, etc.

3 When the shadows lengthen,
Show us, Lord, Thy way;
Through the darkness lead us

To the heavenly day;
When our course is finished,
Ended all the strife,
Grant us with the faithful,
Palms and crowns of life.
Jesus, King of glory, etc.

W. H. Davison.

290.

8.7.8.7.8.8.7.

1 THE little while I linger here
Should grief and fear o'ertake me?
No; Jesus is my Shepherd dear,
He never will forsake me.
He gave His life to save the herd,
And with His Spirit and His Word,
Is present with us always.

2 I hear Him speak, I know His voice,
I go where'er He beckons.
His own He knows, they are His choice,
Their numbers, too, He reckons.
And He will seek the straying sheep,
The feeble in His bosom keep,
And gently raise the fallen.

3 He strengthens me with living bread,
With waters sweet and gracious,
Which flow from life's great fountain-head,
With peace and joy most precious.
Though rough and thorny is my way,
If from His path I do not stray,
I shall not be discouraged.

4 O Thou who saidst, "Away from me
No one shall snatch them ever."
Thee I implore, to Thee I flee,
Ah leave, forsake me, never!
The world allures; oh, guide me through,
That with the blessed I may view
Thy Father's glorious mansions.

5 How vain the wordling's pomp and show,
How brief His joys and pleasures!
The night approaches now, and lo!
We leave all earthly treasures.
And then what is all earthly bliss
To that blest promise, Where He is
We shall be with Him also!

F. M. Franzen.

291.

11.11.11.6.6.11.

1 HOW blest are the hours that Jesus bestows,
When wonders of grace to the spirit He shows!
His Word lights the way to the heavenly goal,
His Spirit is near us,
His Spirit is near us,
To rouse us, and teach us, and comfort our soul!

2 Lord Jesus, our Savior, Thy Spirit us give
To quicken, and strengthen, and cause us to live;
Grant faith and give love, and in mercy bestow

Whatever is needed,
Whatever is needed,
To exercise faith in our hearts here below.

3 Our hearts are so cold, yea, as hard as a stone;
Such are they by nature, and Thou art alone,
On earth and in heaven, the Savior who can,
A new heart creating,
A new heart creating,
A new heart creating, make each a new man.

4 From sorrows of earth wilt Thou now turn our mind,
For days that are coming, oh, help us to find
Our joy and our comfort in what Thou hast wrought;
For we are Thy people,
For we are Thy people,
With death, wounds, and anguish so preciously bought.

5 Lord, therefore, remember in mercy and love
Thy people, and grant us Thy help from above;
Thy law cause to wake us, Thy grace give us cheer,
And lead us Thy Spirit,
And lead us Thy Spirit,
So that we may know that Thy presence is near.

From Hemlandssånger.

292.

10.10.5.5.10.

1 RISE from thy stupor, heart so uneasy;
Why so completely forget what thou hast?
Christ is forever
Thy loving Savior,
He's still the same as He was in the past.

2 Pause and consider, earnestly ponder
What thou possessest in Him, not in thee:
Righteous and holy,
Perfect most truly
Art thou in Christ, who from sin sets thee free.

3 Though thou at times can not feel it, nor see it,
Though so unholy and sinful within,
Jesus hath bought thee,
And mercy brought thee,
And still upholds thee, and saves thee from sin.

4 Right in the midst of sin's daily affliction,
Justification eternal thou hast.
That thou art holy
Thou ow'st Him solely,
Him upon whom all thy burdens were cast.

5 God is in Christ now thy Friend and thy Father;
Jesus thy Brother on Calvary died;

And by His merit
Has sent His Spirit,
To be thy Strength, and thy Comfort, and
Guide. *C. O. Rosenius.*

293.

8.8.7.8.8.7.7.

1 JESUS, Thou my heart's Desire,
Blesséd Lord and only Savior,
Let my soul find rest in Thee.
Let Thy weary dove retire
To Thy bosom safe forever,
Flying o'er this restless sea
Home to rest in peace with Thee.

2 Thou alone canst satisfy me,
And assuage my thirst so burning
With the water from life's well.
Savior, Thou canst sanctify me;
For Thy grace my heart is yearning;
With Thy fulness in me dwell,
Blessed Lord, and all is well.

Lina Sandell.

294.

9.8.9.8.8.8.

1 DEAR Savior, in Thy bosom hide me,
There make the weary wanderer blest;
In all the word there's none beside Thee
To give my soul the longed-for rest.
Dear Jesus, I would come to Thee,
Be Thine throughout eternity.

2 The world to me is dark and dreary:
My evil heart doth cause me grief.
Redeemer, I am sad and weary,
Give Thou my troubled soul relief.
Come, precious Jesus, lead Thou me,
And keep me ever near to Thee.

3 With Thee I'm safe from every danger,
But only, Lord, when in Thy care;
For here on earth I'm but a stranger,
And prone to fall in every snare.
Thou art the true and living Way,
Blest Jesus, keep me Thine alway.

From Hemlandssånger.

295.

8.8.7.8.8.7.8.8.8.8.8.8.

1 O LORD, devoutly love I Thee,
Come, Jesus, and abide with me,
And grant me e'er Thy favor.
In this wide world of anxious care,
Vain glory find I everywhere.
But peace with Thee, my Savior.
E'en though, in woful agony,
My soul and body pine away,
Thou art my Comfort, ever blest,
I safely on Thy bosom rest.
Lord Jesus Christ, my Savior dear,
Thy saving hand is ever near.

2 Almighty God, for what I own,
Receive, and am, to Thee alone
I ought my thanks to render.

Teach me to use Thy gifts, I pray,
To aid the poor, and never stay,
O Lord, Thy mercies tender.
Make known to me, O God, Thy will,
And purge my soul of every ill;
Yea, make me patient and content,
Nor let my soul to earth be bent,
Lord Jesus Christ, for Thy death's sake
The bonds of my affliction break.

Send, Lord, Thine angels forth at last
To bear my soul, when life is past,
Where heavenly joy aboundeth;
And let my weary body rest
In peace, where'er Thou seest best,
Until Thy voice resoundeth.
Then lo! in holy vesture clad,
I shall behold my Lord and God;
His grace and glory then shall be
My joy in all eternity.
Lord Jesus Christ, my prayer fulfill;
In life, in death Thine am I still.

M. Schalling. J. O. Wallin.

296.

8.7.8.7.8.7.7.

1 JESUS keep in memory ever
Wouldst thou be God's child and friend;
Let thy heart forget Him never,
Still thy gaze on Jesus bend.
In thy rest and in thy labor
Look to Him with every breath,
Look to Jesus' life and death.

2 Look to Jesus, till reviving
Faith and love thy bosom swell;
Strength for all things good deriving
From Him who did all things well;
Work as He did, in thy season,
Works which shall not fade away,
Work while it is called to-day.

3 Look to Jesus, praying, waking,
When thy feet on roses, tread;
Follow, worldly pomp forsaking,
With thy cross, where He hath led.
Look to Jesus in temptation;
Baffled shall the tempter flee,
And God's angels come to thee.

4 Look to Jesus, when dark lowering
Perils thy horizon dim;
Unlike His disciples cowering,
Calm 'mid tempests look on Him.
Trust in Him who still rebuketh
Wind and billow, fire and flood;
Forward! then, and trust in God.

5 Look to Jesus when distresséd,
See what He, the Sinless, bore;
Is thy heart with conflict presséd?
Is thy soul still harassed sore?
See His bloody sweat, His conflict,
Watch His agony increase,
Hear His prayer, and taste His peace!

6 Art thou by sore want surrounded?
Do thy pains press forth thy sighs?
Art thou wronged and deeply wounded?
Does a scornful world despise?
Friends forsake thee or deny thee?
See what Jesus must endure,
He who as the light was pure!

7 Look to Jesus still to shield thee
When this dwelling thou must leave
In that last need He will yield thee
Peace the world can never give.
Look to Him, thy head low bending;
He, who finished all for thee,
Takes thee then with Him to be.

F. M. Franzen.

297.

9.8.9.8.9.9.8.

1 WE Christians should ever consider
What Christ hath so graciously taught;
For He, who hath made us His children,
Would have us retain in our thought
How little things earthly do merit,
Lest we, who should heaven inherit,
The heavenly prize leave unsought.

2 All nature a sermon may preach thee;
The birds sing thy murmurs away;
The birds, which nor sowing nor reaping,
God fails not to feed day by day;
And He, who those creatures doth cherish,
He never will leave thee to perish;
Or art thou not better than they?

3 The lilies, nor toiling nor spinning,
Their clothing how gorgeous and fair!
What tints in their tiny robes woven,
What wondrous devices are there!
All Solomon's stores could not render
One festival robe of such splendor
As the modest field lilies do wear.

4 If God o'er the grass and the flowers
Such delicate beauty hath spread,
The flowers which to-day are so fragrant,
To-morrow are faded and dead;
Oh, why, then, should earthly cares fret thee?
Thy Father will never forget thee,
Nor fail to provide thee with bread.

H. Spegel.

298.

11.10.11.10. Iambic.

1 I HAVE a Friend so patient, kind, forbearing,
Of all my friends this Friend doth love me best;
Though I am weak and sinful, yet when sharing
His love and mercy I am ever blest.

2 He is my Lord, my Friend, yea, He's my Brother;
And Jesus Christ is His most blessed Name.
He loves more tenderly than any mother;
To rest in Him is more than wealth and fame.

3 My poor and wretched soul He bought so dearly,
And freed from condemnation, death, and hell;
The old and bitter foe He crushed completely.
My soul, rejoice and sing, for all is well!

4 Thus I'm redeemed; no more the law prevaileth,
For Christ, the Lord, is my Redeemer's Name;
His precious blood more than my sin availeth;
His merit covers all my guilt and shame.

5 With hallelujahs here I'd tell the story,
My Lord to praise, to laud and magnify;
And praise His Name for evermore in glory,
Before His throne with all the saints on high.

C. O. Rosenius.

299.

L. M.

1 JESUS, and shall it ever be,
A mortal man ashamed of Thee?
Ashamed of Thee, whom angels praise,
Whose glories shine through endless days!

2 Ashamed of Jesus! sooner far
Let evening blush to own a star;
He sheds the beams of light divine
O'er this benighted soul of mine.

3 Ashamed of Jesus! just as soon
Let midnight be ashamed of noon;
'Tis midnight with my soul, till He,
Bright Morning Star, bid darkness flee.

4 Ashamed of Jesus! that dear Friend
On whom my hopes of heaven depend!
No; when I blush, be this my shame,
That I no more revere His Name.

5 Soon shall He come with power to bless
All who do here His Name confess;
And then may this my glory be,
That He is not ashamed of me!

Joseph Grigg. a.

300.

L. M. 6 lines.

1 THEE will I love, my Strength, my Tower,
Thee will I love, my Joy, my Crown;
Thee will I love with all my power,
In all my works, and Thee alone:
Thee will I love, till the pure fire
Fill my whole soul with chaste desire.

2 I thank Thee, uncreated Sun,
That Thy bright beams on me have shined;
I thank Thee, who hast overthrown
My foes, and healed my wounded mind;
I thank Thee, whose enlivening voice
Bids my freed heart in Thee rejoice.

3 Uphold me in the doubtful race,
Nor suffer me again to stray;

Strengthen my feet, with steady pace
Still to press forward in Thy way;
That all my powers, with all their might,
In Thy sole glory may unite.

4 Thee will I love, my Joy, my Crown;
Thee will I love, my Lord, my God!
Thee love beneath Thy smile or frown,
Beneath Thy scepter or Thy rod.
What though my flesh and heart decay?
Thee shall I love in endless day.

John Scheffler.

301.

8.7.8.7.7.7.

1 JESUS, Lord and precious Savior,
All my comfort and my joy!
Graciously extend Thy favor,
Let Thy Word my soul employ.
Jesus, come, abide with me,
Let me ever be with Thee.

2 What I do, oh, let me ever
Jesus, in Thy Name begin;
Give success to my endeavor,
Final victory therein.
Jesus, come, abide with me,
Let me ever be with Thee.

3 Let my words and thoughts, O Savior,
To Thy praise and glory tend;
Help me, Lord, that I may gather
Treasures that shall never end.

Jesus, come, abide with me,
Let me ever be with Thee.

4 When my days on earth are over,
Let me gladly take my rest;
May the time come, blessed Savior,
When to Thee it seemeth best.
Jesus, come, abide with me,
Let me ever be with Thee.

J. Arrhenius. J. O. Wallin.

302.

8.7.8.7.D.

1 JESUS is my Friend most precious,
Never friend doth love as He;
Should I leave this Friend so gracious,
Spurn His wondrous love for me?
No! nor friend nor foe shall sever
Me from Him who loves me so;
His shall be my will forever,
There above, and here below.

2 Bitter death for me He suffered;
From all guilt He set me free;
To His Father He hath offered
Everlasting prayers for me.
Who is he that would condemn me?
Christ hath saved me by His grace;
Who can from my Savior draw me?
I am safe in His embrace.

3 And I am persuaded ever,
Life nor death shall tear me from

Christ my blessed Lord and Savior;
Present things nor things to come,
Height, nor depth, nor fear, nor favor,
Aught that heaven and earth afford,
Can me from God's love e'er sever,
Love revealed in Christ our Lord.

J. Arrhenius.

303.

C. M.

1 SHINE on our souls, eternal God!
With rays of beauty shine;
Oh, let Thy favor crown our days,
And all their round be Thine.

2 Did we not raise our hands to Thee,
Our hands might toil in vain;
Small joy success itself could give,
If Thou Thy love restrain.

3 With Thee let every week begin,
With Thee each day be spent,
For Thee each fleeting hour improved,
Since each by Thee is lent.

4 Thus cheer us through this toilsome road,
Till all our labors cease;
And heaven refresh our weary souls
With everlasting peace.

Philip Doddridge. a.

304.

S. M.

1 THE Lord my Shepherd is,
I shall be well supplied:
Since He is mine, and I am His,
What can I want beside?

2 He leads me to the place
Where heavenly pasture grows,
Where living waters gently pass,
And full salvation flows.

3 If e'er I go astray,
He doth my soul reclaim,
And guides me in His own right way,
For His most holy Name.

4 While He affords His aid,
I cannot yield to fear:
Though I should walk through death's dark shade,
My Shepherd's with me there.

5 The bounties of Thy love
Shall crown my following days;
Nor from Thy house will I remove,
Nor cease to speak Thy praise.

Isaac Watts.

305.

7.6.7.6.D.

1 IF God Himself be for me,
I may a host defy;
For when I pray, before me

My foes confounded fly.
If Christ, the Head, befriend me,
If God be my support,
The mischief they intend me
Shall quickly come to naught.

2 I build on this foundation,
That Jesus and His blood
Alone are my salvation,
The true eternal good:
Without Him, all that pleases
Is valueless on earth:
The gifts I owe to Jesus
Alone my love are worth.

3 His Holy Spirit dwelleth
Within my willing heart,
Tames it when it rebelleth,
And soothes the keenest smart.
He crowns His work with blessing,
And helpeth me to cry
"My Father!" without ceasing
To Him who reigns on high.

4 To mine His Spirit speaketh
Sweet words of soothing power,
How God to him that seeketh
For rest, hath rest in store.
How God Himself prepareth
My heritage and lot,
And though my body weareth,
My heaven shall fail me not.

Paul Gerhardt.

306.

7s. 6 lines.

1 WHAT our Father does is well:
Blessed truth His children tell!
Though for plenty He send want,
Though the harvest store be scant,
Yet we rest upon His love,
Seeking better things above.

2 What our Father does is well;
Shall the wilful heart rebel
If a blessing He withhold
In the field, or in the fold?
Is He not Himself to be
All our store eternally?

3 What our Father does is well:
Though He sadden hill and dell,
Upward yet our praises rise
For the strength His Word supplies.
He has called us sons of God;
Can we murmur at His rod?

4 What our Father does is well:
May the thought within us dwell
Though nor milk nor honey flow
In our barren Canaan now,
God can save us in our need;
God can bless us, God can feed.

2 Therefore unto Him we raise
Hymns of glory, songs of praise;
To the Father and the Son

And the Spirit, Three in one,
Honor, might, and glory be,
Now and through eternity.

Benjamin Schmolk.

307.

S. M. D.

1 COMMIT thou all thy griefs
And ways into His hands,
To His sure truth and tender care
Who earth and heaven commands:
Who points the clouds their course,
Whom winds and seas obey,
He shall direct thy wandering feet,
He shall prepare thy way.

2 Thou on the Lord rely,
So safe shalt thou go on;
Fix on His work thy steadfast eye,
So shall thy work be done.
No profit canst Thou gain
By self-consuming care;
To Him commend thy cause; His ear
Attends the softest prayer.

3 Thy everlasting truth,
Father, Thy ceaseless love,
Sees all Thy children's wants, and knows
What best for each will prove.
And whatsoe'er Thou will'st,
Thou dost, O King of kings!
What Thine unerring wisdom chose,
Thy power to being brings.

4 Thou everywhere hast sway,
And all things serve Thy might;
Thy every act pure blessing is,
Thy path unsullied light.
When Thou arisest, Lord,
What shall Thy work withstand?
When what Thy children want Thou giv'st,
Who, who shall stay Thy hand?

Paul Gerhardt.

308.

C. M.

1 HOW happy is the man who hears
Instruction's warning voice,
And who celestial wisdom makes
His early only choice!

2 For she has treasures greater far
Than east or west unfold;
And her rewards more precious are
Than all their stores of gold.

3 She guides the young with innocence
In happy paths to tread;
A crown of glory she bestows
Upon the hoary head.

4 According as her labors rise,
So her rewards increase;
Her ways are ways of pleasantness,
And all her paths are peace.

Michael Bruce.

309.

7.7.8.8.7.7.

1 I AM Jesus' little lamb,
Therefore glad at heart I am;
Jesus loves me, Jesus knows me,
All that's good and fair he shows me,
Tends me every day the same,
Even calls me by my name.

2 Out and in I safely go,
Want and hunger never know;
Soft green pastures he discloseth,
Where His happy flock reposeth;
When I faint or thirsty be,
To the brook He leadeth me.

2 Should not I be glad all day
In this blessed fold to stay?
By this holy Shepherd tended,
Whose kind arms, when life is ended,
Bear me to the world of light?
Yes! oh yes, my lot is bright.

Henrietta Louisa von Hayn.

310.

11s.

1 Though troubles assail us and dangers affright,
Though friends should all fail us and foes all unite,
Yet one thing secures us, whatever betide,
The promise assures us—"The Lord will provide."

2 The birds, without garner or storehouse are
fed;
From them let us learn to trust God for our
bread:
His saints what is fitting shall ne'er be denied
So long as 'tis written, "The Lord will
provide."

3 When Satan assails us to stop up our path,
And courage all fails us we triumph by faith.
He cannot take from us, though oft he has
tried,
This heart cheering promise "The Lord will
provide."

4 No strength of our own, or goodness we
claim;
Yet, since we have known the Savior's great
Name,
In this our strong tower for safety we hide:
The Lord is our power, "The Lord will provide."

John Newton. a.

311.

C. M.

1 GOD moves in a mysterious way,
His wonders to perform:
He plants His footsteps in the sea,
And rides upon the storm.

2 Deep in unfathomable mines
Of never-failing skill,
He treasures up His bright designs,
And works His sovereign will.

3 Ye fearful saints, fresh courage take:
The clouds ye so much dread
Are big with mercy, and shall break
In blessings on your head.

4 Judge not the Lord by feeble sense,
But trust Him for His grace;
Behind a frowning Providence
He hides a smiling face.

5 His purposes will ripen fast,
Unfolding every hour.
The bud may have a bitter taste,
But sweet will be the flower.

6 Blind unbelief is sure to err,
And scan His works in vain.
God is His own interpreter,
And He will make it plain.

William Cowper.

312.

9.8.9.8.8.8.

1 LET, O my soul, thy God direct thee,
And trust in Him through all thy days;
In every danger He'll protect thee,
And crown thy years with peace and grace.
He doth not build upon the sand
Who trusts in God's almighty hand.

2 Of what avail is all our sorrow?
What profit all our sighs and tears?
Why should we grieve for each to-morrow?
Why thus begin and end our years?
Our sighs and sorrows but increase
Our burdens and disturb our peace.

3 Be still, in faith and hope abiding,
Trust in thy God and be content;
In His unfailing love confiding,
Take what His gracious hand hath sent,
To God who chose thee as His own
Thy every need and care is known.

4 The time to comfort thee He knoweth,
He giveth thee whate'er is best;
The prayer that from thy bosom goeth
He heareth ere it is expressed.
With gifts He cometh unawares
In answer to thy fervent prayers.

5 Think not when tried and tempest driven,
Thou art forsaken by thy God;
For those who are the heirs of heaven
Must pass beneath the chastening rod.
Thy night of weeping may ere long
Be changed into the morn of song.

6 What does it cost the Lord Almighty
To raise the humble and the low?
Or to abase the high and mighty,
And cause their utter overthrow?

For He whose wonders none can trace,
He lifteth up; He doth abase.

7 Walk in His truth, be firm and fearless,
And do thy duty day by day;
Trust in His Word when sad and cheerless,
Make it thy comfort and thy stay.
The Lord thy God thy refuge make,
And He will never thee forsake.

G. Neumarck. J. O. Wallin.

313.

S. M.

1 WHAT cheering words are these!
Their sweetness who can tell?
In time and to eternal days,
"'Tis with the righteous well."

2 In every state secure
Kept by Jehovah's eye,
'Tis well with them while life endure,
And well when called to die.

3 'Tis well when joys arise;
'Tis well when sorrows flow;
'Tis well when darkness veils the skies,
And strong temptations blow.

4 'Tis well when on the mount
They feast on dying love:
And 'tis as well in God's account,
When they the furnace prove.

5 'Tis well when Jesus calls,
"From earth and sin arise,
Join with the hosts of ransomed souls,
Made to salvation wise."

John Kent. a.

314.

11.10.11.10.

1 COME, ye disconsolate, where'er ye languish;
Come to the mercy-seat, fervently kneel;
Here bring your wounded hearts, here tell your anguish;
Earth has no sorrow that heaven cannot heal.

2 Joy of the desolate, light of the straying,
Hope, when all others die, fadeless and pure!
Here speaks the Comforter, tenderly saying,
Earth has no sorrow that heaven cannot cure.

3 Here see the Bread of Life; see waters flowing
Forth from the throne of God, pure from above;
Come to the feast of love; come, ever knowing
Earth has no sorrow but heaven can remove.

Thomas Moore.

315.

7.6.D. Trochaic, and Chorus.

1 SAFE in the arms of Jesus,
Safe on His gentle breast,
There by His love o'ershaded,
Sweetly my soul shall rest.
Hark! 'tis the voice of angels,
Borne in a song to me,
Over the fields of glory,
Over the jasper sea.

Chorus—Safe in the arms of Jesus,
Safe on His gentle breast,
There by His love o'ershaded,
Sweetly my soul shall rest.

2 Safe in the arms of Jesus,
Safe from corroding care,
Safe from the world's temptations,
Sin cannot harm me there.
Free from the blight of sorrow,
Free from my doubts and fears;
Only a few more trials,
Only a few more tears!

Chorus—Safe in the arms of Jesus, etc.

3 Jesus, my heart's dear refuge,
Jesus has died for me;
Firm on the Rock of Ages
Ever my trust shall be.
Here let me wait with patience,
Wait till the night is o'er;

Wait till I see the morning
Break on the golden shore.
Chorus—Safe in the arms of Jesus, etc.

Fanny J. Crosby (Mrs. Van Alstyne.)

316.

10.9.10.9.10.9.10.7.

1 WHERESOE'ER I roam through valleys dreary,
Over mountains, or in pathless wood,
Ever with me is a Friend to cheer me,
Warning, comforting as none else could.
'Tis the Shepherd, who once dying, bleeding,
Still through all eternity shall live;
Following His flock, protecting, feeding,
He the tenderest care doth give.

2 All my needs eternally supplying,
All in all to me that Friend shall be;
Everything for which my heart is sighing
He perceives, and helps me lovingly.
Though I often feel forsaken, lonely,
He is ever near, for He did say:
"I am with you alway", and this only
Gives me courage on my way.

3 Piercéd Heart with love o'erflowing, guide me,
Help me through life's desert find my way;
Let my faith, no matter what betide me,
Find assurance in Thy wounds for aye.
To Thy bosom, for this life is fleeting,

Take me, wash my garments in Thy blood,
And arising may I at Thy meeting
Cry with joy: My Lord and God.

C. O. Rosenius.

DEATH AND RESURRECTION.

317.

11s.

1 I WOULD not live alway; I ask not to stay
Where storm after storm rises dark o'er the way:
The few lurid mornings that dawn on us here
Are enough for life's woes, full enough for its cheer.

2 I would not live alway, thus fettered by sin,
Temptation without, and corruption within:
E'en the rapture of pardon is mingled with fears,
And the cup of thanksgiving with penitent tears.

3 I would not live alway; no, welcome the tomb;
Since Jesus hath lain there, I dread not its gloom:
There sweet be my rest, till He bid me arise
To hail Him in triumph descending the skies.

4 Who, who would live alway, away from His
God?
Away from yon heaven, that blissful abode,
Where the rivers of pleasure flow o'er the
bright plains,
And the noontide of glory eternally reigns:

5 Where the saints of all ages in harmony
meet,
Their Savior and brethren transported to
greet;
While the songs of salvation unceasingly roll,
And the smile of the Lord is the feast of the
soul!

William Augustus Muhlenberg.

318.

S. M. D.

1 A FEW more years shall roll,
A few more seasons come,
And we shall be with those that rest,
Asleep within the tomb:
Then, O my Lord, prepare
My soul for that great day;
Oh, wash me in Thy precious blood,
And take my sins away!

2 A few more storms shall beat
On this wild, rocky shore,
And we shall be where tempests cease,
And surges swell no more.
A few more struggles here,
A few more partings o'er,

A few more toils, a few more tears,
And we shall weep no more.

3 'Tis but a little while
And He shall come again,
Who died that we might live, who lives
That we with Him may reign:
Then, O my Lord, prepare
My soul for that glad day;
Oh, wash me in Thy precious blood,
And take my sins away!

Horatius Bonar.

319.

L. M. 6 lines.

1 MY God, I know that I must die:
My mortal life is passing hence;
On earth I neither hope nor try
To find a lasting residence.
Then teach me by Thy heavenly grace
With joy and peace my death to face.

2 My God, I know not when I die;
What is the moment or the hour;
How soon the clay may broken lie,
How quickly pass away the flower:
Then may Thy child preparéd be
Through time to meet eternity.

3 My God, I know not how I die;
For death has many ways to come,
In dark mysterious agony,
Or gently as a sleep to some.

Just as Thou wilt, if but it be
To bring me, blessed Lord, to Thee!

4 My God, I know not where I die,
Where is my grave, beneath what strand;
Yet from its gloom I do rely
To be delivered by Thy hand.
Content, I take what spot is mine,
Since all the earth, my Lord, is Thine.

5 My gracious God, when I must die,
Oh, bear my happy soul above,
With Christ, my Lord, eternally
To share Thy glory and Thy love:
Then comes it right and well to me,
When, where, and how my death shall be.

Benjamin Schmolk.

320.

L. M. 6 lines.

1 LORD Jesus Christ, true Man and God,
Who borest anguish, scorn, the rod,
And diedst at last upon the tree,
To bring Thy Father's grace to me:
I pray Thee, through that bitter woe,
Let me, a sinner, mercy know.

2 When comes the hour of failing breath,
And I must wrestle, Lord, with death,
When from my sight all fades away,
And when my tongue no more can say,
And when my ears no more can hear,
And when my heart is racked with fear,

3 When all my mind is darkened o'er,
And human help can do no more;
Then come, Lord Jesus! come with speed,
And help me in my hour of need;
Lead me from this dark vale beneath,
And shorten then the pangs of death.

4 Joyful my resurrection be,
Thou in the judgment plead for me,
And hide my sins, Lord, from Thy face,
And give me life, Lord, by Thy grace!
I trust Thee utterly, my Lord,
For Thou hast promised in Thy Word!

5 Dear Lord, forgive us all our guilt;
Help us to wait until Thou wilt
That we depart; and let our faith
Be brave, and conquer e'en in death:
Firm resting on Thy sacred Word,
Until we sleep in Thee, our Lord.

Paul Eber.

321. S. M.

1 ONE sweetly solemn thought
Comes to me o'er and o'er:
I'm nearer to my home to-day
Than e'er I've been before:

2 Nearer my Father's house,
Where many mansions be,
Nearer the throne where Jesus reigns,
Nearer the crystal sea.

3 Nearer the bound of life
  Where burdens are laid down,
Nearer leaving the cross of grief,
  Nearer gaining the crown.

4 But lying dark between,
  And winding through the night,
Flows on the deep and unknown stream
  That leads me to the light.

5 Jesus, perfect my trust,
  Strengthen my hand of faith,
And be Thou near me when I stand
  Upon the shore of death.

Phoebe Cary.

322.

L. M.

1 I FALL asleep in Jesus' wounds,
There pardon for my sin abounds;
Yea, Jesus' blood and righteousness
My jewels are, my glorious dress,

2 In which before my God I'll stand,
When I shall reach the heavenly land.
So now in peace I yield my breath,
I am God's child in life and death.

3 'Tis well, O death, thou takest me
To dwell with Christ eternally;
Through Jesus Christ I am made whole;
Receive, O Lord, my ransomed soul!

Paul Eber.

323. L. M.

1 HOW blest the righteous when he dies!
When sinks a weary soul to rest!
How mildly beam the closing eyes!
How gently heaves the expiring breast!

2 A holy quiet reigns around,
A calm which life nor death destroys;
And naught disturbs that peace profound
Which his unfettered soul enjoys.

3 Farewell, conflicting hopes and fears,
Where lights and shades alternate dwell;
How bright the unchanging morn appears!
Farewell, inconstant world, farewell!

4 Life's labor done, as sinks the clay,
Light from its load the spirit flies,
While heaven and earth combine to say,
"How blest the righteous when he dies!"

Anna L. Barbauld.

324. L. M.

1 ASLEEP in Jesus! blessed sleep,
From which none ever wakes to weep:
A calm and undisturbed repose,
Unbroken by the last of foes.

2 Asleep in Jesus! oh, how sweet
To be for such a slumber meet!
With holy confidence to sing
That death has lost his venomed sting!

3 Asleep in Jesus! peaceful rest,
Whose waking is supremely blest:
No fear, no woe, shall dim that hour
That manifests the Savior's power.

4 Asleep in Jesus! oh, for me
May such a blissful refuge be!
Securely shall my ashes lie,
And wait the summons from on high.

Margaret Mackay.

325.

11.11.11.5.

1 WHERE is the Friend for whom I'm ever yearning?
My longing grows when day to night is turning;
And though I find Him not as day recedeth,
My heart still pleadeth.

2 I know He's there in every force and power,
Where waves the harvest and where blooms the flower;
I'm ever in my breath and sighs so burning,
His love discerning.

3 When summer winds blow gently, then I hear Him;
Where sing the birds, where rush the streams I'm near Him;
But better far when in my heart He blesses
Me with caresses.

4 And yet to hide Him oft a cloud prevaileth;
My prayer can reach Him, but my vision faileth.
Would I could see His face and heart so loving,
And cease my roving.

5 Oh, where such beauty is itself revealing
In all that lives, through all creation stealing,
What must the source be whence it comes, the Giver?
Beauty forever.

6 O Fount of peace, whose rills with light are beaming,
When shall Thy waters come upon me streaming?
In Thy fresh waters what shall end my crying?
A peaceful dying.

7 My soul, be strong! Hope, pray with self-denial!
Thy heavenly Friend submits Himself to trial:
So shalt thou find in Him, on Him depending,
Mercy unending.

8 Soon, in the harbor, where no waves are breaking,
Or like the weary dove her refuge taking,

Thou, timorous lamb, shalt by thy Shepherd's favor
Find rest forever.

J. O. Wallin.

326.

11.11.5.5.11.

1 IN hope my soul, redeemed to bliss unending,
By faith to heaven's glorious height ascending,
Is mindful ever
That Christ did sever
The chains of death, that I might live forever.

2 With Him I have salvation's way discovered,
The heritage for me He hath recovered.
Though death o'ertakes me,
Christ ne'er forsakes me,
To everlasting life He surely wakes me.

3 More radiant there than sun e'er shone in brightness,
My soul shall shine before God's throne in whiteness.
My God, who knows me,
In glory clothes me,
As He declared when for His own He chose me.

4 Oh, may I come where strife and grief are ended,
Where all Thy saints shall meet, with peace attended!

Grant, Lord, Thy favor
And mercy ever,
And turn my sorrow into joy forever.

5 Lord Jesus Christ, keep me prepared and waking,
Till from the vale of tears Thy bride Thou'rt taking
To dwell in heaven,
Where joy is given,
And clouds of darkness are forever riven.

Elle Andersdotter. J. O. Wallin.

327.

6.4.6.4.6.6.6.4.

1 FADE, fade, each earthly joy;
Jesus is mine,
Break, every tender tie;
Jesus is mine.
Dark is the wilderness,
Earth has no resting-place,
Jesus alone can bless;
Jesus is mine.

2 Tempt not my soul away;
Jesus is mine.
Here would I ever stay;
Jesus is mine.
Perishing things of clay,
Born but for one brief day,
Pass from my heart away;
Jesus is mine.

3 Farewell, ye dreams of night;
Jesus is mine.
Lost in this dawning bright,
Jesus is mine.
All that my soul has tried,
Left but a dismal void;
Jesus has satisfied;
Jesus is mine.

4 Farewell, mortality;
Jesus is mine.
Welcome, eternity;
Jesus is mine.
Welcome, O loved and blest,
Welcome, sweet scenes of rest,
Welcome, my Savior's breast:
Jesus is mine.

Mrs. Jane C. Bonar.

328.

8.7.8.7.D. and Chorus.

1 We shall sleep, but not for ever,
There will be a glorious dawn;
We shall meet to part—no, never,
On the resurrection morn!
From the deepest caves of ocean,
From the desert and the plain,
From the valley and the mountain,
Countless throngs shall rise again.

Chorus—We shall sleep, but not forever,
There will be a glorious dawn;
Weshall meet to part—no, never,
On the resurrection morn!

2 When we see a precious blossom
That we tended with such care
Rudely taken from our bosom,
How our aching hearts despair!
Round its little grave we linger,
Till the setting sun is low,
Feeling all our hopes have perished
With the flower we cherished so.
Chorus—We shall sleep, etc.

3 We shall sleep, but not for ever,
In the lone and silent grave;
Blessed be the Lord that taketh,
Blessed be the Lord that gave.
In the bright, eternal city
Death can never, never come!
In His own good time He'll call us
From our rest to home, sweet home.
Chorus—We shall sleep, etc.

Mrs. Mary A. Kidder.

JUDGMENT.

329.

8.7.8.7.4.7.

1 DAY of judgment, day of wonders,
Hark! the trumpet's awful sound,
Louder than a thousand thunders,
Shakes the vast creation round!
How the summons
Will the sinner's heart confound!

2 See the Judge our nature wearing,
Clothed in majesty divine!
Ye who long for His appearing,
Then shall say, "This God is mine!"
Gracious Savior,
Own me in that day for Thine!

3 At His call the dead awaken,
Rise to life from earth and sea;
All the powers of nature, shaken
By His looks, prepare to flee:
Careless sinner,
What will then become of thee?

4 But to those who have confesséd,
Loved, and served the Lord below,
He will say, "Come near, ye blesséd!
See the kingdom I bestow!
You forever
Shall my love and glory know."

John Newton.

330.

8.7.8.7.8.8.7.

1 THE day is surely drawing near,
When He, the Lord's Anointed,
Will with great majesty appear,
As Judge of all appointed.
All mirth and laughter then shall cease,
When flames on flames will still increase,
As the Apostle teacheth.

2 A trumpet loud will then resound,
And all the earth be shaken;
Then all who in their graves are found
Will from their sleep awaken.
But all that live will in that hour,
By the Almighty's boundless power,
And at His word be changéd.

3 Then woe to those who scorned the Lord,
And sought but carnal pleasures,
Who here despised His precious Word,
And loved their earthly treasures.
With shame and trembling will they stand,
And at the Judge's stern command
Must leave the Lord forever.

4 Oh, may my name, dear Lord, be found,
Free from all condemnation,
For Thy death's sake, Thy pains and wounds,
In Thy book of salvation.
I will not doubt:—I trust in Thee;—
From Satan Thou hast made me free,
And from all condemnation.

5 Therefore my Intercessor be,
And for Thy death and merit
Declare my name from judgment free,
With all who life inherit;
That with my brethren I may stand
With Thee in heaven, our fatherland,
Which Thou for us hast purchased.

6 Lord Jesus Christ, do not delay,
Oh, hasten our salvation!
We often tremble on our way,
In fear and tribulation.
Then hear us when we cry to Thee;
Come mighty Judge, come, make us free
From every evil. Amen!

B. Ringwald.

331.

8.7.8.7.8.8.7.

1 GREAT God, what do I see and hear!
The end of things created!
The Judge of man I see appear,
On clouds of glory seated.
The trumpet sounds: the graves restore
The dead which they contained before;
Prepare my soul to meet Him.

2 The dead in Christ shall first arise,
At the last trumpet's sounding,
Caught up to meet Him in the skies,
With joy their Lord surrounding;
No gloomy fears their souls dismay;
His presence sheds eternal day
On those prepared to meet Him.

3 But sinners, filled with guilty fears,
Behold His wrath prevailing,
For they shall rise, and find their tears
And sighs are unavailing,
The day of grace is past and gone;
Trembling they stand before the throne,
All unprepared to meet Him.

4 O Christ, who diedst and yet dost live,
To me impart Thy merit;
My pardon seal, my sins forgive,
And cleanse me by Thy Spirit.
Beneath Thy cross I view the day
When heaven and earth shall pass away,
And thus prepare to meet Thee.

W. B. Collyer.

ETERNITY.

332. 8.8.7.8.8.7.8.8.

1 ETERNITY! most awful word!
Within the heart a piercing sword!
Beginning without ending!
Eternity, unmeasured time!
I sink beneath the thought sublime
That I to thee am tending:
Deep horrors fill my quaking heart,
My lips in speech refuse to part.

2 Eternity! oh what a pang!
Eternity! No serpent's fang
Could send that thrill of terror;
When I revolve Thy clanking chains,
The dark abyss of deathless pains,
My soul is filled with horror.
Oh, search this universe around,
No equal terror can be found.

3 Awake, O man, from sinful sleep;
Henceforth thy feet from wandering keep:
Seek God by true repentance!
Awake, behold thy wasting sand,
Eternity is just at hand,
And brings thine awful sentence.
This is perchance thy final day;
This hour thy soul may haste away.

4 Eternity! most awful word!
Within the heart a piercing sword!
Beginning without ending!
Eternity! unmeasured time!
I sink beneath the thought sublime,
That I to thee am tending:
Lord Jesus, when it pleaseth Thee,
Grant me Thy blest eternity!

John Rist.

333.

11.10.11.10.8.8.7.

1 ABODE of peace, my Father's home forever!
My weary soul in faith doth yearn for Thee.
I homeward look to Thee, my Lord and Savior,
To Thine abode of peace, eternally.
There is on earth no peaceful rest;
Our faith is weak, our souls oppressed,
Our vision dim and failing.

2 The Lord be praised that time so swiftly flieth;

God's promise is fulfilled for evermore.
Who on God's Word and promises relieth
Shall find at last the choicest wine in store.
Forgotten then is all distress,
Eternal peace and happiness
Shall then be ours forever.

3 Then, keep my heart forever, O my Savior,
And let me never, Lord, from Thee depart.
In joy, in pain, in sorrow, now and ever,
Thou only givest solace to my heart.
For when, O Lord, I am with Thee,
All other comforts well may flee;
With Thee I'm ever blessèd.

Agatha Rosenius.

334.

C. M.

1 WHEN I can read my title clear
To mansions in the skies,
I bid farewell to every fear,
And wipe my weeping eyes.

2 Should earth against my soul engage,
And hellish darts be hurled;
Then I can smile at Satan's rage,
And face a frowning world.

3 Let cares like a wild deluge come,
And storms of sorrow fall,
May I but safely reach my home,
My God, my heaven, my all!

4 There shall I bathe my weary soul
In seas of heavenly rest;
And not a wave of trouble roll
Across my peaceful breast.

Isaac Watts.

335.

8.7.8.7. Iambic, and Chorus.

1 THERE is a gate that stands ajar,
And through its portals gleaming,
A radiance from the cross afar,
The Savior's love revealing.
Chorus—Oh, depth of mercy! can it be
That gate was left ajar for me?
For me, for me?
Was left ajar for me?

2 That gate ajar stands free for all
Who seek through it salvation;
The rich and poor, the great and small,
Of every tribe and nation.
Chorus—Oh, depth of mercy! etc.

3 Press onward, then, though foes may frown,
While mercy's gate is open;
Accept the cross, and win the crown,
Love's everlasting token.
Chorus—Oh, depth of mercy! etc.

4 Beyond the river's brink we'll lay
The cross that here is given,
And bear the crown of life away,
And love Him more in heaven.
Chorus—Oh, depth of mercy! etc.

Mrs. Lydia Baxter.

336.

10s. D.

1 JOYFULLY, joyfully, onward we move,
Bound to the land of bright spirits above;
Jesus, our Savior, in mercy says, Come,
Joyfully, joyfully, haste to your home.
Soon will our pilgrimage end here below,
Soon to the presence of God we shall go,
Then, if to Jesus our hearts have been given,
Joyfully, joyfully, rest we in heaven.

2 Death with its arrows may soon lay us low,
Safe in our Savior, we fear not the blow;
Jesus hath broken the bars of the tomb,
Joyfully, joyfully, we will go home.
Bright will the morn of eternity dawn,
Death shall be conquered, his scepter be gone;
Over the plains of sweet Canaan we'll roam,
Joyfully, joyfully, safely at home.

William Hunter.

337.

11.10.11.10. and Chorus.

1 COME, O my soul, my every power awaking,
Look unto Him whose goodness crowns thy days;
While into song angelic choirs are breaking,
Oh, let thy voice its thankful tribute raise.

Chorus—Tell how alone the path of death He trod;
Tell how He lives, thy Advocate with God;

Lift up thy voice, while heaven's triumphant throng
Swell at His feet the everlasting song.

2 Think, O my soul, how patiently He sought thee
Far, far away upon the mountains steep,
Then in His arms how tenderly He brought thee
Home to His fold, a weary, wandering sheep.
Chorus—Tell how alone, etc.

3 Sing, O my soul, and let thy pure devotion
Rise to His throne, thy Savior, Friend, and Guide;
Sing of His love, that, like a mighty ocean,
Flows unto thee and all the world beside.
Chorus—Tell how alone, etc.

4 Soon, O my soul, thine earthly house forsaking,
Soon shalt thou rise the better land to see;
Then will thy harp, a nobler strain awaking,
Praise Him who died to purchase life for thee.
Chorus—Tell how alone, etc.

Lizzie Edwards.

338.

9.11.10.10.9.11.

1 I'm a pilgrim, and I'm a stranger,
I can tarry, I can tarry but a night;
Do not detain me, for I am going
To where the fountains are ever flowing:
I'm a pilgrim, and I'm a stranger,
I can tarry, I can tarry but a night.

2 There the glory is ever shining;
Oh, my longing heart, my longing heart is there;
Here in this country so dark and dreary
I long have wandered, forlorn and weary:
I'm a pilgrim, and I'm a stranger,
I can tarry, I can tarry but a night.

3 Of the city to which I'm going
My Redeemer, my Redeemer is the light;
There is no sorrow, nor any sighing,
Nor any sinning, nor any dying:
Of the city to which I'm going
My Redeemer, my Redeemer is the light.

Mrs. Mary S. B. Shindler.

339.

8.7.8.7.D. Iambic, and Chorus.

1 OH, what has Jesus done for me?
He came from the land of Canaan;
He died for me upon the tree,
That I might go to Canaan:

A glorious crown appears in view
  In that bright land of Canaan;
A palm of royal victory too;
  Come, let us go to Canaan.

Chorus—Canaan, bright Canaan,
    The glorious land of Canaan;
  Our Canaan is a happy place,
    Come, let us go to Canaan.

2 When I shall join that blessed throng
  In the glorious land of Canaan,
I'll sing the great Redeemer's song
  With the happy saints of Canaan:
There Jesus sits upon His throne,
  Exalted high in Canaan;
Inviting all His children home,
  To dwell with Him in Canaan:

Chorus—Canaan, bright Canaan, etc.

3 Come, sinner, turn, and go with me,
  For Jesus waits in Canaan,
With angels bright to welcome thee
  To all the joys of Canaan:
Come freely to salvation's streams,
  They sweetly flow in Canaan;
There everlasting glory beams
  Around His throne in Canaan:

Chorus—Canaan, bright Canaan, etc.

John Curwen.

340.

8.6.6.5. and Chorus.

1 WHEN He cometh, when He cometh
To make up His jewels,
All His jewels, precious jewels,
His loved and His own.

Chorus—Like the stars of the morning,
His bright crown adorning,
They shall shine in their beauty,
Bright gems for His crown.

2 He will gather, He will gather
The gems for His kingdom:
All the pure ones, all the bright ones,
His loved and His own.

Chorus—Like the stars of the morning, etc.

3 Little children, little children
Who love their Redeemer
Are the jewels, precious jewels,
His loved and His own.

Chorus—Like the stars of the morning, etc.

W. O. Cushing.

341.

11.8.12.9.

1 I THINK, when I read that sweet story of old,
When Jesus was here among men,
How He called little children as lambs to His fold,
I should like to have been with them then.

2 I wish that His hand had been placed on my
head,
That His arm had been thrown around
me,
And that I might have seen His kind look
when He said,
"Let the little ones come unto Me."

3 Yet still to His footstool in prayer I may go,
And ask for a share in His love;
And if I only earnestly seek Him below,
I shall see Him and hear Him above.

4 In that beautiful place He has gone to pre-
pare
For all who are washed and forgiven;
Full many dear children are gathering there,
"For of such is the kingdom of heaven."

5 But thousands and thousands who wander
and fall,
Never heard of that heavenly home:
I wish they could know there is room for
them all,
And that Jesus had bid them to come.

6 And oh, how I long for that glorious time,
The sweetest and brightest and best,
When the dear little children of every clime,
Shall crowd to His arms and be blest!

Jemima Luke.

342.

8.6.8.6.6.7.

1 AROUND the throne of God in heaven,
Thousands of children stand;
Children whose sins are all forgiven,
A holy happy band,
Singing Glory, Glory,
Glory be to God on high.

2 In flowing robes of spotless white,
See every one arrayed;
Dwelling in everlasting light,
And joys that never fade,
Singing Glory, Glory, etc.

3 What brought them to that world above,
That heaven so bright and fair,
Where all is peace and joy and love?
How came those children there?
Singing Glory, Glory, etc.

4 Because the Savior shed His blood
To wash away their sin:
Bathed in that pure and precious flood,
Behold them white and clean!
Singing Glory, Glory, etc.

5 On earth they sought the Savior's grace,
On earth they loved His Name;
So now they see His blessed face,
And stand before the Lamb,
Singing Glory, Glory, etc.

Mrs. Anne Shepherd.

343.

6.4.6.4.6.7.6.4.

1 THERE is a happy land,
  Far, far away,
Where saints in glory stand,
  Bright, bright as day.
Oh, how they sweetly sing,
Worthy is the Savior King,
Loud let His praises ring,
  Praise, praise for aye!

2 Come to that happy land,
  Come, come away;
Why will ye doubting stand,
  Why still delay?
Oh, we shall happy be,
When, from sin and sorrow free,
Lord, we shall live with Thee,
  Blest, blest for aye.

3 Bright, in that happy land,
  Beams every eye;
Kept by a Father's hand,
  Love cannot die.
Oh, then, to glory run,
Be a crown and kingdom won,
And, bright above the sun,
  We reign for aye.

Andrew Young.

344.

8.7.8.7. and Chorus.

1 IN the Christian's home in glory,
  There remains a land of rest;

There my Savior's gone before me,
To fulfill my soul's request.
Chorus—There is rest for the weary,
There is rest for the weary,
There is rest for the weary,
There is rest for you;
On the other side of Jordan,
In the sweet fields of Eden,
Where the tree of life is blooming,
There is rest for you.

2 He is fitting up my mansion,
Which eternally shall stand,
For my stay shall not be transient,
In that holy, happy land.
Chorus—There is rest, etc.

3 Pain and sickness ne'er shall enter;
Grief nor woe my lot shall share;
But in that celestial centre
I a crown of life shall wear.
Chorus—There is rest, etc.

Samuel Young Harmer.

345.

C. M. and Chorus.

1 I LOVE to think of the heavenly land,
Where white robed angels are;
Where many a friend is gathered safe,
From fear and toil and care.

Chorus—There'll be no parting,
There'll be no parting,

There'll be no parting,
There'll be no parting there.

2 I love to think of the heavenly land,
Where my Redeemer reigns,
Where rapturous songs of triumph rise,
In endless, joyous strains.
Chorus—There'll be no parting, etc.

3 I love to think of the heavenly land,
The saints' eternal home,
Where palms, and robes, and crowns ne'er fade,
And all our joys are one.
Chorus—There'll be no parting, etc.

4 I love to think of the heavenly land,
That promised land so fair,
Oh, how my raptured spirit longs
To be forever there!
Chorus—There'll be no parting, etc.

L. Hartsough.

346.

8s.

1 WE speak of the realms of the blest,
That country so bright and so fair,
And oft are its glories confessed;
But what must it be to be there!

2 We speak of its pathways of gold,
Its walls decked with jewels so rare,
Its wonders and pleasures untold;
But what must it be to be there!

3 We speak of its freedom from sin,
From sorrow, temptation, and care,
From trials without and within;
But what must it be to be there!

4 We speak of its service of love,
The robes which the glorified wear,
The church of the first-born above;
But what must it be to be there!

5 Do Thou, Lord, 'mid sorrow and woe,
Still for heaven my spirit prepare,
And shortly I also shall know,
And feel what it is to be there.

Mrs. Elizabeth Mills.

347.

8.7.8.7. and Chorus.

1 SHALL we meet beyond the river,
Where the surges cease to roll?
Where, in all the bright forever,
Sorrow ne'er shall press the soul?

Chorus—Shall we meet, shall we meet,
Shall we meet beyond the river!
Shall we meet beyond the river,
Where the surges cease to roll?

2 Shall we meet in that blest harbor?
When our stormy voyage is o'er?
Shall we meet and cast the anchor
By the fair celestial shore?

Chorus—Shall we meet, etc.

3 Shall we meet in yonder city,
Where the towers of crystal shine?
Where the walls are all of jasper,
Built by workmanship divine?
Chorus—Shall we meet, etc.

4 Shall we meet with Christ our Savior,
When He comes to claim His own?
Shall we know His blessed favor,
And sit down upon His throne?
Chorus—Shall we meet, etc.

H. L. Hastings.

348.

8.7.8.7. and Chorus.

1 SHALL we gather at the river,
Where bright angel feet have trod;
With its crystal tide forever,
Flowing by the throne of God?

Chorus—Yes, we'll gather at the river,
The beautiful, the beautiful river;
Gather with the saints at the river,
That flows by the throne of God.

2 On the margin of the river,
Washing up its silver spray,
We will walk and worship ever
All the happy, golden day.
Chorus—Yes, we'll gather at the river, etc.

3 Ere we reach the shining river,
Lay we every burden down;

Grace our spirits will deliver
And provide a robe and crown.
Chorus—Yes, we'll gather at the river, etc.

4 At the smiling of the river,
Mirror of the Savior's face,
Saints whom death will never sever,
Lift their songs of saving grace.
Chorus—Yes, we'll gather at the river, etc.

5 Soon we'll reach the silver river,
Soon our pilgrimage will cease;
Soon our happy hearts will quiver
With the melody of peace.
Chorus—Yes, we'll gather at the river, etc.

Robert Lowry.

349.

9s. and Chorus.

1 THERE'S a land that is fairer than day,
And by faith we can see it afar;
For the Father waits over the way,
To prepare us a dwelling place there.
Chorus—In the sweet by and by,
We shall meet on that beautiful shore,
In the sweet by and by,
We shall meet on that beautiful shore.

2 We shall sing on that beautiful shore
The melodious songs of the blest,
And our spirits shall sorrow no more,
Not a sigh for the blessing of rest.
Chorus—In the sweet by and by, etc.

3 To our bountiful Father above,
We will offer our tribute of praise,
For the glorious gift of His love,
And the blessings that hallow our days.

Chorus—In the sweet by and by, etc.

S. F. Bennett.

350.

C. M.

1 THERE is a land of pure delight,
Where saints immortal reign;
Infinite day excludes the night,
And pleasures banish pain.

2 There everlasting spring abides,
And never-withering flowers:
Death, like a narrow sea, divides
This heavenly land from ours.

3 Sweet fields, beyond the swelling flood,
Stand drest in living green:
So to the Jews old Canaan stood,
While Jordan rolled between.

4 But timorous mortals start and shrink
To cross this narrow sea,
And linger, shivering on the brink,
And fear to launch away.

5 Oh, could we make our doubts remove,
Those gloomy doubts that rise,
And view the Canaan that we love,
With unbeclouded eyes!

6 Could we but climb where Moses stood,
And view the landscape o'er,
Not Jordan's stream, nor death's cold flood,
Should fright us from the shore.

Isaac Watts.

351.

7.6 4.4.7.6.7.6.

1 MY heart is yearning ever
To reach a place of rest,
Jerusalem,
My happy home,
In Thee my heart shall never
By sin or grief be pressed.
My heart is yearning ever
To reach that city blest.

2 Within its radiant portals
None ever sheds a tear.
God's city bright
Gives all delight;
No grief nor wail of mortals
Is where the Lamb is near.
Within its radiant portals
None ever sheds a tear.

3 Their blessed Lord and Savior
Doth rule and govern them
In peace and joy,
Without alloy,
For sin can enter never
The new Jerusalem.

Their blessed Lord and Savior
Doth rule and govern them.

4 Behold the goal in glory,
Now shining from afar;
Oh, city of
The God of love,
Where no more earthly worry
My happiness shall mar!
Behold the goal in glory,
Now shining from afar!

5 And even I shall conquer
In Jesus' Name and might.
Though weak and faint,
Still as a saint,
I'll in the haven anchor,
Sweet haven of delight.
Yea, even I shall conquer
In Jesus' Name and might.

From Hemlandssånger.

352.

7 6.7.6.D.

1 JERUSALEM the golden,
With milk and honey blest,
Beneath thy contemplation
Sink heart and voice opprest:
I know not, oh, I know not,
What social joys are there!
What radiancy of glory,
What light beyond compare!

2 And when I fain would sing them
My spirit fails and faints,
And vainly would it image
The assembly of the saints,
They stand, those halls of Zion,
Conjubilant with song,
And bright with many an angel,
And all the martyr throng:

3 There is the throne of David;
And there, from care released,
The song of them that triumph,
The shout of them that feast;
And they who, with their Leader,
Have conquered in the fight,
Forever and forever
Are clad in robes of white!

Bernard de Morlaix.

353.

C. M.

1 JERUSALEM, my happy home,
Name ever dear to me!
When shall my labors have an end
In joy, and peace, and thee.

2 When shall these eyes thy heavenbuilt walls
And pearly gates behold?
Thy bulwarks with salvation strong,
And streets of shining gold?

3 Oh, when, thou city of my God,
Shall I thy courts ascend,

Where evermore the angels sing,
Where sabbaths have no end?

4 There happier bowers than Eden's bloom,
Nor sin nor sorrow know:
Blest seats! through rude and stormy scenes
I onward press to you.

5 Why should I shrink from pain and woe,
Or feel at death dismay?
I've Canaan's goodly land in view,
And realms of endless day.

6 Apostles, martyrs, prophets there
Around my Savior stand;
And soon my friends in Christ below
Will join the glorious band.

7 Jerusalem, my happy home!
My soul still pants for thee;
Then shall my labors have an end,
When I thy joys shall see.

Composite.

354.

C. M. D.

1 JERUSALEM, Jerusalem,
Thou city ever blest,
Within thy portals first I find
My safety, peace, and rest.
Here dangers always threathen me,
My days in strife are spent,
And labor, sorrow, worry, grief,
That is at best their strength.

2 No wonder, then, that more and more
  My longings do increase,
Jerusalem, Jerusalem,
  For thee, and never cease.
My lineage, too, to thee I trace,
  A stranger in the earth,
In thee my burghership I have,
  In thee I have my birth.

3 No wonder, then, that I do long,
  O blessed home, for thee,
Where finally I shall have rest,
  From sin and sorrow free;
Where tears and weeping are no more,
  Nor death, nor pain, nor night,
For former things are passed away
  In yonder home of light.

4 Now all for me has lost its charm
  Which here so much is praised,
Since on the cross, through faith, I saw
  My Savior, Jesus, raised,
My goal is fixed, one thing I ask,
  Whate'er the price may be,
Jerusalem, Jerusalem,
  Soon to arrive in thee.

Lina Sandell.

355.

10.6.10.6.7.6.7.6.

1 JERUSALEM, thou city fair and high,
  Would God I were in thee!
My longing heart fain, fain to thee would fly!

It will not stay with me;
Far over vale and mountain,
Far over field and plain,
It hastes to seek its Fountain
And quit this world of pain.

2 O happy day, and yet far happier hour,
When wilt thou come at last?
When fearless to my Father's love and power,
Whose promise standeth fast,
My soul I gladly render,
For surely will His hand
Lead me with guidance tender
To heaven my fatherland.

3 O Zion, hail! bright city, now unfold
The gates of grace to me!
How many a time I longed for thee of old,
Ere yet I was set free
From yon dark life of sadness,
Yon world of shadowy naught,
And God had given the gladness,
The heritage I sought.

4 Unnumbered choirs before the shining throne
Their joyful anthems raise,
And th' heavenly halls re-echo with the tone
Of that great hymn of praise,
And all its host rejoices,
And all its blessed throng
Unite their myriad voices
In one eternal song. *J. M. Meyfart.*

DOXOLOGIES.

1. C. M.

TO Father, Son, and Holy Ghost,
The God, whom we adore,
Be glory, as it was, is now,
And shall be evermore.

2. C. M. D.

TO praise the Father, and the Son,
And Spirit all-divine,
The One in Three, and Three in One,
Let saints and angels join.
Glory to Thee, Blest Trinity,
The God, whom we adore,
As was, is now, and e'er shall be,
When time shall be no more.

3. S. M.

TO God the Father, Son,
And Spirit, One in Three,
Be glory, as it was, is now,
And shall forever be.

4. S. M. D.

PRAISE, as in ages past,
Praise, as is now in heaven,
Praise, while eternity shall last,
To Thee, O God, be given;

Whom all the angelic host
And saints on earth adore,
To Father, Son, and Holy Ghost,
Be glory evermore.

5.

L. M.

PRAISE God, from whom all blessings flow;
Praise Him, all creatures here below;
Praise Him above, ye heavenly host;
Praise Father, Son, and Holy Ghost.

6.

L. M. 6 lines.

TO God the Father, God the Son,
And God the Spirit, Three in One,
Be glory in the highest given,
By all on earth, and all in heaven,
As was through ages heretofore,
Is now, and shall be evermore.

7.

H. M. or 6.6.6 6.8.8.

TO God, the Father, Son,
And Spirit, ever blest,
Eternal Three in One,
All glory be addressed,
As heretofore it was, is now
And so shall be for evermore.

8.

5.5.8.8.5.5.

GLORY be to Thee,
Endless One in Three,
Father, Son, and Holy Spirit,
Through the Savior's boundless merit:

God in Unity,
Blessed Trinity.

9. 6.4.6.4.6.6.4.

TO God the Father, Son,
And Spirit be
The highest honor done,
Now and for aye.
My song shall ever be,
Glory, my God, to Thee,
Glory to Thee.

10. 6.6.4.6.6.6.4.

TO God the Father, Son,
And Spirit, Three in One,
All praise be given:
Crown Him in every song,
To Him our hearts belong,
Let all His praise prolong,
On earth, in heaven.

11. 6.5.6.5.

NOW, henceforth, forever,
Glory be to Thee,
Father, Son, and Spirit,
Blessed One in Three.

12. 7s.

HOLY Father, holy Son,
Holy Spirit, Three in One,
Glory, as of old, to Thee,
Now and evermore shall be.

13. 7s. 6 lines.

PRAISE the Name of God most high;
Praise Him, all below the sky;
Praise Him, all ye heavenly host,
Father, Son, and Holy Ghost:
As through countless ages past,
Evermore His praise shall last.

14. 7s.D.

HOLY Father, Fount of light,
God of wisdom, goodness, might;
Holy Son, who cam'st to dwell,
God with us, Immanuel;
Holy Spirit, heavenly Dove,
God of comfort, peace, and love;
Evermore be Thou adored,
Holy, holy, holy, Lord.

15. 7.6.7.6.

TO Father, Son, and Spirit,
Eternal One in Three,
As was, and is forever,
All praise and glory be.

16. 7.6.7.6.D.

TO God the ever-glorious,
The father, and the Son,
And Spirit all-victorious,
Thrice holy Three in One;
The God of our salvation,
Whom earth and heaven adore,
Praise, glory, adoration,
Be now and evermore.

17. 7.8.7.8.7.7.

HOLY Father, Holy Son,
  Holy Spirit, we adore Thee,
Everlasting Three in One;
  Let all creatures bow before Thee,
Saints and angels bless Thy Name,
Earth and heaven Thy praise proclaim.

18. 7.8.7.8.8.8.

HOLY Father, Holy Son,
  Holy Spirit, we adore Thee,
Everlasting Three in One;
  Let all creatures bow before Thee,
Let Thy people here confess Thee;
Earth and heaven unite to bless Thee.

19. 8.7.8.7.

PRAISE the Father, earth and heaven;
  Praise the Son, the Spirit praise;
As it was, and is, be given
  Glory through eternal days.

20. 8.7.8.7.D.

PRAISE the God of all creation;
  Praise the Father's boundless love;
Praise the Lamb, our expiation,
  Priest and King enthroned above;
Praise the Fountain of salvation,
  Him by whom our spirits live;
Undivided adoration
  To the One Jehovah give.

21.

8.7.8.7.4.7

GREAT Jehovah, we adore Thee,
God the Father, God the Son,
God the Spirit, joined in glory
On the same eternal throne:
Endless praises
To Jehovah, Three in One.

22.

8.7.8.7.7.7.

GLORY be to God the Father.
Glory be to God the Son,
Glory be to God the Spirit,
Everlasting Three in One:
Him let heaven and earth adore,
Now, henceforth, and evermore.

23.

8.7.8.7.8.8.

PRAISE the God of all creation;
Praise the Father's boundless love;
Praise the Lamb, our expiation;
Praise the Spirit, throned above;
Praise the God of our salvation;
His be endless adoration.

24.

8.7.8.7.8.8.7.

NOW to the holy Three in One,
Who o'er creation reigneth,
Be everlasting honor done,
To Whom all praise pertaineth.
All blessing be to God Most High,
All glory to His Majesty,
Who all the world sustaineth.

INDEX.

The authors of the hymns are given in the text at the end of each hymn. The translators are given in the following index. An *a* at the end of the name indicates that the hymn or translation has been more or less changed.

INDEX

of hymns found in *Svenska Psalmboken*, *Hemlandssånger*, and *Söndagsskolboken*.

Hymnal.	Psalmboken.	Hemlands-sånger.	Söndagsskol-boken.
No. 91......	511	......	......
93......	......	117	83
94......	113	......	......
102......	134	......	......
110......	133	......	......
111......	22	......	......
112......	17	......	......
113......	23	......	......
118......	21	......	......
121......	24	......	......
132......	268	......	196
133......	272	......	197
134......	......	......	251
136......	......	......	22
140......	......	......	185
143......	......	302	134
144......	......	304	173
146......	......	164	171
147......	260	......	......
149......	......	152	9
150......	330	......	3
151......	328	......	......
156......	......	363	......
158......	500	......	29
162......	......	373	31
164......	332	......	......
170......	420	......	......
180	......	355	......
181......	443	......	......
182......	434	......	18
183......	......	400	......
189......	......	145	......
190......	378	......	......
192......	118	......	......
193......	124	......	91
194......	120	......	......
195......	......	141	33

Hymnal.	Psalmboken.	Hemlands-sånger.	Söndagsskol-boken.
No. 196......	......	139	136
202......	......	200	92
203......	......	201	......
214......	......	179	......
216......	......	128	......
217......	......	129	......
221......	528	171	......
222......	154	......	......
223......	150	......	......
226......	152	......	......
227......	158	......	......
228......	151	......	......
233......	165	......	......
234......	......	244	......
235......	......	235	147
236......	......	245	......
237......	......	221	150
245......	194	......	......
247......	......	303	153
248......	192	......	143
249......	187	......	116 & 121
250......	......	246	......
254......	......	248	179
255......	......	311	163
256......	......	65	63
265......	......	497	......
267......	46	......	130
268......	147	......	126
276......	......	......	95
281......	......	88	74
283......	......	431	176
284......	......	312	......
285......	......	313	......
290......	119	......	......
291......	......	163	10
292......	......	421	......
293......	......	292	......

Hymnal.	Psalmboken.	Hemlands-sånger.	Söndagsskol-boken.
No. 294......	......	288	......
295......	221	......	......
296......	127	......	......
297......	298	......	......
298......	......	258	140
301......	204	......	25
302......	213	......	141
309......	......	......	138
310......	......	15	178
312......	239	......	......
315......	......	264	164
316......	......	103	135
320......	469	......	......
322......	480	......	......
325......	481	413	......
326......	487	......	209
327......	......	257	159
328......	......	470	......
330......	498	......	......
332......	463	......	......
333......	......	465	......
335......	......	478	......
336......	......	476	231
338......	......	443	215
339......	......	450	64
340......	......	387	210
341......	......	......	188
342......	......	491	211 & 216
343......	......	......	214
345......	......	488	221
347......	......	169	......
349......	......	487	220
351......	......	496	......
353......	......	......	222
354......	......	489	......
355......	......	498	......
142	71	67	63

www.ingramcontent.com/pod-product-compliance
Lightning Source LLC
Chambersburg PA
CBHW032309280326
41932CB00009B/754